THE LAST 40 YEARS
BEFORE DEVASTATING JUDGMENT
ARE ALREADY
MORE THAN HALF OVER!

THE END OF THE AGE is not like any other book. It concerns times that will soon steamroll right over us whether we are ready or not. Since the very near future is firmly rooted in the past, **THE END OF THE AGE** contains a wide angle view of time from Adam to the Great White Throne of Judgment, plus the momentous events that will take place. *We need to be forewarned.*

From the Introduction

THE END OF THE AGE

M.J. AGEE

(Previously published as *Exit 2007*)

AVON BOOKS ◆ NEW YORK

Dedicated to Ed who has so patiently endured my studying, and Bob for his encouragement, when he said, "Go ahead and write that book for the world to read, it just may be that you have the key that can unlock so much mystery about the Bible."

"Nothing is secret, that shall not be made manifest: neither any thing hid, that shall not be known and come abroad."   Luke 8:17

All Biblical quotations are from the King James Version unless otherwise noted.

AVON BOOKS
A division of
The Hearst Corporation
1350 Avenue of the Americas
New York, New York 10019

Copyright © 1987, 1991 by Marilyn J. Agee
Published by arrangement with Archer Press
Library of Congress Catalog Card Number: 91-22936
ISBN: 0-380-72181-3

First Avon Books Printing: January 1994

AVON TRADEMARK REG. U.S. PAT. OFF. AND IN OTHER COUNTRIES, MARCA REGISTRADA, HECHO EN U.S.A.

Printed in the U.S.A.

RA 10 9 8 7 6 5 4 3 2 1

"O EARTH, EARTH, EARTH,
HEAR THE WORD OF THE LORD"
Jeremiah 22:29

JESUS SAID, "I HAVE FORETOLD YOU **ALL** THINGS"
Mark 13:23

"SURELY, THE LORD GOD WILL DO NOTHING, BUT HE
REVEALETH HIS SECRET UNTO HIS SERVANTS THE
PROPHETS."
Amos 3:7

"OH THAT GOD WOULD SPEAK...AND THAT HE WOULD SHEW
THEE **THE SECRETS OF WISDOM**, THAT THEY
ARE DOUBLE TO THAT WHICH IS!"
Job 11:5,6

"NONE OF THE WICKED SHALL UNDERSTAND; BUT
THE WISE SHALL UNDERSTAND."
Daniel 12:10

Contents

List of Charts

What will we know if we watch?

"IF THEREFORE THOU SHALT NOT WATCH, I WILL COME ON THEE AS A THIEF, AND THOU SHALT NOT KNOW WHAT HOUR I WILL COME UPON THEE."
Revelation 3:3

Introduction

The "time of the end" has come.

Daniel was told to "shut up the words, and seal the book, even to the time of the end: many shall run to and fro, and knowledge shall be increased."[1] Little did we realize that this surge in knowledge would extend even to the understanding of Bible prophecy.

It is exciting to live during these final years as our age winds down for only in this particular time slot can some scriptures be understood clearly. At first, the Church saw through a glass darkly, knowing only in part. Knowledge of the meaning of prophecy gained momentum slowly over the years but is now accelerating faster for we will soon see face to face.[2]

The last 40 years before devastating judgment jars our entire planet are already more than half over. The Rapture may be only a few years away. It is imperative that we take a good fresh look at what Scripture says, because time for research and validation is getting short.

Do you have an inquiring mind? an insatiable curiosity, a need to know? Are you honestly searching for truth no matter which theories might prove to be untenable? Are you unafraid of new ideas, serenely confident in your own innate ability to separate the gold from the sand? This book is for you to whom the search for knowledge is exciting and the possibilities boundless.

Exit: 2007 is not like any other book. It is strong meat for the mature Church at the end of the Church Age. It concerns times that will soon steamroll right over us whether we are ready or not.

Since the very near future is firmly rooted in the past, *Exit: 2007* contains a wide-angle view of time from Adam to the Great White Throne Judgment plus a telephoto picture of things that will take place near the end of this age. Since these latter events are so momentous that they will shake, juggle and rearrange our whole world economy more than once, we need to be forewarned.

Along the way, many questions that have wanted answers for many years are satisfied. For instance, what are the wheels within wheels of Ezekiel, chapters 1 and 10, the flaming sword of Genesis 3:24 that was placed to the east of Eden and turned every way, and the curse of Zechariah 5?

The future of this generation has been prewritten. Specific events and clues to their precise dates are foretold in the Bible. The dates of end time events were not meant to be understood until the Sign of the End of the Age appeared and locked them into their place in time. This sign was the Six-day War between Egypt and Israel. That was the first time the newly established branch of Israel grew leaves that endured.

The new graft had to take before it could grow. At first, Israel had to fight to establish her borders. According to the fig tree parable in Matthew 24, she was to grow leaves while young. She was nineteen in 1967 when she sprouted leaves: the Gaza Strip, the Golan Heights, the West Bank and the Sinai. She ended that war with over four times the territory she had when it began. The Times of the Gentiles ended as she took possession of Jerusalem and the Temple area.

The last generation, born in 1967, will see the Sign of the Son of Man and the return of our Lord Jesus Christ. I believe this age will expire with an explosive catastrophic holocaust in 2007 as the Day of the Lord begins. This burnt sacrifice on the Feast of Trumpets was foretold long ago.

Interpreting prophecy is not always easy, but very rewarding. Although there are many types and symbols to identify, there are keys in God's Word to unlock their meanings. Scripture must be interpreted by Scripture and prophecy compared with prophecy to piece together the entire picture. All must be considered together. A thorough understanding of any one passage depends on adequate knowledge of the entire Bible. The more you know, the more you can know. "For whosoever hath, to him shall be given."[3]

My more than 30 years of intensive Bible study have made me a strong Pretribulationist. I believe the Rapture will precede the seven year Tribulation.

Biblical quotations are from the King James Version unless otherwise noted. For clarity, the first letter in a quotation is not capitalized unless capitalized in the original. Italics in the original are usually omitted so they will not be confused with the bold emphasis I have added throughout.

As you read, "Prove all things; hold fast that which is good."[4] Be sure to compare everything with the scriptures. I may make mistakes, but God never does.

M. J. Agee

Chapter 1

The Wise Shall Understand

The secret of secrets is no secret any more.

God's cleverly concealed timetable of end of the age events, including when Christ will actually return, can now be revealed. When this truth finally grabs you, the thrill racing along your skin may stand the hair up on your arms.

Why now? because the Times of the Gentiles ended when Israel took Jerusalem, and the Sign of the Age has already appeared. These make a tremendous difference. Luke 21:24 said, "Jerusalem shall be trodden down of the Gentiles, until the times of the Gentiles be fulfilled." Israel will be in distress during the last half of the seven year Tribulation, but their troubles will be brought on by the Israeli False Prophet.

At the end of the shortened Tribulation, a multi-nation army will attack from the north. However, when Israel blows the alarm on the trumpet, the Lord will fight for her with what Scripture calls the Sword of the Lord. A natural catastrophe will fell the invading army on the mountains of Israel the same day. The Lord has some unusual weapons in his armoury.

You can't hide behind Jesus' declaration during his Olivet Discourse that no one knew the day or hour of his return. That was before the Crucifixion. It applied only to that particular time. His apostles were having difficulty understanding why he had to die and were not ready for anything else. The church did not yet exist. The Revelation [*Apokalupsis*, coming, revealing, disclosure] had not yet been written.

If I say today that I do not know something, I could learn it tomorrow. My statement about not knowing would be true when stated, but would not necessarily be true forever.

Jesus' statement was true at the time, but it was not meant to stand forever. Since dates can be figured out during the Tribulation, why not now, a short time before the Rapture?

In chapter six, you will see that when Jesus said, "But of that day and hour no one knows" (NASB), **the present tense applies only to that particular time, not to some future time. Clear clues revealing the month and day of both advents were already in the Old Testament,** but not yet recognized. Those clues plus the Sign of the End of the Age lock in the year for us.

Imagine making a scale drawing on clear acetate of events from the beginning of the Tribulation to the millennial peace. Add every known restricting condition to events. Then slide it back and forth over a scale drawing of our calendar with the Jewish calendar superimposed and see where it fits. There isn't but **one place** in the near future where it will fit.

After you have your scale drawing, what would it take to lock the whole thing in place in time? One simple tie-in would suddenly drop the whole block into its proper slot.

The Sign of the End of the Age was the tie-in that bridged the gap and pegged the whole block into place. It truly was the Key of Knowledge. God's timetable is now so simple to figure out, you will wonder why it has been such a well kept secret for so long. (More about the Sign in chapter eight.)

The Last Days

Today the puzzle can finally be worked because we are near the end of two of the "last days" of Hebrews, the days that had already started when Jesus died that we might be saved. At that point, man had already passed the mid-point of Time. Over 4,000 years had gone by. Hebrews 1:2 says,

> GOD, who at sundry times and in divers man-
> ners spake in time past unto the fathers by the
> prophets, Hath in these **last days** spoken
> unto us by his Son.

Jesus' ministry lasted three and one half years, not just a few days, so these were not 24 hour days, but the great 1,000 year days Peter referred to when he said, "But, beloved, be not ignorant of this one thing, that one day is with the Lord as a thousand years, and a thousand years as one day."[1] Since "last days" is plural, there were two or more still to come. Actually, four days were past; three were to come. We are now nearing the end of the sixth millennial day.

12

The seventh is the Sabbath ("*sabbatismos*," translated "rest" in Hebrews 4:9), the 1,000 year Day of the Lord that completes the great week. The Millennium is the last day.

Order of Events

Between now and Christ's peaceful millennial kingdom, five major events will take place in this order:

(1) **The Rapture**, when Christ takes the believers to heaven to escape the coming terrible Tribulation

(2) **The beginning of the Tribulation**, the last seven years of Satan's evil reign

(3) **The beginning of the Millennium**, the 1,000 year Day of the Lord

(4) **Christ's return** to Earth as Prince of Peace, King of kings and Lord of lords

(5) **The battle of Armageddon**, which cannot take place until Christ is on Earth

Failure of the Year Day Theory

Some have tried to set dates for the Second Advent and failed. For instance, William Miller thought Christ would return in 1844. How did he go wrong?

First, he assumed that the 2,300 days of Daniel 8:14 stood for years. In verses 13 and 14, Daniel said,

How long shall be the vision concerning the daily sacrifice, and the transgression of desolation, to give both the sanctuary and the host to be trodden under foot? And he said unto me, Unto two thousand and three hundred days; then shall the sanctuary be cleansed.

These days are not years. They are the exact number of 24 hour days in the shortened Tribulation. Israel will sacrifice daily during the first half of the Tribulation. The sacrificing will stop after 1,260 days because the False Prophet will set an idol in the Temple and sit there pretending that he is God.

During the last half of the seven years, called the Great Tribulation, the days between the desecration of the Temple and the end of the age are to be shortened. Jesus said,

> For then shall be great tribulation, such as was not since the beginning of the world to this time, no, nor ever shall be. And except those days should be shortened, there should no flesh be saved: but for the elect's sake those days shall be shortened.[2]

The 2,300 day countdown begins when Israel and Rome sign a peace treaty and ends as this age expires in earthly agony.

Since William Miller thought that the 2,300 years would probably start at the same time as the Seventy Weeks of Daniel, he counted 2,300 years from B.C. 457 and came up with the Day of Atonement in 1844. None of this is correct, though B.C. 457 is not far off the mark.

Charles Russell expected the church to be Raptured before October, 1914. What was wrong with his reasoning?

In Leviticus 26:28, the Lord said, "I, even I, will chastise you seven times for your sins."

Charles Russell thought the seven times were seven years. Thus far, he was correct. Compare Revelation 12:6 with 12:14. The 1,260 days are equal to "a time, and times, and half a time," or three and one half years. The seven times represent the seven year Tribulation that is coming upon the world in the near future.

Then he converted these seven years to 2,520 days, which was still all right. A prophetic year is often counted as having 360 days like the Babylonian year. In Revelation 12, the 1,260 days equal three and one half years (360 x 3 1/2 = 1,260). In the 11th chapter, 42 months equal 1,260 days. There a month has 30 days and a year 360. It was probably a lunar calendar for there are about 29 1/2 days between new moons.

But, in his next step, Charles Russell made a big mistake. He changed these literal 2,520 days to 2,520 years. He added them to B.C. 606, when he thought Israel went into captivity in Babylon, and came up with 1914. Martin Anstey found an 82 year mistake in Ptolemy's chronology, so 606 B.C. was 82 years too early. However, thinking that seven literal years were really 2,520 years was his major error.

14

There are times when days do stand for years, as when Ezekiel bore the iniquity of Judah forty days to represent 40 years. We have to analyze Scripture very carefully to know when this applies and when the days are literal 24 hour days.

Recently, many people, including Edgar Whisenant, thought the Rapture might take place in 1988. They started counting one 40 year generation in 1948, when Israel became a nation again. They did not read the parable of the fig tree in Matthew 24:32 carefully enough. When a scion is grafted into an old rootstock, it does not immediately begin to grow. The new graft must take. Sap must begin to flow. Later, it will "put forth leaves" and grow. People like Mr. Whisenant forgot to watch for Israel's growth before starting the countdown. The Berkeley Bible is clear: "the fig tree: As soon as her branch becomes tender **and puts out leaves** . . . all this will happen before this present generation passes on."

Applied Logic

Just because some have made mistakes in trying to discern the date of the Second Advent, it does not automatically follow that the timetable presented in this book is also wrong. According to the study of logic, even if 1,000 people have been wrong so far, it does not make this wrong.

Be fair to yourself. Keep an open mind and do not prejudge. No matter what you have heard in the past, no matter what someone else says now, please read the **Biblical evidence** first, then decide what you think about it.

The time is short. You do not have many years left to figure it out. It will not take long to prove this timetable right or wrong. If it is correct, there is not much time to earn crowns and other heavenly rewards doing the King's business in preparation for the Rapture. If it is not, remember, the scriptures are true, even if our understanding is faulty.

The Time of The First Advent was Foretold

When Christ came the first time, people should have figured out from Daniel 9:24-26 when to expect him. They were to count 483 years after the commandment to rebuild Jerusalem. As explained in detail later, I agree with the outstanding and highly respected Biblical chronologist, Martin

Anstey, that the decree was given in B.C. 454. According to Jewish inclusive reckoning, where the first year is counted as number one, the 483 years ended in 29 A.D. After that, the Messiah was to "be cut off, but not for himself."

The Hebrew word *karath*, translated "cut off," is used in the Mosaic Law and means to perish or be killed. The Messiah was cut off, crucified, killed to save us from the deadly penalty of our sins. Jesus' death as our Passover sacrifice was "not for himself" but as a substitute for us. According to Isaiah 53:3-6 in the Old Testament,

> He is despised and rejected of men, a man of sorrows . . . he hath borne our griefs, and carried our sorrows: yet we did esteem him stricken, smitten of God, and afflicted. But **he was wounded for our transgressions**, he was bruised for our iniquities: the chastisement of our peace was upon him; and **with his stripes we are healed**. All we like sheep have gone astray; we have turned every one to his own way; and **the LORD hath laid on him the iniquity of us all**.

In all of history, this is the only thing that has ever happened that gives us any chance at all. Without him, and without his perfect sacrifice, we are totally lost, hurtling downward on a slick slide, unable to catch on to anything to stop being dumped in a fiery hell prepared for Satan and his wicked angels, called demons.

Daniel 9:26 also shows that the Messiah had to come before Jerusalem and the Temple were destroyed by the Romans in 70 A.D. **If Jesus was not the Messiah, there will be none**. Since the Temple genealogical records were burned, no one today except Jesus could prove his decent from king David. The genealogy of Jesus has been preserved in the Bible. No matter how long we wait, **no one else can ever qualify**. The Jewish people still waiting for a messiah should consider that fact.

In spite of having Daniel's prophecy, most neither discerned the time nor recognized that *Y'shua* (Joshua in Hebrew, Jesus in Greek) was the Messiah. Therefore, he scolded, "Ye hypocrites, ye can discern the face of the sky and of the earth; but **how is it that ye do not discern this time?**"[3]

Jesus told them the temple would be destroyed "because thou knewest not the time of thy visitation," Luke 19:44.

It is now our turn at bat. Will we also strike out? We are in the same position. There are enough clues in Scripture to figure out when he will come the second time. (If he's to return, he had to be resurrected. Return proves resurrection.) Will we do any better than they did? Or will he scathingly say, **"How is it that ye do not discern this time?"**

The Wise Shall Understand

Daniel recorded many time clues, but they were sealed until the **time of the end**, these days in which we are now living. Yet, even in the book of Daniel, the Lord told us that

> none of the wicked shall understand; but **the wise shall understand.**[4]

We are living in "the time of the end." Today our depth of perception is speedily being increased under the tutorage of our omnipotent God. The time is right. The blinding scales are dropping from our eyes so we can find and interpret the time clues hidden among the leaves of Scripture.

The Key to Understanding

All along, we were supposed to watch for new developments. Remember when Jesus admonished Peter, James, John, and Andrew to watch? He also said, "And what I say unto you **I say unto all, Watch**."[5] It must be important. Scripture records that he said, "Watch," 23 times.

Watching was essential. Why? because it was the key that would unlock God's secrets. It was so supremely important that Jesus warned the church, saying,

> If therefore thou shalt not watch, I will come on thee as a thief, and thou shalt not know what hour I will come upon thee.[6]

What an astonishing statement. Do you realize what it implies? Reread it and think about it. A secret is hidden there.

If we do not watch, we will not know when Christ will come upon us. But, what will we know if we do watch?

Startling, isn't it? Inherent in Jesus' declaration is the reverse, that **if we do watch, we will know when he will come** upon us. Doesn't that give you a thrill?

This is so plain, it is incredible that we missed it for so long. It is like a trick question on an exam. You have to examine it closely or you will not fully understand everything it says. If you scan it fast, you could miss its hidden message time after time after time.

This means that **we can know ahead of time exactly when the Rapture will occur**, when

> the Lord himself shall descend from heaven
> with a shout, with the voice of the archangel,
> and with the trump of God: and the dead in
> Christ shall rise first: Then we which are alive
> and remain shall be **caught up** together with
> them in the clouds, to meet the Lord in the air:
> and so shall we ever be with the Lord.[7]

The word for "caught up" in my Latin translation is *rapiemur*. Our English word Rapture, used to describe the departing, is derived from *rapiemur*.

Rapture is a perfect word for the occasion. We will be ecstatic with joy when we are gathered up to be with the great God and our Saviour Jesus Christ forever, when the expected "blessed hope"[8] becomes reality and we don't have to die.

Don't have to die! Now that's exciting. That's a little more personal. Those believers who please God will be translated before the Tribulation judgment just as Enoch was taken to heaven before the Flood.

> By faith **Enoch was translated that he
> should not see death**; and was not found,
> because God had translated him: for before his
> translation he had this testimony, that he
> pleased God.[9]

Enoch was a gentile type of the church, the *ecclesia*, or called out ones. As he was kept from the Flood Judgment, those **who please God** will be kept from the Tribulation.

According to scripture, there are three groups of mankind, gentiles, Jews and the church.[10] Anyone who accepts Jesus Christ as their own personal Saviour is a member of the church. Within the church are both gentile Christians and Jewish or Hebrew Christians.

Milk or Meat

Before the Sign of the End of the Age appeared, I assumed that neither the date of the Rapture, when Christ comes for his church and meets them in the air, nor the date of the Second Advent, when he returns with his church to literally walk on the Earth the second time, could be known before the Rapture took place. This was a false assumption based on the fact that the early church did not know.

However, the infant church was never meant to fully understand the times and seasons. When young, it was fed milk, the "first principles of the oracles of God."[11] Only after some time had elapsed, could it be fed meat.

Paul said that the "strong meat belongeth to them that are of full age."[12] That is the church of today, 1,961 years old.

Isaiah asked, "Whom shall he teach knowledge? and whom shall he make to understand doctrine?" and answered, "Them that are weaned from the milk, and drawn from the breasts."[13] Now snowy-headed with age, the church can assimilate strong meat.

What is the strong meat? Have you ever wondered about that? It must be something that was not known in the early days after the Crucifixion, but nourishment intended for the church of our days.

Since **nothing can be added to the Bible**, it must be new light shed on existing scriptures. In this time of the end, God is teaching us knowledge and making us understand doctrine. Be alert. Open your heart and mind and let him show you. If you pray sincerely and ask for his help, he will open the eyes of your understanding.

The last thing Jesus told the apostles before he ascended to heaven was,

It is not for you to know the times or the seasons, which the Father hath put in his own power. **But ye shall receive power**, after

that the Holy Ghost is come upon you: and ye
shall be witnesses unto me both in Jerusalem,
and in all Judaea . . . and unto the uttermost
part of the earth. And when he had spoken
these things . . . he was taken up.[14]

The Holy Spirit came upon the church on Pentecost ten
days after this discussion. The situation is different today.
The church is mature, the generation that will see the return of
the Lord has already been born, and the wise have the power
to understand because of the indwelling Holy Spirit. It is now
time for the church to receive **"their portion of meat in
due season."**[15] The Sign of the End of the Age heralded the
beginning of the "due season" in which the church is to receive
her strong meat."To every thing there is a season, and a time
to every purpose under the heaven."[16]

John 16:13 says that when "the Spirit of truth, is
come, he will guide you into all truth . . . and **he will shew
you things to come**." You can know what is coming.

The Last Hour

John, the beloved apostle, wrote a letter bridging the
chasm of time. In it he addressed today's generation, saying,

Little children, **it is the last hour**.[17]

Peter said that "one day is with the Lord as a thousand
years, and a thousand years as one day,"[18] so an hour of a
thousand year day of heaven[19] is 41 2/3 years.

I believe John was referring to the last generation who
will see the return of Christ before the 41 2/3 years following
the Sign of the End of the Age are over.

These latter years are exciting if you are a Christian
looking forward to the Rapture. I believe it is only a few years
away. Continuing his message to us, John said,

But ye have an unction [anointing] from the
Holy One, and **ye know all things**. . . . But
the anointing which ye have received of Him
abideth in you, and ye need not that any man
teach you: but . . . the same anointing teacheth

you of **all things,** and is truth, and is no lie.[20]

The Holy Spirit is now teaching this generation the latent meaning of certain scriptures. Though not understood in other ages, the necessary clues to reveal the mysteries of God's timetable to this elite group were planted in the Bible long ago. They were just easy to overlook until God was ready for us to find them.

All Things are Foretold

No wonder the Lord said, "But take ye heed: behold, **I have foretold you all things.**"[21] He actually meant "**all**" things. Not one clue is missing. If you want to know when an important event will occur, start looking for clues.

Thanks to my previous intensive Bible study and the Lord's help, I have not only been able to find enough clues to sketch God's blueprint of time, from Adam to the Great White Throne Judgment, but to date the main events precisely.

The prophets who dutifully recorded the time clues did not necessarily understand them. But, they

> prophesied of the **grace that should come to you: searching what, or what manner of TIME the Spirit of Christ which was in them did signify** [make plain by words], when it testified beforehand the sufferings of Christ [the First Advent, when he was crucified], and the glory [the Second Advent, when he comes in glory] that should follow. Unto whom it was revealed, that not unto themselves, but **unto us** they did minister the things which are now reported unto you.[22]

This anointing of the Holy Spirit will help you in your search for these time clues in the scriptures. The exact month and day of both Advents were indicated by the prophets. These are plain enough once you understand, but couched in terms that make them easy to miss. After you find them, you will wonder how they could have remained such a mystery for so long. Only God could have blinded us to their significance over such an extended period of time. He prevented our understanding until the time of the end began. Now it is easy.

21

Clear or Obscure

Some things in the Bible are so clear that anyone can understand them easily. Others are so obscure that the indwelling Holy Spirit must teach us their full meaning.

For instance, when Paul and Silas were asked by the Philippian jailer, "Sirs, what must I do to be saved?", the answer was an excellent example of clarity. They replied,

Believe on the Lord Jesus Christ, and thou shalt be saved, and thy house.[23]

Paul expanded this a bit in his letter to the Romans, making the way of salvation explicit. He said,

If thou shalt confess with thy mouth the Lord Jesus, and shalt believe in thine heart that God hath raised him from the dead, thou shalt be saved. For with the heart man believeth unto righteousness; and with the mouth confession is made unto salvation.[24]

Although the way of salvation is clear, times and seasons are not. The various time clues are scattered throughout the pages of the Bible like unmined silver is dispersed through the rock in irregular clumps and broken veins, but like small slivers of silver, they are precious, hard to find, but worth the effort. God, mastermind that he is, deftly wove the clues into passages where they would not be noticed until he was ready to give us new eyes to see with.

Scripture says, "The words of the LORD are pure words: as silver tried in a furnace of earth, purified seven times."[25] We have to find the pure silver before we can figure out God's timetable.

Do you know why he made his timing so hard to figure out? Before you suspect him of purposefully trying to confuse us, let Isaiah explain to you why the good Lord did not make everything in the scriptures as clear as possible.

Isaiah explained to those that would not hear that

the word of the LORD was unto them precept upon precept, precept upon precept; line upon

line, line upon line; **here a little, and there
a little**; that they might go, and fall backward,
and be broken, and snared, and taken.[26]

God has a purpose for everything he does. Believers
are judged for rewards, and those who do not believe must be
judged for their unbelief and awarded what they deserve.

Prerequisites

Without the Holy Spirit, much of the Bible would
seem like so much nonsense, because the "natural man
receiveth not the things of the Spirit of God for they are
foolishness unto him: neither can he know them, because they
are spiritually discerned."[27]

Unless you believe in Christ, and therefore have the
indwelling Holy Spirit, you may not understand enough to
know whether the timetable presented here is correct or not.
So, if you have never asked Jesus Christ (*Y'shua Mashiyach*
to the Hebrews) to be your own personal Saviour, you owe it
to yourself to do so right now.

Pray. Tell him you believe in him and accept him as
your personal Saviour. That is all you have to do. It is so
simple. Salvation is a free gift. It is offered to you without
your having to do anything to earn it, but you do have to
accept it for it to apply to you.

If you truly believe in him, your past sins, including
the deadly sin of unbelief, will be forgiven. Then, when you
are clean and perfect in God's sight, his Spirit will flow in,
filling your inner being with his tremendous love, joy, and
peace. It only takes an instant to be born into God's family.

Your capacity for comprehending spiritual things will
then increase. The Lord said,

Turn you at my reproof: behold, I will pour out
my spirit unto you, I will make known my
words unto you.[28]

Formula for Finding Hidden Treasure

Do you truly want to understand? Finding answers to
your questions involves praying and searching the scriptures.

Digging the answers out is work. Are you willing? Solomon, the wisest of men, gave us the formula to follow for success. He declared,

> Yea, if thou criest after knowledge, and liftest up thy voice for understanding; If thou seekest her as silver, and searchest for her as for **hid treasures**; Then shalt thou understand the fear of the Lord, and find the knowledge of God.[29]

Prayer works. After seven years of constantly reading man's books about the Bible, I almost despaired of ever learning what some difficult passages in Scripture meant.

For instance, in Ezekiel 1 and 10, **cherubim** and **wheels within wheels** are mentioned. What are they? What is the **flaming sword** that God placed to the east of Eden that we read about in Genesis 3:24? What is "**the curse that goeth forth over the face of the whole earth**" described in Zechariah 5:3? What is **the whirlwind** that we are to understand all about in these "latter days" in which we are now living? Is this knowledge part of our strong meat? Jeremiah said,

> Behold, a whirlwind of the LORD is gone forth in fury, even a **grievous whirlwind**: it shall fall grievously upon the head of the wicked. The anger of the LORD shall not return, until he have executed, and till he have performed the thoughts of his heart: **in the latter days ye shall consider it perfectly.**[30]

I know now what these things are, but I did not know then. Even in seven years of searching among the wealth of books in the library at the Bible Institute of Los Angeles, I could find no authors who explained these to my satisfaction.

A dilemma; what to do?

Not being one to give up easily, in desperation I opened my Bible, laid my hands on it and prayed. I said, "Lord! you'll have to show me what it means! I want to know all the deep things, everything you intend man to understand in the Bible, everything!"

From that time on, I began to be able to work through the more difficult problems and find a solution. Understanding and knowledge tumbled in on each other's heels. It has now been at least 31 years since I began to study the scriptures in earnest, and I am still learning.

The Lord has honored my prayer far beyond anything I had ever dreamed or even dared hope for. As much as I had already studied, I still had no idea how much information was packed in that one small book. It was as if he was waiting for me to ask before really pouring it on.

When you pray for understanding and wisdom, ask in unswerving faith, leaving no room for the slightest flicker of doubt. James, half-brother of Jesus, said,

> If any of you lack wisdom, let him ask of God,
> that giveth to all men liberally, and upbraideth
> not; and it shall be given him. But let him ask
> in faith, nothing wavering. For he that wa-
> vereth is like a wave of the sea driven with the
> wind and tossed. For let not that man think that
> he shall receive any thing of the Lord.[31]

After praying, patiently embark on your great treasure hunt. Like a prospecting miner, examine each piece of scripture as carefully as you would silver ore. You have to look closely for the narrow twisting ribbon of silver before you can hope to find it. Try to look at each verse as if you had never seen it before. Remain alert to the possibility that there may be more meaning there than is apparent at the first quick glance. Compare Scripture with Scripture diligently.

Only God, who had his complete timetable in mind, could have planted the clues to time in the various books of Scripture in such a way that they would not be recognized too soon or too late. The prophets did not understand all that they wrote. The Bible contains a great number of hidden treasures for those of us in this time of the end who will search with an open mind. Proverbs 2:7 makes this clear:

> He layeth up [*tsaphan*, hides] sound wis-
> dom for the righteous.

Types and Similitudes

There are many types and similitudes, shadows of what is to come. They help us understand prophecy. Job said,

For enquire . . . of the former age, and prepare
thyself to the search of their fathers: (For we
are but of yesterday, and know nothing, because **our days upon earth are a shadow:**) Shall not **they teach thee**, and tell
thee, and utter words out of their heart.[32]

Therefore, Job 11:5, 6 is a real eye opener.

But oh that God would speak and . . . shew
thee **the secrets of wisdom**, that they **are
double to that which is!**

The secrets of wisdom are double to that which is.
What does that mean? The Hebrew *kephel*, translated
"double," means to repeat or duplicate. The secrets of wisdom
are duplicates of history. No wonder people say that history
repeats itself. Some of it certainly does, and not by accident. It
is all part of God's plan.

Suddenly, that dry old history in the Bible becomes
vitally interesting when we realize that it was recorded to help
us understand Biblical prophecy. Some prophecies in the Old
Testament also had a double application, one to a near event
and the other to a similar event at the end of this age, which
will be almost a carbon copy of a portion of history.
Sometimes the latter fulfillment is greater than its preview.

The seven feasts God ordained and a few other things
were portents of impending prophesied events. You can tell
that Paul understood this. He knew that the seven Feasts, the
new moon (important end time events will happen on the new
moon) and the sabbaths were all foreshadows. He told the
Colossians,

Let no man therefore judge you in meat, or in
drink, or in respect of an holyday [the feasts],
or of the new moon, or of the sabbath days:
which are a **shadow of things to come.**[33]

Watch One Hour

Do not let Jesus,' "But of that day and hour knoweth
no man"[34] blind you now that the time of the end has begun.

26

That was **the Lord's delay switch** to keep us from searching for time clues too soon. It referred to the time before **the Holy Spirit descended and filled the disciples on Pentecost, giving the church the power to understand, but not the insight.**

Do pay attention to Jesus', "Watch therefore, for ye know neither the day nor the hour wherein the Son of man cometh."[35] **Why were we to watch if we could not find out the day and hour by watching?** If it was impossible to know, what difference would it make if we watched or not?

Mark 13:35-37 hints that **if we watch, we can know when to expect Christ.** "Watch ye therefore: for ye know not when the master of the house cometh . . . Lest coming suddenly [*exaiphne*s, **unexpectedly**] he find you sleeping. And what I say unto you I say unto all, Watch."

For me, watching made the difference between knowing and not knowing. Soon after the Sign of the End of the Age appeared, things just fell into place, and I understood God's Timetable of End Time Events. God's whole Plan of the Ages seems so simple and logical after you understand it.

We were to watch very carefully during these "latter days," this last 41 2/3 years. Don't let the Lord come and find you sleeping as he found the disciples slumbering. Jesus said to Peter,

What, could ye not watch with me one hour?[36]

Why one hour? because we are to watch one hour of a 1,000 year day. Like many other things in history, this little dramatization not only applied then, but is also a shadow of things to come and has another application at the end of this age.

This adds a new dimension to the responsibility to watch that already rests on our shoulders. The general command, "Watch," is focused down to the final "**watch with me one hour.**" One hour is roughly equivalent to one generation. It is important to watch during this last generation.

Many Scriptures Especially Written for Us

It's easy to see that many things in Israel's history were meant to apply to us when we read I Corinthians 10:11:

Now all these things happened unto them for ensamples [examples]: and **they are written for our admonition** [warning], upon whom the ends of the world [*aionon*, ages] are come.

The scriptures were penned for all mankind, but much of the Bible was especially written for us because we are facing events that men of other ages have not had to face. Never again will the scriptures be needed like they are needed now as we approach the dreadful end of this age. We need to know what is coming, when it will take place, and how to avoid it. We need to make some sound plans.

Because many scriptures were especially written for us, the whole Bible can be brought to bear on end of the age events. Not everything has an end of the age application, but so much more does than is generally realized that we should search with this in mind.

Jesus continued to Peter, "Watch and pray, that ye enter not into temptation."[37] Try applying this to us. We are to watch and pray that we do not enter into the temptation that we call the Tribulation, seven years during which the Beast and False Prophet rule, a time of an especially difficult temptation. Satan has planned a neat little **trap** for people during that time and he is busy herding them into it.

During those years, men will have to take the Mark of the Beast or be denied the privilege of buying or selling anything. And if they do break down and take "the mark, or the name of the beast, or the number of his name,"[38] they will have no more chance at all to avoid the wrath of God. It will be an exceptionally hard decision to make. Scripture says,

If any man worship the beast [the Satanic False Prophet] and his image, and receive his mark in his forehead, or in his hand, The same shall drink of the wine of the wrath of God . . . he shall be tormented with fire and brimstone in the presence of the holy angels, and in the presence of the Lamb: And the smoke of their torment ascendeth up for ever and ever: and they have no rest day nor night, who worship the beast and his image, and whosoever receiveth the mark of his name.[39]

We have said in the Lord's prayer "lead us not into temptation, but deliver us from evil." This too could have a special application at the end of this age.

Can't it also mean that we are asking not to be led into the Tribulation with its great temptation, but to be delivered from its evil by being taken to heaven in the Rapture that precedes it?

The Secret Shall be Revealed

Surely, the Lord GOD will do **nothing**, but **he revealeth his secret** unto his servants the prophets.[40]

All clues to help us understand his secret were written into the existing scriptures. God has set a precedent before by warning the world of coming judgments. He told Noah of the flood that would come. He knew exactly when it would happen, for in Genesis 6:3 the Lord said, "My spirit shall not always strive with man . . . yet his days shall be an hundred and twenty years."

The Lord warned Abraham and Lot that Sodom and Gomorrah would be destroyed. He told Joseph there would be a seven year famine, Moses of the plagues that would destroy Egypt, Jonah that Nineveh would be destroyed, and Amos of the destruction not only of Tyre but of several other nations.

God is fair, just and consistent. Therefore, he is helping us understand the nature of the judgment that is coming at the end of this age and when it will take place.

Since the **time of the end** began, all can be known, even when Christ will return. You can safely believe, trust in, and rely on the carefully chosen words of our Lord. After all, "God was in Christ, reconciling the world unto himself."[41]

Take Heed Therefore How Ye Hear

In Luke 8:17,18, Jesus said,

For **nothing is secret, that shall not be made manifest**; neither any thing hid, that shall not be known and come abroad. Take heed therefore how ye hear.

29

In 12:2, he said, "For there is **nothing** covered, that shall not be revealed; neither hid, that shall not be known."

He kept saying this. Matthew 10:26 says, "Fear them not therefore: for there is **nothing covered, that shall not be revealed**; and hid, that shall not be known." He repeated it over and over because it is very important. In the parable of the candle in Mark 4:22, it was revealed that **these things that are to be brought to light should be told**, not kept to oneself:

> And he said unto them, Is a candle brought to be put under a bushel, or under a bed? and not to be set on a candlestick? For there is **nothing** hid, which shall not be manifested; neither was any thing kept secret, but that it should come abroad. **If any man have ears to hear, let him hear** . . . Take heed what ye hear; with what measure you mete, it shall be measured to you: and unto you that hear shall more be given. For he that hath, to him shall be given: and he that hath not, from him shall be taken even that which he hath.

The Hidden is Brought to Light

It is exciting to realize that there is no secret that can remain secret, nothing hidden that can remain hidden. All is meant to be revealed at the proper time, and that time is the present. During this last hour, "**the thing that is hid bringeth he forth to light**."[42]

Solomon, the wisest of men, told us, "**A wise man's heart discerneth both time and judgment**."[43] Here are two things we can figure out.

It is important to search carefully and thoughtfully to find out exactly what he meant by "**time**" and "**judgment**." When we comprehend the meaning of these, other pieces of our puzzle will fall into place easily.

Do you class yourself among the wise? The wise virgins are the Bride of Christ that are going in the Rapture. If we are the wise, we must understand before the Rapture takes place. We won't be here after the Tribulation begins. The wise shall understand, and a wise man's heart discerneth **time**.

Chapter 2

A Pacific Moon?

The future is like a tree firmly rooted in the past.

To thoroughly understand the top growth, we must also examine the rest of the tree. A study of the roots enables us to date God's timetable from the creation of Adam.

By extrapolating both ours and the Jewish calendar back to the first day of Adam, we find that he was probably created on Elul 29 (Friday, September 18, B.C. 4043). Thus, the Lord rested on the Sabbath, Tishri 1 (Saturday, September 19), the Jewish New Year and the Feast of Trumpets.

The opening verses of the Bible begin with the original creation of this Earth, not with the creation of Adam. Our omnipotent God created this blue and white orb our astronauts called the prettiest thing in space, and it is older than mankind.

"By the word of the LORD were the heavens made; and all the host of them by the breath of his mouth. . . . he spake, and it was done; he commanded, and it stood fast."[1] In awe, David said, "When I consider thy heavens, the work of thy fingers, the moon and the stars, which thou hast ordained; What is man, that thou art mindful of him?"[2]

Before Adam, the Earth was inhabited by strange animals that wandered at will through lush vegetation. It was not a desolate waste for Scripture says that God "created it not in vain [tohu, waste], he formed it to be inhabited."[3]

Among smaller species roamed animals of extraordinary size: dire wolves, dirk-toothed cats, camels, deer, ground sloths, sabre-toothed tigers, etruscan rhinos, imperial elephants, mastodons, woolly mammoths, and dinosaurs.

Sudden Death

Quickly, death grabbed that world with icy fingers. Earth became an uninhabited waste, a dark-shrouded whirling ball zipped up tight in an overcoat of frost, snow and ice.

31

The Earth "was [*hajah*, had become] without form [*tohu*, waste] and void [*bohu*, empty]; and darkness [from dust/smoke/water] was upon the face of the deep" (Gen. 1:2).

No fact in geologic history is so startling as the abrupt extermination of earth's inhabitants. There are cuttlefish that were overcome so quickly they did not release their ink, bivalves that did not have time to close their shells, sharks that were obviously swimming at burial, fish that could not have been dead when closely packed in burial for they are curled with spread fins as if drawn up in horror. Predators and their prey, young and old alike, were destroyed, quickly stratified in layers of mud or gravel and covered with ice, snow or frost. Sea creatures are found with land animals. Some bones were broken by the dashing by which they were deposited. All were buried by the same paroxysmal cataclysm that killed them.

Everywhere, Earth shows evidence of that catastrophe. Broken strata of continental and oceanic crust dumped on Alaska and along the western edges of Canada, United States, Mexico and South America where it did not originate, great bedrock faults, shatter cones, shocked quartz, glassy microspherules scattered over the entire Earth, extreme volcanism, ruffled mountains, deep water-cut canyons, interbedded sandstone, siltstone, shale, coal and clay, large bone cemeteries, shells on all land masses that are products of distant seas, and fossil trees extending up through multiple stratified layers laid down quickly by moving water, all bear mute testimony to the effects of a terrible cataclysm.

Siberian mammoths were frozen so quickly that some are standing or kneeling, with grass, sedge, and buttercups still in their mouths, their flesh fresh enough for dogs to eat. The temperature necessary to prevent decomposition in the center or crystals in their flesh would have had to be more than 150° below zero. That this intense cold was accompanied by other forces of a catastrophic nature is proved by the presence in hard hit Alaska of mammoths that were literally torn in pieces while fresh and immediately frozen. Professor Brandt of Berlin Academy examined their skin microscopically and found evidence from red blood corpuscles in the skin that they died from suffocation, either by water or gas.

Earth's axis shifted abruptly during the catastrophe. When fluid rock, lava or water borne sediment, is deposited, microscopic magnetized iron oxide particles align themselves toward north. These tiny compass needles recorded the shift.

A Pacific Moon?

Extensive ash beds indicate a violent explosion in one area of the Earth during geologic history. False bottom soundings in our Pacific Ocean were found by Lamont Geological Observatory to be caused by ash beds covering 472,500 square miles. The ashes are mainly curved and crumpled glass that would have settled slowly. Their presence suggests volcanic action on a scale beyond our knowledge.

There are other strange facts about that area. The crust is much thinner than anywhere else, especially around French Polynesia. The crust is 2-6 km at the East Pacific Rise and 7-13 at the Mid-Atlantic Ridge. The Pacific has the deepest trenches on Earth; the Mariana is 336,198 feet deep. There are rock chimneys from which hot jets emerge. Gigantic fractures run north-south in the South Pacific and east-west in the north. Hot spots in the North Pacific are moving north as a group. Those in the South Pacific are moving south. Crust is moving north about 5.3 centimeters a year along the oceanic East Pacific Rise, taking with it Baja California and all land west of the San Andreas Fault up to Point Arena, California.

The seismic activity around the edges is unusual. The faults rimming the Pacific Basin slip and shake regularly as if orchestrated by an unseen hand. The Ring of Fire, called the circum-Pacific belt by seismologists, gets 80% of all earthquakes and 75% of Earth's 600 active volcanoes.

The continents are inexorably inching away from the Mid-Atlantic rift valley and moving toward the Pacific basin, shuffling along at about 17 millimeters a year. South America is slowly swinging its tail toward the Pacific.

A large asteroid probably dashed in at an oblique angle, exploded on both land and sea in the Pacific area in prehistoric times and caused a portion of earth's crust to reach escape velocity of 7 1/2 miles per second and become our moon. The moon rotates at the same rate as the Earth and is still moving away from us about an inch a year.

Apollo 11 brought back the first lunar soil and basaltic rocks from a maria on July 24, 1969. Apollo 12, 14, 15, 16 and 17 also brought back rocks. Earth and moon rocks are not totally different as had been thought. Chemical breakdown shows the similarity. The ingredients are the same; the proportions vary. None have organic matter or show signs of life, but all elements necessary for life were identified in them.

All moon rocks are considered igneous (relating to or resulting from fire), with the easily vaporized elements sodium, potassium, lead and rubidium relatively depleted. Found almost everywhere except the basaltic marias are loosely formed breccias made up of **shattered pieces** of other rocks.

There is evidence of pronounced shock and large amounts of different kinds of rare gas. The greatest surprise was the presence of abundant **glass beads** in the soil and rocks. They are small with many forms, colors, and chemical properties. There are both spherical and angular shapes and lustrous brown, yellow and clear colors. Vaporized rock could have condensed into these beads.[4] Were they formed at the same time as the glassy microspherules we find sprinkled all across the Earth and the glass ash in our Pacific Basin?

I believe an asteroid hit the Earth, exploded the moon material off into space, and caused the extinction of earth's inhabitants when the tons and tons of water, vaporized rock, and dust ejected into the atmosphere shut out the light.

After the Berkeley, California, "Origin of the Earth" meeting sponsored by the Lunar and Planetary Institute in December, Richard A. Kerr's article, "Making the Moon, Remaking Earth," was published in *Science* March 17, 1989. He wrote, "**It now seems likely that the impact of a Mars-size object somehow formed the moon.**" He said that a giant off-center impact could knock Earth into its 23° axial tilt, account for the angular momentum of both its rotation and the moon's orbit and explain the nickel/cobalt ratio of Earth's upper mantle. Alternative explanations, fission, capture and coaccretion, all fail. Giant impact in our solar system could account for the planets not orbiting in perfect circles in exactly the same plane. John Jones, Johnson Space Center, found giant impact "a very attractive hypotheses" of our moon's formation. Geochemist Jeffrey Taylor, University of New Mexico, saw it as the leading contender.

Since the volume of shattered rock excavated is 60 to several hundred times that of the impact body and there would also have been explosive volcanism, enormous steam force and change in the magnetic field, I think the impacting body was smaller than Mars. Our rocks don't reveal that much heat.

Luis Alvarez, professor of physics who won the Nobel Prize in physics in 1968 (now deceased), and his son, Walter Alvarez, professor of geology, both of University of California at Berkeley, examined sediment layers from Gubbio,

Italy. They found that half an inch of red clay, laid down between a layer of Cretaceous limestone with fossils and a layer of Tertiary limestone with no fossils, contained **30 times as much iridium** as normal rock. There are only a few sources of high concentrations of this rare element, in the earth's core, or in extraterrestrial objects such as asteroids.

They decided that an **asteroid** about 10 kilometers wide and traveling 25 kilometers per second must have hit Earth and kicked so much dust up into the stratosphere that **night lasted several years. The darkness suppressed photosynthesis, collapsing food chains.** Dramatic mass extinctions, including dinosaurs, occurred at the Cretaceous-Tertiary boundary, which they date at 65 million years ago. The foraminifera and nannoplankton extinction took place in a geomagnetic reversed polarity zone.

Corroborating samples of iridium from sites in Denmark and New Zealand seemed like overwhelming evidence. The two Alvarez's, F. Asaro and H. V. Michel published "Extraterrestrial Cause for the Cretaceous-Tertiary Extinction" in *Science*, June 6, 1980.[5]

In "The End of the Cretaceous: Sharp Boundary or Gradual Transition?" in *Science*, March 16, 1984, the Alvarez group reported that they found the iridium anomaly in Montana within the **reversed-polarity interval when the dinosaurs became extinct.** They added that extinction did not have to be instantaneous in all groups everywhere.

Iridium highs have been found on land and sea worldwide in at least **100 locations,** concrete proof of catastrophe.

James S. Trefil, in *Space Time Infinity*, his 1985 Smithsonian Institution book, said that the last extinction of earth's inhabitants took place 11,000 years ago. He described the Alvarez study and said, **"It is hard to argue against the reality of the asteroid impact."**[6]

On July 1, 1988, the Orange County Register ran an article with this attention getting headline and first paragraph:

Huge asteroid hit the Pacific eons ago, UCLA study says.
An asteroid measuring more than a quarter-mile across smashed into the South Pacific with a force of 12 billion tons of TNT about 2.3 million years ago and might have contributed to the cooling in the Earth's last glacial age.

Frank T. Kyte, one of the three man team investigating it, said the asteroid's size could have been larger. They calculated its size by studying six Pacific Ocean cores. This only confirms minimum size. Some samples are unmelted asteroid material laced with salt.

Traveling about 12,000 mph., **the asteroid**, Kyte indicated, **hit the ocean southwest of South America** with the force of 12 billion tons of TNT, spraying into the upper stratosphere billions of tons of water and vaporized asteroid as the velocity and energy of the mass were converted into an instant explosion that makes the Hiroshima atomic bomb (a mere force of 20,000 tons of TNT) seem like a toy.

He speculated that this water and vaporized material could have reflected sunlight away from the Earth, causing a rapid decrease in temperature. Glaciation, he thought, started in the Northern Hemisphere about the same time the asteroid hit and continued until about 10,000 years ago.[7]

Radiocarbon formation is increasing faster than it's decay. Calculating C-14 back to zero gives a 10,000 year age for the atmosphere. Dr. Thomas G. Barnes, professor of physics at University of Texas, says that based on magnetic decay, 10,000 years is the outside limit for earth's age.[8]

It was a shock to discover that Earth's magnetic field is decreasing so rapidly (backed by over 140 years of record keeping). Extrapolating the decay backward, the magnetic field would have been 142 times what it is today only 10,000 years ago. **After 21,000 years, it could have been enough to blow Earth apart.**[9]

It is not easy to calculate the real age of the Earth for the catastrophe may have reset the clocks. Whatever Earth's age, it seems that we did have a great asteroid impact, an Ice Age and mass extinction. Do we have a Pacific Moon?

If the moon was explosively expelled from the Earth by asteroid impact, the quick change in balance would have hauled the seas from their beds and dashed them in disorderly patterns back and forth across the face of the Earth until the dynamic equilibrium had become established and the globe had settled on its new axis. Gigantic tides would have deposited layer upon layer of mud and gravel as it rocked, burying creatures and plants helter-skelter in the confused strata of the Earth, forming fossil bearing layers quickly instead of slowly. This is exactly what we find as we examine our planet. There are large deposits of disjointed skeletons of many species all jumbled together plus laminated layers of rock and fossils.

Characteristic of all coal fields, we find alternating beds of coal, shale and sandstone. Petroleum is found in sedimentary layers of rock. All life forms found in Dominican amber are extinct. This amber was originally the resin of certain types of trees in which small life forms, such as insects and frogs, were trapped and preserved intact for us. In mine tunnels, miners follow amber rich veins of lignite coal in sandstone or limestone deposits, exactly the kind of stratified and fossilized deposits we would expect to find if watery debris dashed madly to and fro across the face of the Earth.[10]

Both the shift of Earth's axis and the sudden plunge in temperature could have been brought about by the forces unleashed by the removal of a section of crust. Western North America was shoved northward. Alaska took the brunt of it.

Nearly three fourths of the earth's surface is water. If the land were smooth, it would be drowned in a sea two miles deep. Without considering the rocking motion, can you imagine the cutting force of this much water if a portion of crust was gouged out? Water would pour into the cavity so rapidly that canyons like our Grand Canyon could have been eroded in a very short time, effectively aging Earth quickly.

The first water cascading into the basin and hitting the exposed superheated magma would instantly flash into steam. Steam, gas, ash, vaporized rock and debris would hiss forth as from a planetary volcanic steam turbine. The initial heat of the blast would sterilize some of the surface of the Earth.

As the Earth rotated, the vaporized rock, water, dust, and smoke clouds would have spread in a wide belt around it, shutting out both light and heat. As temperatures plummeted, steam in the lower atmosphere would soon blanket the Earth with frost, freezing sleet, hail and snow. Between the shutting out of the warmth of the sun, the dashing overflowing seas, and the descending frost, sleet, snow, and ice, the Earth would quickly become an icy ball whirling along in darkness. Sooner or later, all life, except that found in some seeds, roots and spores, would be exterminated by the initial heat sterilization, volcanic blast, extremely poisonous gas, mud, water, tidal waves, impact debris, freezing, starvation, or darkness. Almost all life ultimately depends on photosynthesis.

In 1883, Krakatoa's mighty blasts shot out a dense volcanic cloud 17 miles high, blocking out so much sunlight that the world temperature dropped 13 degrees that year. This is a miniature picture of what happened if the moon was swiftly shucked out of the Earth by an asteroid impact.

Did it actually happen? There was a catastrophe. The magnetic poles did flip-flop. Iridium, microtectites, shocked quartz, sanidine, stishovite (formed only by impact) and soon were deposited. Coal, petroleum and fossils were formed.

It would explain why lunar rocks are magnetized when there is no source of magnetism on the moon, why sea-levels fell dramatically, why pillow lava formed in the ocean ended up on top of the ground in Wyoming, why limestone at Laytonville, California was originally formed at 17° SOUTH latitude, why Peruvian rock is found in Baja California, why the Earth cracked at the East Pacific Rise and why California has many earthquakes. The Earth did become dark, desolate and empty, and the Lord did break up a place for the sea.

> Who shut up the sea with doors when it brake
> forth, as if it had issued out of the womb?
> When I made the cloud the garment thereof,
> and thick darkness a swaddlingband for it, And
> **brake up for it my decreed place** (Job
> 38:8-10).

Dating the Catastrophe

Radiocarbon dating may or may not give us a clue to when this catastrophe took place. The mammoths test out more than 10,000 years old. In Two Creeks, Wisconsin, a fossil forest was found with all the trees pushed over. Dates figured for the trees average 11,523 years ago.

Cores from the Arctic Ocean show that minute animal life that had multiplied there for many years suddenly ceased to exist around 11,000 years ago. The extinct animal bones in the La Brea Tar Pits in Los Angeles also date back about 11,000 years.[11] Paul S. Martin, professor of geosciences at the University of Arizona, declared that the animals were gone by 11,000 years ago in every dated site of extinct mammals.[12]

Adam was, I believe, created in B.C. 4043. Therefore, if these dates are reliable, the previous inhabitants of this planet would have been exterminated by about 7,000 years before Adam was created. Whether this happened 65 million years ago or 13,000 years ago doesn't matter. It happened.

In the ice pack or out of it, there was no chance for evolution to take place, no remote possibility for any organism to become man, no way for a prehistoric horse to evolve into the horse we know today. There was nothing left after the judgment of those days but an uninhabited icy morgue of fossils rotating inside a voluminous cloud envelope that made it darker than an arctic night on the surface.

God will cause a great death-blow in one area of Earth at the end of our age. Again, the sun will become dark as sackcloth of hair, the moon will become red as blood and the stars will not shine through the dark cloud cover.[13]

Escape from Chaos

God incubated the surface of the ice, or as Moses said, "the face of the waters," probably by the greenhouse effect. By the equivalent of the Jewish Elul 24 (Sunday, September 13, B.C. 4043), God began restoring the Earth. **Remember September 13, the dark day** when God said, "Let there be light." It ties in later. (The Bible provides enough information to date the years from the creation of Adam to the Crucifixion with exactness. Martin Anstey, the noted Biblical chronologist, put that story together for us.[14])

It was Sunday, the first day of the week, when the first diffused light bathed the Earth in its glow. It was a literal twenty four hour day for there was both night and day. Genesis 1:5 says, "And the evening and the morning were the first day." If those days of creation had been 1,000 year days, the plants would have died again during the 500 year night.

By Monday, the heavy cloud began to rise up from the Earth, leaving an expanse of space between the water on Earth and the vapor above. On Tuesday, after the water had run into the sea beds and the exposed land surface drained and dried, God caused the former vegetation to renew itself. "And every plant of the field [world, Matthew 13:38] **before** it was in the earth, and every herb of the field **before** it grew."[15] No animal made it through the catastrophe, but the plants did. Their seeds, roots and spores survived the long hard winter.

Wednesday, the sun, moon, and stars were seen in the heavens as the heavy vapors coalesced into separate clouds. The Earth was ready to support animal life. Thursday, God began to create a new order on Earth. He created a whole new fauna, starting with creatures that live in water or fly in the air.

On Friday, Elul 29 (our September 18), after creating all the land creatures, God created Adam (according to Jewish tradition, a man equal to 30 years old) then Eve.

Jewish tradition regards the Feast of Trumpets, their New Year, as the anniversary of the beginning of the world.[16] That New Year Day was the Saturday Sabbath, **Tishri 1, when the Lord rested**. (This ties in again also.) By that time all the necessary parts were finished, and the new world [Gr. *kosmos*, orderly arrangement] could began to operate.

God planted a garden in the temperate zone near the Euphrates River.[17] Mist watered the plants. The atmosphere was now so warm from the greenhouse effect of the material still in the stratosphere that it did not rain until Noah's day.

The Lord brought the animals for Adam to name. From the very first, God gave Adam command of a language with which he could communicate with Eve and with the Lord himself, and he didn't speak in grunts. Can you imagine the difficulty of naming all the animals in grunts? or of remembering or recording their names? The serpent and sheep are mentioned by their correct names right away.

The human brain is a wonderful invention. It is as if God created a wireless computer terminal in Adam's head that was God-conscious and could broadcast it's information to God's mainframe computer upon demand.

First, he programmed it with subconscious instructions to keep the body functioning whether conscious thoughts were turned off or on. This basic program is automatically copied to the brain of all progeny. Each of us has a similar computer terminal brain in our head, still able to be read at will by God's mainframe brain. Then, he programmed Adam with the language, knowledge and reasoning ability of a 30 year old.

Adam was not like the the animal kingdom. They did not have God-consciousness, and he was not descended from them. His flesh was not like theirs. "All flesh is not the same flesh: but there is **one kind of flesh of man, another flesh of beasts**, another of fishes, and another of birds."[18]

Just as God had commanded the animals to be fruitful, and multiply, he told Adam and Eve to "Be fruitful, and multiply, and **replenish** the earth."[19] They understood and began to fill the world with children, both sons and daughters.

"Having made known unto us the mystery of his will...That in the dispensation of the fulness of times he might gather together in one all things in Christ, both which are in heaven, and which are on earth." Ephesians 1:10

Chapter 3

Seven Part Test

Adam's Forty Years in Paradise

Adam had 890 years to regret his disobedience after leaving the Garden of Eden near where the Euphrates River pours into the Persian Gulf. **The ground in that area was cursed**.

That's not hard to believe after seeing the wasteland in southern Iraq and Kuwait on Cable Network News. The United Nations' armed forces fought to liberate Kuwait in that general area. The ground is mostly flat desolate desert. The Lord told Adam,

> Because thou hast hearkened unto the voice of thy wife, and hast eaten of the tree, of which I commanded thee, saying, Thou shalt not eat of it: **cursed is the ground** for thy sake; in sorrow shalt thou eat of it all the days of thy life; Thorns also and thistles shall it bring forth to thee; and thou shalt eat the herb of the field; In the sweat of thy face shalt thou eat bread, till thou return unto the ground; for out of it wast thou taken: for dust thou art, and unto dust shalt thou return.

Adam and Eve lived in the Garden of Eden 40 years because they were being tested. Throughout Scripture, the number 40 means testing or probation. The Israelites searched the land 40 days. Failing to believe God during that test, they had to wander in the wilderness 40 years while all that generation except Caleb and Joshua died off. The Lord said,

"After the number of the days in which ye searched the land, even forty days, each day for a year, shall ye bear your iniquities, even forty years, and ye shall know my breach of promise."[1]

Three successive monarchs, Saul, David and his son Solomon, each ruled 40 years, an inexplicable phenomenon unless controlled by God. Out of this test, David earned the right to rule again after the resurrection. The Lord said, "they shall serve the LORD their God, and David their king, whom I will **raise up** unto them."[2] David will rule under Christ.

The first Adam was tempted by Satan during 40 time periods just as Jesus Christ, called "the last Adam" in I Corinthians 15:45, was tempted by Satan 40 time periods [days].

Dispensations and Ages are two types of chronological sequences indicated in Scripture. When you make a scale drawing of the seven dispensations on clear acetate and lay it over a scale chart of the ages, you will see that the only way it will fit is if the **Dispensation of Innocence is before the beginning of the ages.** You will also find out that the Dispensation of Innocence lasted 40 years. (See chapter 5, Age of Time, for information on the ages.)

Adam lived in two different economies, one during the 40 years before he was expelled from the garden and another the remainder of his 930 year life.

There are seven different dispensations, or economies, in all, and there is good reason for no more than that. God does things in sevens because seven means complete.

Meaning of Numbers

Many numbers have meanings in Scripture. One represents unity, two stands for union and three indicates the Trinity, a single Godhead, consisting of a plurality of eternal persons, the Father, Son and Holy Spirit.

Both the Old and New Testaments bear witness to both the singularity and plurality of the Godhead. In Deuteronomy 6:4 the great commandment is "Hear, O Israel: The LORD [Jehovah, singular] our God [Elohim, plural] is one LORD [Jehovah, singular]." The word used for "one" is *echad*, a unity, as when man and wife become "one" flesh or when several soldiers become "one" troup. In Matthew 28:19, the command is "Go ye therefore, and teach all nations, baptizing them in the name [singular] of the Father, and of the Son, and of the Holy Ghost." The Trinity is a unity of Father, Son and Holy Spirit, three persons in one Godhead, all partakers of the same nature.

Two are seen in Matthew 22:44, where Jesus quoted Psalms 110:1: "The LORD [God the Father] said unto my [David's] Lord [God the Son], sit thou on my right hand, till I make thine enemies thy footstool."

Three are mentioned in Isaiah 48:16: "Come . . . hear ye this . . . from the beginning . . . there am I [Christ]: and now the **Lord GOD**, and his **Spirit**, hath sent **me** [Christ]. Thus saith the LORD [**Christ**], **thy Redeemer**, the Holy One **of Israel** [Jesus was an Israelite as the Messiah must be]."

The New Testament says in I Corinthians 8:6, "there is but one God, the Father, of whom are all things, and we **in** him; and one Lord Jesus Christ [the creator], by whom are all things, and we **by** him. [We are **in** the Father **by** means of our Lord and Saviour Jesus Christ.] Speaking of Adam and Jesus Christ, 1 Corinthians 15:47 explains, "The first man is of the earth, earthy: **the second man is the Lord from heaven**." Second Corinthians 5:19 distills it all into simple language that cannot easily be misunderstood: "**God was in Christ reconciling the world unto himself**."

Four is the number of the Earth, fourth from the center of our solar system. Five denotes division. Six stands for man, who was created on the sixth day. Seven means perfection or completion and is God's number. Eight indicates a new order. Nine typifies rebellion. Ten is the complete earthly number, and twelve the complete heavenly number. **Thirteen is Satan's number**. Thirty is the Jewish age of maturity. Forty draws our attention to special times of testing and probation. Fifty is the number of restoration and is therefore the Jubilee year.[3] Knowing these special meanings will help us understand some of God's dealings with humans.

The Seven Part Test: Dispensations

God's plans are perfect. Since seven means perfection and completion, he divided the testing of mankind into seven unequal chunks of time. During each one, humans are required to obey some definite revelation of the will of God. Every time, they fail the test. Therefore, **a Saviour is necessary**.

Time, from the creation of Adam to the Great White Throne Judgment at the end of the Millennium, consists of these seven unequal periods, which we call dispensations, during which man is tested under different conditions. Some instructions given by God apply to all of time, but others apply only to certain dispensations.

Five segments are past, one is and the other is yet to come. The seventh is called "the dispensation of the fulness of times," in Ephesians 1:10.

We are living very near the end of the sixth dispensation, the longest one. Soon after the seventh begins, Christ will return and rule as KING OF KINGS AND LORD OF LORDS during the Millennium. When the seventh is over, the test is complete and eternity will begin.

The conditions under which man is tried and the number of years I believe God allotted to each dispensation are:

Innocence	40	Law	1,559
Conscience	1,616	Grace	1,977
Human Government	427	Kingdom	1,000
Promise	430	Total	7,049

The total years set aside for this test run from the time of Adam's creation through A.H. 7,049 (3007 A.D.).

A.H. means Anno Hominus, year of man. B.C. is Before Christ. A.D. means Anno Domini, year of our Lord, i.e., Jesus Christ. Therefore, when you write today's date, whether you believe in him or not, you affirm the birth of our Lord Jesus Christ, who has two natures, both God and man. You can't escape it. This one man's life changed the course of human events.

Time seems to be 7,049 years long [7,000 + (7 x 7)]. Scripture describes in detail the main events that take place during this block of time carved out of eternity. Rounded off, it is easy to remember that the Bible covers about 7,000 years. It only hints at many things before and after this, the testing of the angels, the splitting apart of Satan's planet and the wonderful things that will be ours in eternity.

"Eye hath not seen, nor ear heard, neither have entered into the heart of man, the things which God hath prepared for them that love him."[4]

44

Adam to the Expulsion: Dispensation of Innocence

The Dispensation of Innocence extended from that balmy **Friday, September 18th, B.C. 4043 when man was created** just before the autumnal equinox to the time he was driven from his Edenic paradise 40 years later on Tishri 1.

How do we know it was a nice day when Adam was created? Because he was naked and had no need of clothing. It is simple, but you have to stop and think about it. In searching the Scriptures, think like a detective. Look for clues as carefully as if with a magnifying glass. A monumental amount of information is packed into that one small book.

Adam was created innocent, set in an ideal environment, given dominion, tested for obedience to God and judged a failure. Eve was deceived, but not Adam. He willfully decided to disobey and eat of the forbidden fruit. Thus, Satan regained dominion over the Earth and will keep it until Christ, whose right it is, takes dominion after the Second Advent. Satan has a throne and is the one Amos referred to as "him that holdeth the sceptre from the house of Eden."[5]

Man both gained dominion and lost it at Eden. Christ will take sovereignty from Satan after The Curse literally strikes Eden and Babylon immediately after this age expires.

Babylon, in Iraq, is being rebuilt. Saddam Hussein has even rebuilt Nebuchadnezzar's palace. It is about 162 miles northwest of the traditional site of the Garden of Eden.

According to evidence, **the garden was near Eridu** (Abu Sharem), 12 miles south of Ur, Iraq, where Abraham came from, near the Persian Gulf. Halley's Bible Handbook quotes an ancient Babylonian inscription that says, "Near Eridu was a garden, in which was a mysterious Sacred Tree, a Tree of Life, planted by the gods . . . and no man enters." The Weld Prism, found 40 miles away at Larsa, lists the first two kings of pre-flood history as reigning at Eridu. The **earliest writing** was found at Larsa. Man had language and writing skills much earlier than many have thought.

What is The Curse? God cursed the ground, and "drove out the man; and he placed at the east of the garden of Eden Cherubims, and a flaming sword which turned every way, to keep the way of the tree of life."[6] What are Cherubim? and what is the flaming sword that turns in all directions?

45

The cherubim are real. They are still there. The flaming sword that glitters as it rotates is still there too. Both are visible if you know what they are, where they are, and how to look for them. Ezekiel saw them in a vision and described them for us.

The sword is poised ready for a strike. It is prepared for the Day of Slaughter, when "the sword of the LORD shall devour from the one end of the land even to the other end of the land."[7] God drove Adam out of that area for the good of mankind. When the flaming sword descends on that cursed ground, the split Earth will bear the mark of its slash forever. (The cherubim and Sword of the Lord will be identified later.)

Expulsion to Flood: Dispensation of Conscience

The second dispensation, Conscience, lasted 1,616 years. It ran from A.H. 40 (B.C. 4003), after Adam and Eve reluctantly trudged out of the garden they lost, to A.H. 1656 (B.C. 2387), when the great flood destroyed all flesh that moved upon the Earth except that which was preserved in the ark that Noah built. At that time, "all the high hills, that were under the whole heaven, were covered."[8]

During this dispensation, under the Adamic Covenant, man was to do what he knew to be good and avoid what he knew to be wrong. Could he do it? What happened? extreme degeneration. Again man failed the test, an easy simple test.

The flood was necessary because Satan had attempted to corrupt the human race so that the Messiah could not come in the body of pure man to redeem us.

Hybrids, part man and part angel, populated the Earth. These were the "angels which kept not their first estate, but left their own habitation . . . reserved in everlasting chains under darkness unto the judgment of the great day."[9]

Angels seem to be taller than ordinary men. Genesis 6:4 indicates this. Their progeny were giants:

> There were giants in the earth in those days; **and also after that**, when the sons of God came in unto the daughters of men, and they bare children to them, the same became mighty men which were of old, men of renown.

These "sons of God" are angels, individually created by God and always referred to in the masculine gender. Satan is an angel and is one of the "sons of God" in Job 1:6 and 2:1.

Your choice today really boils down to which son of God will you choose; Satan, a created being, an angel; or Jesus Christ, the creator who took on himself a human body and became God's "only begotten Son," our Saviour.

> In the beginning was the Word [Christ, whose name is called The Word of God in Revelation 19:13], and the Word was with God, and **the Word was God**. . . . **And the Word was made flesh**, and dwelt among us (John 1:1,14).

> And without controversy great is the mystery of godliness: **God was manifest in the flesh**, justified in the Spirit, seen of angels, preached unto the Gentiles, believed on in the world, received up into glory (I Timothy 3:16).

The Philistine giant, Goliath, was one of the hybrid creatures. By the time the Hebrews were about ready to enter the promised land,

> only Og king of Bashan remained of the . . . giants . . . his bedstead . . . of iron . . . nine cubits [13 1/2 feet] was the length thereof, and four cubits [6 feet] the breadth of it.[10]

But Noah, who tradition says lived 70 miles north of Eridu (Eden) at Fara, where a flood deposit has been found, was "perfect in his generations"[11] and walked with God, so the Lord kept him, his three sons and all four of their wives, eight people, alive to repopulate the Earth after the flood subsided.

Noah's belief in God paid off. Others died for their wickedness. They couldn't even believe it would rain. Noah's household was the only one saved, and by their families "were the nations divided in the earth after the flood."[12]

Has Noah's Ark been found preserved in ice and snow? Probably, but whether or not the wood found by French industrialist Fernand Navarra in 1955 at the 13,500 foot level of Mt. Ararat in Turkey is part of Noah's Ark does not matter. Without the actual Ark, even without the scriptures, there is ample proof that the Flood took place.

God said that knowledge would increase in the latter days.[13] It certainly has, especially since the development of modern computers. By using one to do the computations that would have taken more than one man's lifetime to do by hand, it has been proved that according to the rate of increase in world population, man did start with eight in Noah's time.

Sir Leonard Woolley, English archaeologist who directed the Joint Expedition of the British Museum and the Museum of the University of Pennsylvania, made yearly excavation trips to Mesopotamia, 150 miles southeast of Babylon in what is now modern Iraq, from 1922 to 1934. Near the Garden of Eden, in Ur, where Abraham was born, he found 11 feet of clean flood-laid silt between layers holding remains of civilization. Under the silt were remnants of houses.

At the time, his find excited the archaeological world. Here was proof of the Noachic flood. Wooley stated that this was a land of floods, but nothing like this occurred in their later history. For that silt to form, he said that there must have been 20 to 25 feet of water.[14]

At Kish, first city rebuilt after the flood, five feet of water-laid clay was found between layers of ancient relics. In Noah's city, Fara, a similar layer was found. Above it was rubbish. Below it were skeletons and stratified rubbish from civilization, including cylinder seals, pottery, pots and pans.[15]

Before the flood, did God warn of coming judgment? or indicate when it would take place? Yes, just as he is warning us today of judgment to come and showing us when it will take place, he warned them in those days. Both Enoch and Noah understood. We know that Enoch, whose name means "teacher," knew when the Flood was coming, for he named his son Methuselah, which means "when he is dead, it will be sent." It happened when Enoch thought it would. Noah was born when Methuselah was 369 years old and was 600 when the flood wiped out the wicked antediluvian civilization. Since Methuselah lived 969 years, it began to rain the year he died (369 + 600 = 969) (Genesis 5:25-29; 7:6). You will see the significance of Noah's going up at the age of 600 later on.

Unlike today, it was easy for Noah to figure out how much time he had left to build the Ark. The Lord said plainly that man's days would be "an hundred and twenty years."[16]

When the rain began to fall, Noah's son, Japeth, was 100 years old. Ham was 99 and Shem 98. They would have helped Noah build the Ark. Scripture does not tell us how long it took. It could have been anything up to 120 years. The apocryphal Book of Jasher, mentioned in Joshua 10:13 and 2 Samuel 1:18, says it was built in five years.

Noah knew what was coming and when to expect it. He would have told his family also. We can also know what is coming and exactly when to expect it.

Flood to Abraham: Dispensation of Human Government

The Dispensation of Human Government began in A.H. 1656 (B.C. 2387) and lasted 427 years. The Noachic Covenant put man to a new test. He was to govern the world for God. This sounds easy enough, but failure stuck to humanity during this time also. It takes a lot of wisdom to be a good leader, more than some can muster.

During this Dispensation that followed the great flood, stress within the earth's crust reached the breaking point. I believe this tension began when the Pacific Basin was gouged out to form the moon. Finally, the continents split their seams and started their slow drift toward the Pacific Basin.

The Atlantic Rift Valley is earth's largest geological feature, stretching 72,000 kilometers and covering 28% of Earth's surface. The movement was probably rapid as the continents ripped apart for there are large quantities of volcanic rock on the sea floor in mid ocean, but the size and weight of the mass to be moved soon slowed the continents to a creep.

Many geologists ignore the Bible and go on endlessly speculating about when continental drift began, but Scripture tells us that the division of the Earth took place during the life span of one man. He was born in A.H. 1757 (B.C. 2286), just 100 years after the great flood ended.

This man was aptly named Peleg, for it means "divided," and "in his days was the earth divided."[17] He lived 239 years and died in A.H. 1996 (B.C. 2047), twelve years before Abram was born and ten years before Noah died. Therefore, continental drift also began in the days of Noah.

Had you figured out when the continents broke apart? Scripture tells it in just seven words. It would be easy to skip over it. By this you can see that if we are to recognize time clues in the scriptures, we must pay the closest attention for every word in the original language was God-breathed and meaningful. This great God of ours is the omniscient King of the whole universe. Not only does he know everything, but his communications are exceptionally revealing. Every fact or action recorded is for a reason. As we read, we should continually ask ourselves why God would want us to know that particular thing. Why is it important? It was not just to fill up space.

The judgment at the Tower of Babel also took place during Peleg's lifetime. He was probably 40 years old. Not only was the Earth divided while Peleg was alive, but mankind was divided into different nations. Genesis 10:32 says,

> These are the families of the sons of Noah, after their generations, in their nations: and by these were the nations divided in the earth after the flood.

From Adam to the Tower of Babel, mankind had only one language. Do you realize that, because of Adam's 930 year life span, Adam, Enoch, Methuselah and Noah's father, Lamech, were contemporaries and spoke the same language?

Adam could have discussed things with Enoch for 308 years, Methuselah for 243 years and with Noah's father, Lamech, for 56 years. Lamech could know for sure what had taken place prior to his day for Adam could tell him face to face. Man in that day did not need to make up stories to explain things. They knew how it was.

Noah did not know Enoch, who was translated 69 years before Noah was born, but he learned about Adam and Enoch from his father, Lamech, and his grandfather, Methuselah. Noah lived until two years before Abram was born.

After the Flood, there were some changes. Before the Flood, it did not rain. A mist came up to water the plants. After the Flood, it rained as it does now. Before the Flood, man lived a long time, as much as Methuselah's 969 years, probably so the knowledge God imparted to Adam could be passed on easily to Noah. Following the Flood, the life span of man was cut in half.

After the construction was initiated on the Tower of Babel, the Lord confounded man's speech so that they could

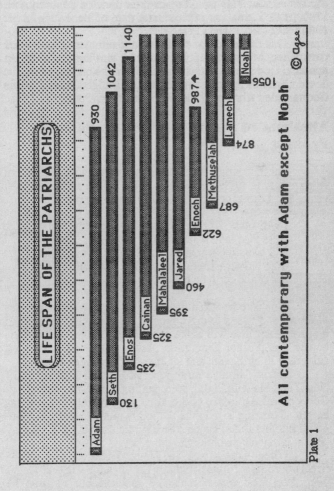

LIFE SPAN OF THE PATRIARCHS

Plate 1

All contemporary with Adam except Noah

Adam 930
Seth 130 1042
Enos 235 1140
Cainan 325
Mahalaleel 395
Jared 460
Enoch 622 987↑
Methuselah 687
Lamech 874
Noah 1056

© القمر

not understand each other. Then man finally followed God's wishes and scattered across the face of the entire Earth.[18]

Since they apparently had no trouble traversing to all parts of the land, the continents must have broken apart after this dispersion. This would place their division between A.H. 1797 (B.C. 2246), the approximate date of Babel, and A.H. 1996 (B.C. 2047) when Peleg died.

This Dispensation of Human Government ended when God called Abram, a gentile, and gave him the promises. At that time God started to deal mainly with one nation, Israel, the descendants of Abram [which means a high father], whom God renamed Abraham [father of a great multitude].

Abraham to the Exodus: Dispensation of Promise

The Dispensation of Promise began with the call of Abram in A.H. 2083 (which is our B.C. 960) and lasted 430 years. The Lord gave him an unconditional promise:

> I will make of thee a great nation, and I will bless thee, and make thy name great . . . And I will bless them that bless thee, and **curse him that curseth thee**: and in thee shall all families of the earth be blessed.[19]

This is to be taken literally. Let any nation that curses the Jews and wants to drive them from their God-given land beware. The Curse will strike debilitating terror to their hearts before this present generation passes. They will hold their sides as if in birth pain, and all knees will be weak as water.

When Abram (ninth generation from Shem, son of Noah) and his wife, Sarai, were getting old, Sarai thought of God's promise to make of Abram a great nation, yet she was barren. Thinking to help the Almighty out, she told Abram to go in unto her maid, Hagar, the Egyptian, saying that "it may be that I may obtain children by her."[20]

When Abram was 86, Hagar (whose name means flight) bore him Ishmael (whom God hears). He and Hagar were later cast out because he mocked, but in time he had twelve sons of whom many Egyptians are descended.

Later, when Abram was 99 years old, the Lord said,

> I will make my covenant between me and thee,
> and will multiply thee exceedingly . . . thy
> name shall be Abraham . . . I will give unto
> thee, and to thy seed after thee . . . all the land
> of Canaan, for an everlasting possession . . .
> As for Sarai [contention] . . . Sarah [princess]
> shall her name be. And I will bless her, and
> give thee a son also of her . . . Then Abraham
> fell upon his face, and laughed, and said in his
> heart, Shall a child be born unto him that is an
> hundred years old? and shall Sarah, that is
> ninety years old, bear?[21]

The Lord, who didn't need any help and who did things according to his own predetermined schedule, continued, "But my covenant will I establish with Isaac [laughter], which Sarah shall bear unto thee at **this set time** in the next year."[22] There was a very good reason why they had to wait.

Between this event and the birth of the child, Sodom and Gomorrah were destroyed because of their wickedness. This foreshadows the destruction of the wicked at the end of the age a short time before Christ returns.

In all of Sodom, there were not ten who were righteous.[23] Only Lot, Abraham's nephew who had come to Canaan with him, and Lot's two daughters were saved. His wife disobeyed the command to not look back and became a pillar of salt (maybe what we would call mineral salts). We will find out later just what kind of destruction hit Sodom and Gomorrah for a similar one will hit Babylon immediately after this present age ends.

The next year (A.H. 2108, B.C. 1935) Isaac was born to Abraham and Sarah, "according to **the time of life**."[24]

What is **"this set time"** or **"the time of life"**? Have you ever wondered? These are not just idle words. Isaac is a type of Christ, and this set time of life is the Feast of Trumpets, the Jewish New Year, on which Jesus was born.

First, Adam's life was created just prior to the start of the Jewish New Year. Later, Isaac was born on the Jewish New Year's Day, then Jesus was born on Isaac's birthday. In the future, all Israel will be born in a day.[25] It will also be on New Year's Day, the Feast of Trumpets, "the time of life."

Sixty years later in this Dispensation of Promise, while man was living under the Abrahamic Covenant, Jacob (which means supplanter) was born to Abraham's son, Isaac. The Lord called his name Israel (which means soldier of God). Israelites were to be soldiers of God. Jacob's 12 sons are the patriarchs of the 12 tribes. They are Reuben, Simeon, Levi, Judah, Issachar, Zebulun, Joseph, Benjamin, Dan, Naphtali, Gad and Asher.

Because of famine in the land of Canaan, Jacob and his family moved to Egypt in A.H. 2298 (B.C. 1745). Yet Abraham was promised that the land from the river of Egypt to the Euphrates River was to belong to his seed.[26] This is still to be fulfilled in the future.

Is this why Iraq wants to wipe Israel off the map? She tried in 1948. On May 25, 1965, President Aref of Iraq issued a statement jointly with Egypt's Nasser saying, "The Arab national aim is the elimination of Israel." Iraq attacked Israel again in the 1967 Six-day War and shot Scud missiles at them this year, 1991.

Could the Israelites have known how long it would be before they returned to their own land? Yes. Again God gave enough information to figure it out before it came to pass.

He told Abraham, "Know of a surety that thy seed shall be a stranger in a land that is not their's, and shall serve them; and they [the Egyptians] shall afflict them four hundred years."[27] This 400 year countdown began when wild Ishmael (born of an Egyptian mother) mocked and was cast out.

The main dispute between Egypt and Israel started here. The Ishmaelites think they should inherit God's land, but God gave it to Isaac and his descendants. He is sovereign and sets up whom he pleases and puts down whom he pleases.

Exactly 400 years after Ishmael was sent away, the Exodus from Egypt began under the leadership of Moses and the coaching of God. It was A.H. 2513 (B.C. 1530), and according to Galatians 3:16,17, was 430 years after Abraham received the promises.

So "the sojourning [*mowshab*, time of continuation of existence] of the children of Israel, who dwelt in Egypt, was four hundred and thirty years."[28] This is much easier to understand in the Septuagint, the Greek translation of the scriptures used during Jesus' ministry, which says that they sojourned in the land of Egypt **and** in the land of Canaan for 430 years.

During the Dispensation of Promise, did humans pass the test? No, they failed to obey God, as they do in every one.

Exodus to the Crucifixion: the Dispensation of Law

The Dispensation of Law began in A.H. 2513 (B.C. 1530) and lasted 1,559 years.

The Israelites lived under the Mosaic Covenant, the laws the Lord gave to Moses on Mount Sinai, during this dispensation. They had to wander in the wilderness 40 years while one generation died off. That generation included all those who were afraid to enter the land of Canaan because of the giants who lived there.

Of all those over 20 years old who left Egypt, only Caleb and Joshua (Jesus in Greek, of whom Joshua was a type) went into the promised land. Not even Moses made it.

When it comes time to go with Jesus in the Rapture to our promised land in a few years do not hesitate, even though you see giant angels. In those days they could have gone into Canaan in 11 days, but they did not because there were giants in the land and they did not believe enough in the power of God. Be a Caleb. Believe. Follow the Messiah, *Y'shua Mashiyach*, our Redeemer, the Lord Jesus Christ.

Who went into the promised land? the children, and their children. In A.H. 2553 (B.C. 1490), after Moses died, they finally entered the promised land.

God gave the world the first democracy. Judges ruled Israel until the people asked for a king.

Saul became Israel's first king in A.H. 3023 (B.C. 1020). He ruled 40 years. Then David was crowned king in A.H. 3063 (B.C. 980). He ruled 40 years. His son, Solomon, succeeded him in A.H. 3103 (B.C. 940), and he also ruled 40 years.

Adam, Moses, Saul, David and Solomon each reigned 40 years. Why? because 40 means probation and testing.

During this fifth dispensation, the Israelites were taken captive by Nebuchadnezzar. Could they have known how long that captivity would last? Yes. The Lord said, "And this whole land shall be a desolation, and an astonishment: and these nations shall serve the king of Babylon seventy years.[29]

This is a type of modern nations (this time, all nations) serving another king of Babylon (leader of world government headquartered at Babylon, first the Roman Beast, then the Israeli False Prophet) during the awful seven year Tribulation.

Daniel understood how long the desolation would last. He said, "I Daniel understood by books the number of the years, whereof the word of the LORD came to Jeremiah the prophet, that he would accomplish seventy years in the desolations of Jerusalem."[30] We can also understand the number of the years of our times if we search the Scriptures as Daniel did.

In A.H. 3589 (B.C. 454), they returned to Israel, exactly on time. God's dates are precise.

(According to Martin Anstey, Ptolemaic dates are out of step with the Bible by 82 years. He made an error in the Persian Empire period, so has 82 years too many.[31])

Babylon was told approximately how long she would rule, into the third generation. It happened exactly as predicted.[32]

Man failed his test in the Dispensation of Law. It lasted until the Crucifixion. At that time the Lord blotted "out the handwriting of ordinances that was against us, which was contrary to us, and took it out of the way, nailing it to his cross."[33] We should thank the Lord for doing this. Not one man was ever saved by obeying the law. All sin and fall short of its perfection.

Crucifixion to the End of Our Age: The Dispensation of Grace

This is our dispensation, the sixth, the one in which we now live. It is the longest one of all. Beginning in A.H. 4072 (30 A.D.), it will end the last day of this age, A.H. 6049 (2007 A.D.), lasting 1,977 years.

God is dealing with us in grace under the New Covenant. The law showed man what sin is. It was our schoolmaster to bring us to Christ.[34] It was such a tough master that even then, men had to be saved by grace or none would have made it.

At the present time, God is dealing with the Church. However, he has begun dealing with Israel again too. During the seven year Tribulation, the Seventieth Week of Daniel will run concurrently with the tail end of this Dispensation.

This Dispensation of Grace is characterized by Ephesians 2:8-10, which says,"For by grace are ye saved through faith; and that not of yourselves: it is the gift of God: Not of works, lest any man should boast. For we are his work-manship, created in Christ Jesus unto good works, which God hath before ordained that we should walk in them."

Salvation is accepting the free gift of God. You cannot work for it; nothing you can ever do can earn it. You cannot receive it by merit; nothing about any of us is good enough. The only way is by appropriating the sacrifice made in our stead by our Lord Jesus Christ.

Pray and tell him that you believe in him, that you accept him as your personal Saviour and that you love him.

You should love him. Look what he has done for you. He has taken upon himself the capital punishment due you for your unbelief. Could you have gone through what he did? And he did it not for himself, but for you and me.

If you do not believe there is a God, you are without excuse, being surrounded by all the wonderful things God has made. The intricacies of your own body alone show you that there is a God. The germ of life in seeds shows you. All of nature shows you.

> For the wrath of God is revealed from heaven against all ungodliness and unrighteousness of men, who hold the truth in unrighteousness; Because that which may be known of God is manifest in them; for God hath shewed it unto them. For **the invisible things of him from the creation of the world are clearly seen, being understood by the things that are made,** even his eternal power and Godhead; so that **they are with-out excuse.**[35]

The next prophesied event on God's calendar is the joyous Rapture, when Christ will come for his bride. In that glorious moment in time, believers will be taken to visit their heavenly home, snatched away from the coming Tribulation.

Day of the Lord: Dispensation of Kingdom

The Dispensation of Kingdom will begin in A.H. 6049 (2007 A.D.) and last 1,000 years. The present dispensation will be ushered out in darkness as the 1,000 year Day of the Lord arrives with a terrible catastrophe, the worst holocaust to take place since man was put on the Earth. During the Miller nium, the seventh and last dispensation will run its cours ending as eternity begins for all humankind.

In the first dispensation, man failed. Adam was tried i a state of innocence in a perfect environment. In the last dis pensation, humans will again fail, as in every one. They wi be tried under the perfect King, the divine Lord Jesus Chris in another perfect environment. This time humans will not b innocent like Adam in Eden, but will know both good an evil. Their failure will adequately demonstrate their inna inability to obey God. **If God had not provided us wit a Saviour, we would all be lost forever.**

There was something marred in Adam when he de cided to disobey God that has been inherited by all men. Thi gives us a bent toward evil. We are not altogether products c our environment; neither does Satan cause all our evil doings.

Since God was his father, Jesus did not inherit Adam sin nature. Jesus is called the second Adam. In him man wa given another chance. And just as we have inherited the imag of the earthy, we can inherit the image of the heavenly.

> And so it is written, The first man Adam was made a living soul; the last Adam was made a quickening spirit. . . . The first man is of the earth, earthy: **the second man is the Lord from heaven**. . . . And as we have borne the image of the earthy, we shall also bear the image of the heavenly.[36]

Christ is the Lord from heaven. **In "him dwelleth the fulness of the Godhead bodily"** (Colossians 2:9).

Fred Meldau, editor of Christian Victory Magazine 1956 when his book, *Messiah in Both Testaments,* was p lished, found an interesting statement in the Hebrew of Psa 72. On page 90 of his book, he said that the English translati of verse 17—"His [Christ's] name shall continue as long as sun"—is in the original Hebrew, **"Before the sun was, l name (was) Yinon."**

Christ [Yinon] not only existed before the sun, but created the sun. Our Lord **and** Saviour Jesus Christ has t complete natures, God and man. No others of his kind have e existed. He alone can save. Trust him. He won't let you dow

Chapter 4

Days of Heaven

_____

Our days are not His days. There are days in time and
days in eternity. In the Septuagint, the Greek translation of the
Old Testament used during Jesus' ministry, Isaiah 30:8 says,
"write . . . for these things shall be for **days in time**."

Two great wheels of time are now running concurrently with the one ticking off the dispensations. Both
began to turn when Adam left Eden, when man began to be
tested knowing both good and evil. One wheel measures off
God's great days, the days of heaven;[1] the other records the
passage of the ages. To properly orient ourselves in time, it is
important to understand how God marks "days in time."

God's Great Days

It is a bit of an oversimplification, but time has been
thought to consist of seven 1,000 year days. The final one is
the millennial Day of the Lord, during which our Lord Jesus
Christ will bring enduring peace to this tortured planet.

Plutarch, the famous Greek writer who died about 125
A.D., wrote that even the Chaldeans believed that the conflict
between good and evil would continue for 6,000 years before
an age of peace [the Millennium] would ensue.

This concept of time was accepted by many Christians
in the first few centuries A.D., by Rabbi Elias, Barnabas and
Irenaeus in the first century, by Hilary in the fourth, by
Cassiodorus and Austin in the sixth, by Andrew of Crete in
the seventh, by John of Damascus in the eighth and by others.

In the 17th century, Thomas Burnet wrote that most of
the church fathers accepted it. He said nothing in either nature
or Scripture was against the supposition of 6,000 years
[before the sabbatical Millennium], which had both the
authority of the fathers and antiquity on its side.[2]

Julius Africanus worked out his Biblical chronology in the third century A.D. He thought Adam was created in B.C. 5500. He believed that six 1,000 year days would end 500 years after Christ's birth, then a sabbath of 1,000 years would follow.

Archbishop Ussher, in the seventeenth century, placed creation in B.C. 4004, four 1,000 year days before he thought Jesus was born in B.C. 4. **He expected Christ to return in 1996 A.D.**, after two more 1,000 year days had passed. Widely accepted, his dates have been printed in the margins of many Bibles. Although in need of refinement, his dates come close enough to the truth to show that he did some good thinking on the subject and deserved his status in the field of Bible chronology.

Many refer to the 6,000 years plus the Millennium as the Great Week of Time. In his book, *Dispensational Truth*, Clarence Larkin called these 7,000 years the "Great Week of Human History."[3] It is surprising that more do not accept the Great Week of Time. Along with Job, I wonder

> Why, seeing times are not hidden from the Almighty, do they that know him not see **his days?**[4]

Some do. A few years ago, I saw Howard C. Estep draw an arc with 7,000 written under it when he was talking about time on his television program, The King is Coming.

It seems very likely that a great day lasts 1,000 years for Adam did not physically die in the same 24 hour period in which he disobeyed God. He was told that he would die in that day and he lived to be 930 years old. If the day spoken of lasted 1,000 years, everything fits into a simple picture, and we are not left wondering if this referred to physical death or spiritual death.

One thing is certain and accepted. The Day of the Lord, when Christ rules as King of kings and Lord of lords, will last a millennium. The Scripture plainly says that "they lived and reigned with Christ a thousand years."[5]

Our 24 hour days, with both evenings and mornings, are as in Genesis 1:5. His days last 1,000 years. Psalm 89:26,29 says, "He shall cry to Me, Thou art my father . . . I will make him my firstborn . . . His seed also will I make to endure for ever, and **his throne as the days of heaven.**"

If the throne of Christ is for a 1,000 years, and his throne is also as the days of heaven, then the days of heaven last 1,000 years. Peter begged us to pay attention to this. In II Peter 3:8, he said, "beloved, be not ignorant of this one thing, that **one day is with the Lord as a thousand years**, and a thousand years as one day." Psalm 90:4 tells us the same thing. "For a thousand years in thy sight are but as yesterday when it is past."

The Bible is consistent. If one day with the Lord is as 1,000 years, then the other days with the Lord would each be 1,000 years. Since seven means completion, a block of seven 1,000 year days set apart for man's testing is not incongruous.

I accept the general concept of a Great Week of Time that consists of seven 1,000 year days. It meshes with all the other information about God's timetable perfectly.

It is very likely that the seven 24 hour days of creation week prefigured the seven great days of time. The Greek word translated "rest" and referring to the Day of the Lord in Hebrews 4:9 is "sabbatismos," strongly suggesting that the seventh day when God rested was a type of the greater sabbath, the Millennium, when there will be peace and rest.

Before the Great Week

The years Adam spent in Eden contrast sharply with those of the Great Week of Time. At first, Adam did not have to die. After he was expelled from Eden, all humans were mortal. At first, Adam was tried in innocence. From the opening of the second dispensation to the closing of the seventh, humans are tried knowing both good and evil. Because of different conditions, the 40 years Adam spent in the garden of bliss are not counted as part of the Great Week.

Adam was given dominion in Eden. Like the three great kings of Israel, Saul, David and Solomon, who each ruled 40 years, I believe Adam ruled in the Garden of Eden 40 years, being tested by Satan. Christ, referred to in Scripture as "the last Adam,"[6] was also tempted by Satan for 40 time periods, in his case 40 days. If the last Adam was tested 40 revolutions of time, the first Adam probably was too.

Since the scriptures are always consistent, the number 40 means testing and probation wherever you find it. There is a striking correlation between Adam's time of testing and this last generation's time of testing. Adam's preceded the Great

61

Week. Our's precedes the millennial Day of the Lord. Like Adam, humans are being given 40 years of probation. They will also fail. They too will be judged and cast out of the literal land of Eden near the Euphrates and the Persian Gulf.

The Great Week of the Mortality of Man

Since man is mortal and can die during the entire Great Week of Time, it is more accurate to call it The Great Week of the Mortality of Man. This Great Week probably began in A.H. 40 (our B.C. 4003) and will last about 7,000 years.

Thinking of this 7,000 year Great Week as the time during which man is mortal makes it much easier to see that Adam's years in Eden are not part of it. If drawn to scale and superimposed upon the chart of the Great Week, the Dispensations will not fit unless **the Dispensation of Innocence is before the beginning of the Great Week.**

So far, we have Adam's 40 years in Eden, plus 7,000 years, for a total of 7,040 years. There are yet nine years to be accounted for. They have to do with judgment. Remember, "A wise man's heart discerneth both **time** and **judgment**."

"Christ...set...in the heavenly places, Far above all principality, and power, and might, and dominion, and every name that is named, not only in this age, but also in that which is to come." Ephesians 1:20,21 lit.

Chapter 5

The Ages of Time

The ages of time began when Adam and Eve regretfully moved from their garden paradise. As the wheel of time measuring the 1,000 year days started to turn like a cylinder seal against paper, another wheel began to revolve. This one counts the ages. There are ages of eternity and ages of time, but we are interested here in those of time.

Before the Ages of Time

Before the ages began, while Adam was still enjoying his garden paradise, God promised him that he could gain eternal life. Titus 1:2 speaks of this "eternal life, which God, that cannot lie, promised before the world began [*pro chronon aionion*, before the ages of time]." Who could he promise but Adam? **If God promised him before the ages of time, Adam had to be present before the ages of time began.**

There are several Scriptures that refer to a time before the ages or to the beginning of the ages. Paul said, "But we speak the wisdom of God in a mystery, even the **hidden wisdom**, which God ordained [*proorisen*, predetermined] before the world [*pro ton aionon*, **before the ages**]."[1]

Second Timothy 1:9 tells of "grace, which was given us in Christ Jesus before the world began [*pro chronon aionion*, before the ages of time]." Christ is the Lord, the creator. He was present before the ages of time began. His "name is called The Word of God."[2]

In the beginning was the Word, and the Word was with God, and the Word was God. The same was in the beginning with God. All things were made by him; and without him was not any thing made that was made ... And the Word was made flesh, and dwelt among us.[3]

Purpose of the Ages

The ages have a definite purpose. Paul wrote,

That the Gentiles should be fellow heirs ... Unto me ... is this grace given ... to make all men see what is the fellowship of the mystery, which from the beginning of the world [*aionon*, ages] hath been hid in **God, who created all things by Jesus Christ**: To the intent that now, unto the principalities and powers in heavenly places might be known by the church the manifold wisdom of God, According to the eternal purpose [*prothesin ton aionon*, **purpose of the ages**] which he purposed in Christ Jesus, our Lord.[4]

This secret Paul revealed was God's purpose to make of Jew and Gentile a new thing, the Church.

Gentiles, Jews and the Church

The Bible only recognizes these three groups of mankind, Gentiles, Jews and the Church. This is why Paul said to the Corinthians, "Give none offense, neither to the Jews, nor to the Gentiles, nor to the church of God."[5] The Lord planned the ages around these three groups.

Christ Planned the Ages

Through faith we understand that the worlds were framed [*katertisthai tous aionas*, the **ages were planned**] by the word of God.[6]

God ... Hath in these last days spoken unto us by [*en*, in] his Son, whom he hath appointed heir of all things, by whom also he made the worlds [Greek, *aionas*, ages].[7]

We Must Recognize the Ages to be Able to Understand God's Plan

Ecclesiastes 3:10,11 literally says that **God has set the [olam, ages] in their heart, without which man cannot find out the work that God maketh from the beginning to the end**. Knowing about the ages enables us to figure out the details of God's plan and place them in their proper time slot.

How Long is an Age?

Here we are not referring to an age as a long time of undetermined length, like an ice age. Scripture is often more precise. An age in time is 2,000 years long, two great days.

"God said, Let there be lights in the firmament of the heaven to divide the day from the night; and let them be for signs, and for seasons, and for days, and years."[8] Knowing this, it is significant that each constellation in the Zodiac moves one space along the ecliptic in about 2,000 years, drifting toward the left. Thus it is easier to see that 2,000 years is one of God's measures. Astrology is of Satan and forbidden, but the stars belong to God. He set them there as his own signs.

There are countless ages stretching across the endless ocean of eternity, but only three on this 7,000 year wave of time. The Millennium is only one great day, half an age.

The Age of the Ages

We are now living in the last complete age in time, the very same age in which our Lord was crucified. Hebrews 9:26 says that once "in the end of the world [*sunteleia ton aionon*, **full end of the ages**] hath he appeared to put away sin by the sacrifice of himself."

We are living in The Age of the ages. Ephesians 3:21 says, To "Him be glory in the church by Christ Jesus throughout all ages, world without end." But, the Greek of the last part is *eis pasas tas geneas tou aionos ton aionon*, literally, to all the generations of **the age of the ages**.

In this age of the ages are the Crucifixion, Resurrection and Ascension, completion of the scriptures, Rapture and 2,299 days of the Tribulation [Daniel's 2,300 days less one].[9]

Things happened to Israel for examples. Paul said "they are written for our admonition, upon whom the ends of the world [*tele ton aionon*, **ends** of the ages] are come."[10] Actually, the ends of two ages, of the Jews and the church, are extended and **run concurrently** during the Tribulation.

Matthew said, "But whoever speaks against the Holy Spirit, it shall not be forgiven him—neither in this age, or in that to come."[11] Notice that he did not specifically state that the next block of time is an age. The Lord is very careful how he words things. Only he can differentiate like this, "rightly dividing the word of truth."[12]

This is also true in Ephesians 1:21, where Christ is said to be "Far above all principality, and power, and might, and dominion, and every name that is named, not only in this world [*aioni*, age], but also in that which is to come." That which is to come is the Millennium, a great day, half an age. Half of that age is in time, the remainder in eternity.

During the three 2,000 year ages of time, God deals with Scripture's three divisions of mankind.[13] He dealt with the gentiles (neither Jews nor members of the church) until the time of Abraham, mainly with the Jews until the time of Christ and is now dealing chiefly with the church.

Each group is given about an age in which to obey God's directions. The Age of the Gentiles began in A.H. 40 (B.C. 4003) and lasted 2,000 years. The Age of the Jews began in A.H. 2040 (B.C. 2003) and lasted 2,000 years. The Age of the Church began in A.H. 4040 (B.C. 3) after Jesus was born. However, the church was not born until 30 A.D.

Does this Age End in Year 6,000?

It seems that this age should also last 2,000 years and the Day of the Lord begin in A.H. 6040, 6,000 years after Adam left his paradise, but it is not that simple. Maybe that would have made it easy to figure out God's timetable too soon. I believe something exciting will happen near the beginning of year 6,000, but it looks like this age will be extended by nine years. The number nine means rebellion. During these nine years, rebellion will increase to such a peak that a Satan possessed man will wage war against Christians and sit in the temple in Jerusalem claiming to be God.

During the first few years of the nine, the Lord will be giving hardhearted Israel one more chance to come to her senses and turn to him. When she doesn't, the Tribulation Judgment will take place. Once rolling, it can't be stopped.

The Lord pleads, "Repent, and turn yourselves from all your transgressions; so iniquity shall not be your ruin. Cast away from you all your transgressions, whereby ye have transgressed; and make you a new heart and a new spirit: for **why will ye die, O house of Israel?**"[14]

This is judgment. Remember, a wise man's heart can discern both "time" and "judgment."[15]

Just as in the book of Revelation there is a parenthetical portion between the sixth and seventh seals, the sixth and seventh trumpets, and the sixth and seventh vials, there is a nine year parenthesis between what should be the normal end of the sixth great day and the seventh one.

Near the morning of each age, the Lord visits man. "What is man, that thou shouldest magnify him? and that thou shouldest set thine heart upon him? And that thou shouldest visit him every morning."[16]

In the beginning of the first age, the Lord visited Adam. Near dawning of the second age, the angel of the Lord visited Abraham. As the third age drew near, a body was prepared for the Lord and Jesus was born on Earth. Though only a great day, soon after the Millennium starts, our Lord Jesus Christ will return to Earth again, this time in glory, as King of kings and Lord of lords.

Jesus' Long Day

Jesus is Greek for the Hebrew Joshua. Joshua's long day was a type of Jesus' long day, which will be the first day of the Millennium, a day of judgment and catastrophe.

Like its prototype, Jesus' long day will be extended until the battle is won. During the 24 hour plus day, the Lord will do a strange thing as at Gibeon in Joshua's time.

> Judgment also will I lay to the line, and right-
> eousness to the plummet: and the hail shall
> sweep away the refuge of lies . . . your cove-
> nant with death shall be disannulled, and your
> agreement with hell shall not stand; when the
> overflowing scourge shall pass through, then
> ye shall be trodden down by it . . . For the
> LORD shall rise up as in mount Perazim [which

means interval, or gap], he shall be wroth **as in the valley of Gibeon**, that he may do his work, his strange work; and bring to pass his act, his strange act . . . **a consumption, even determined upon the whole earth.**[17]

The Lord shall rise up at the end of the nine year interval as he did near Gibeon and tread the winepress of the wrath of God. Both times great **chunks of rock** hail down upon the enemy. When Joshua's men fought the Amorites,

the LORD **cast down great stones from heaven** . . . more . . . died with hailstones [*eben barad*, stone hail, not ice] than they whom the children of Israel slew with the sword.[18]

It will happen again. At the end of the shortened Tribulation, great boulders will be cast down from heaven. The beloved apostle John described it:

"And there fell upon men a great hail out of heaven, every **stone** about the weight of a talent [100 pounds]: and men blasphemed God because of the plague of the hail; for the plague thereof was exceeding great."[19]

Though many people have regarded Joshua's long day a myth, it actually did happen. A few years ago, scientists at the Goddard Space Flight Center in Greenbelt, Maryland, were using a computer to check the positions of the sun, moon and planets in other years so their man-made satellites would not bump into any of them later on. As the computer scanned the centuries back and forth, it uncovered an astonishing fact.

There is one day missing in the elapsed time, 23 hours and 20 minutes in Joshua's time and another 40 minutes in the days of Hezekiah. They referred to the Bible. I wish I had seen their faces then. God's word is true to the tiniest detail. The editor of the Evening World newspaper in Spencer, Indiana said, "Our God is rubbing their noses in His truth."

Joshua referred to the 23 hours and 20 minutes as "about a whole day." Scripture is carefully worded. He said,

The sun stood still, and the moon stayed, until the people had avenged themselves upon their enemies . . . So the sun stood still in the midst of heaven, and hasted not to go down about a whole day.[20]

The other 40 minutes equals ten degrees on the sundial. Isaiah said,

This sign shalt thou have of the LORD, that the LORD will do the thing that he hath spoken: shall the shadow go forward ten degrees, or go back ten degrees? And Hezekiah answered, It is a light thing for the shadow to go down ten degrees: nay, but let the shadow return backward ten degrees. And . . . the LORD . . . brought the shadow ten degrees backward.[21]

No man can prove anything in Scripture's original manuscripts incorrect. If God said it, it's absolute truth. Our understanding may be faulty, but every statement is absolute fact.

Day of the Lord

Many Bible expositors think this age we are living in ends with the Rapture (the translation of the Church to heaven), but Scripture will not support this view. When Jesus explained the parable of the tares of the field, he showed that the consummation of this age actually coincides with the beginning of his kingdom. His kingdom begins at the end of the Tribulation, not before it.

Tares are darnel, plants that look just like wheat in the blade. Only after they come into ear can they be separated easily. Of the four kinds growing in Israel, one, the bearded darnel, is even poisonous.

In Scripture, Christians are called wheat; tares are look-alikes but are not really believers. They do not have the correct "fruit," and some are pure poison. Jesus explained,

The enemy that sowed them is the devil; the harvest is the end of the world [*sunteleia tou*

69

aionos, **consummation of the age**]; and the reapers are the angels. As therefore the tares are gathered and burned in the fire; so shall it be in the end of this world [*sunteleia tou aionos toutou*, **consummation of this age**]. The Son of man shall send forth his angels, and they shall gather out of his kingdom all things that offend, and them which do iniquity; And shall cast them into a **furnace of fire.**[22]

Just as the faithful Shadrach, Meshach, and Abed-nego escaped from the fiery furnace in Daniel's day, the faithful will escape from a furnace of fire at the consummation of this age. It is the Translation of the Tribulation Saints, or Rapture II. Truly, "he himself shall be saved; yet so as by fire" (1 Corinthians 3:15).

There is one point in time when this age ends and his kingdom begins. The Tribulation years cannot separate the two events.

Also, Elijah must come and preach during the Tribulation as one of God's two special witnesses before the Day of the Lord can begin. The Old Testament ends with the Lord's promise:

I will send you Elijah the prophet before the coming of the great and dreadful day of the LORD: And he shall turn the heart of the fathers to the children, and the heart of the children to their fathers, lest I come and **smite the earth with a curse.**[23]

Piecing the Prophetic Puzzle

God spread out an interesting prophetic puzzle for us. Recognizing his divisions of time helps us arrange the pieces correctly. These boundaries are like edge pieces of a jigsaw puzzle. Once in place, other pieces are much easier to fit in.

This is why Timothy taught, "Study to shew thyself approved unto God, a workman that needeth not to be ashamed, **rightly dividing the word of truth.**"[24]

We have seven dispensations, seven of God's great days, and three ages, all running concurrently. If you understand these divisions of time, you can work the puzzle.

Chapter 6

Former and Latter Rain

No one can know when Christ will return—impossible! That's what I thought. But the Lord had a few things yet to teach me.

In my painstaking search for the correct crucifixion day, I unexpectedly struck silver. I found Scripture that indicates the month and day of both advents of Christ.

Unbelievable? Of course! at first. But it is there! It has been there ever since Old Testament times, maybe some seven centuries before Jesus was born.

Jewish Month of Both Advents

Prayerfully open your Bible to Hosea, chapter 4. Ask the Lord to help you discern the truth. Glance at the first verse to see who is talking in this passage. "Hear the word of the LORD, ye children of Israel" almost shouts it's importance.

Then look at the last verse of chapter 5. The Lord is still talking. "I will go," he says, "and return to my place, till they acknowledge their offence, and seek my face."

Echoing this thought in the New Testament, our Lord Jesus Christ said, "Ye shall not see me henceforth, till ye shall say, Blessed is he that cometh in the name of the Lord."[1] It is the same Lord speaking in both cases.

God was in Christ reconciling the world unto himself.[2]

The first man Adam was made a living soul; the **last** Adam [our Lord Jesus Christ] was made a quickening spirit. . . . The first man is of the earth, earthy: **The second man** [Christ] **is the Lord from heaven.**[3]

71

Adam and Jesus are both called sons of God in Scripture.[4] Notice that Jesus is the **last** one in his category. If Jesus was not the Messiah, we are without hope. There will be no other of his kind. Our legacy from the first Adam is death, from the second Adam, salvation from death. His Last Will and Testament (the New Testament) became effective upon his sacrificial death. In it he stipulated the conditions we must observe to become his heirs.

> That if thou shalt confess with thy mouth the
> Lord Jesus, and shalt believe in thine heart that
> God hath raised him from the dead, thou shalt
> be saved.[5]

When Philip asked Christ to show them the Father, Jesus said, "Have I been so long time with you, and yet hast thou not known me, Philip? **he that hath seen me hath seen the Father** . . . the words that I speak unto you I speak not of myself: but **the Father that dwelleth in me**, he doeth the works."[6]

"Verily, verily, I [Jesus] say unto you, Before Abraham was, I am."[7] Hebrews 1:2 says that God "Hath in these last days spoken unto us by [*en*, in] his Son."

In the Old Testament, Jehovah (which can also be transliterated as Yahweh, or Ieue) said that there is

> no God else beside me; a just God and a Sav-
> iour: there is none beside me. Look unto me,
> and be ye saved, all the ends of the earth: for I
> am God, and **there is none else.** I have
> sworn . . . That unto me every knee shall bow.[8]

This scripture will be fulfilled in our Lord Jesus Christ, in whom "**God was manifest in the flesh.**"[9]

> God also hath highly exalted him, and given
> him a name which is above every name: That at
> the name of Jesus every knee should bow, of
> things in heaven, and things in earth, and
> things under the earth; And that **every tongue
> should confess that Jesus Christ is
> Lord**, to the glory of God the Father.[10]

Jesus Christ is Lord. He is both "the root [Jehovah] and the offspring [Jesus] of David,"[11] the "Alpha and Omega, the beginning [Jehovah] **and the end** [Jesus], the first and the last,"[12] both Lord of the Old Testament and Lord of the New Testament. He is both God and man. His name is Jesus [Y'shua in Hebrew], which means **"Jehovah is Saviour."** This is why Scripture said that they would call his name Emmanuel, which being interpreted is, **God with us**."[13]

We can understand this easier if we first think of it as if Jesus inherited two complete natures from his parents. Isaiah explained, "Unto us a child is born [inheriting his human nature from his mother], unto us **a son is given** [inheriting his divine nature from his Father]: and the government shall be upon his shoulder: and his name shall be called Wonderful, Counsellor, The mighty God, The everlasting Father."[14] The difference is, the son was "given," not reproduced."God [himself] was in Christ, reconciling the world unto himself" (II Corinthians 5:19). "For **in him** [Jesus Christ] **dwelleth all the fulness of the Godhead** bodily" (Colossians 2:9).

As chapter six begins, the Jewish remnant of the last days speaks. Here is where the vein of pure silver has been hiding all this time, waiting to be discovered by you and me after the Sign of the End of the Age appeared.

Come, [the remnant says], and let us return unto the LORD: for he hath torn, and he will heal us; he hath smitten, and he will bind us up. After two days [two 1,000 year days] will he revive us: in the third day he will raise us up, and we shall live in his sight.

Jesus Christ was resurrected in the third 24 hour day. The modern nation of Israel was raised up in the third 1,000 year day. This was proved true in 1948; Israel's captivity began 2,470 years before, in B.C. 523. The silver follows:

Then shall we know [the remnant continues], if we follow on to know the **LORD**: his [Christ the Lord's] going forth is prepared as the morning [Christ will come in the morning of the Day of the Lord, but not at dawn] and **he shall come unto us as the rain, as the latter and former rain unto the earth.**

73

He shall come unto us as the rain, as the latter an-
former rain unto the Earth. Can you believe it's this easy
Christ came the first time as the former rain and will return a
the latter rain begins in Israel. It's true. Scripture says it.

First, we saw through the glass darkly as we tried t
look at the future prophetic picture. However, in this time o
the end, light is shining brighter and brighter, illuminating th
scene.

The messianic Psalm 72 told us plainly, "**He sha**
come down like rain upon the mown grass: as shower
that water the earth,"[15] but did we understand?

In Scripture, God is symbolized by a river[16] and by
fountain of living waters.[17] Therefore, it is not too aston
ishing to find that Christ is symbolized by the rain. He is Go
incarnate. He will splash down as "the great rain of hi
[God's] strength."[18]

The Lord said, "I will be as the dew unto Israel." The
a little farther on, he said, "**Who is wise**, and he sha
understand these things? Prudent, and he shall know them?"
You of the last generation, you shall know them.

In Deuteronomy 11:14, God told us plainly,

I will give you the rain of your land **in his**
due season, the first rain and the latter rain.

Through the years, God quietly worked a miracle t
show us his truth today. In Israel, the former and latter rain
are such definite seasons that they are marked on those Jewisl
calendars which include harvest seasons and feast dates.

The former rain is a light autumn sprinkling that begin:
in **Tishri, the first month of the Jewish civil year**
The latter rain is "the great rain," a heavy spring deluge tha
begins in **Nisan, the first month of the Jewish sacred**
year and the first month of the Jewish regnal year.
Tishri begins their rainy season. Nisan ends it. From Nisan tc
Tishri, roughly the summer season, is dry.

No mistake can be made in determining these season:
for both the Greek and Hebrew words used in the scriptures
for these rains indicate the seasons in which they fall.

James, the half-brother of Jesus, gave us a clue: "Be
patient therefore, brethren, unto the coming of the Lord
Behold, the husbandman waiteth for the precious fruit of the

DIVISIONS OF TIME

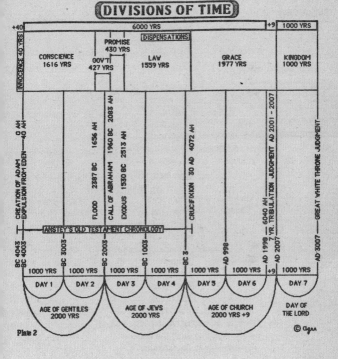

Plate 2

© agee

Jewish Calendar with the Seven Feasts

Sacred Year	Civil Year				Seasons
1	7	**Nisan**		(Mar.-Apr.)	**Latter Rain**
			1	New Moon	
			14	Passover	
			15	Feast of Unleavened Bread begins	
			16	Feast of Firstfruits	Barley harvest begins
2	8	Iyar		(Apr.-May)	Barley harvest
3	9	Sivan		(May-June)	Wheat harvest
			6	Pentecost/ Feast of Weeks	Grapes begin to ripen
4	10	Tamuz		(June-July)	Figs begin to ripen
5	11	Av		(July-Aug.)	Grapes, figs, walnuts, olives ripe
6	12	Elul		(Aug.-Sept.)	Vintage begins
7	1	**Tishri**		(Sept.-Oct.)	**Former Rain**
			1	New Year/Feast of Trumpets	Plowing, sowing
			10	Day of Atonement	
			15	Feast of Tabernacles begins	
8	2	Cheshvan		(Oct.-Nov.)	Wheat, barley sown
9	3	Kislev		(Nov.-Dec.)	
10	4	Teveth		(Dec.-Jan.)	
11	5	Shevat		(Jan.-Feb.)	
12	6	Adar		(Feb.-Mar.)	Almonds blossom
13		Adar II		Intercalary Month added when necessary to keep the seasons aligned with the Calendar	

Plate 3

earth, and hath long patience for it, until he receive the early and latter rain."[20]

The word used for the early rain is *proimon*, which means autumnal showering. *Opsimon* is used for the latter rain and means spring showering.

Jeremiah said, "Neither say they in their heart, Let us now fear the LORD our God, that giveth rain, both the former and the latter, **in his season**."[21] The Hebrew word used for the former rain is *yowreh*, which means autumnal sprinkling rain. *Malqowsh* is the word for the latter rain. It means gathered spring rain. Both rains are to come in "his season."

Therefore, **the Lord has two due seasons, two advents**, two appointments to meet with man. Instead of there being two Messiahs as some Jews have taught, there is one Messiah who comes twice. He came as the suffering Messiah the first time and will come the second time in glory to set up his kingdom.

Can you believe the Lord told us the month and day as plainly as this, and we still did not see it? We've been blind. Jesus' statement about no man knowing the day or hour was **the Lord's delay switch** so we would not understand too soon, before the time of the end began. He wanted people to think Christ could come at any time along the way. Yet, he planted clues in Scripture that would reveal it to this last generation. He had to open our eyes when the time was right.

Tishri, the first month of the Jewish civil year, falls in our September or October, never in December. Bible scholars have long known that December 25 was not the most likely date for the birth of Jesus. However, that date has been kept ever since 354 A. D., when Bishop Liberius of Rome ordered the celebration to be observed on that day.[22]

This was after the reign of Constantine, who proclaimed Christianity the religion of the Roman Empire. Some claim that he marched his army through the river to baptize them. Whether he did or not, by making Christianity the state religion, he was instrumental in bringing pagans into the Christian church.

Bishop Liberius may have thought it would be good for Christians to celebrate the birthday of their Saviour, the Son of God, on the same day that the birthday of the heathen sun god (Satan's counterfeit saviour in the Mystery Religion of Babylon) was being observed, on the Feast of Saturn.

Both times, Christ arrives in a first month. The Lord told us what he would do at the end of this age:

> I will remove far off from you [modern Israel] the northern army [a multi-nation force] . . . rejoice in the LORD your God: for he hath [past tense] given you the former rain moderately, and he will [future tense] cause to come down for you the rain, the former rain, and the latter rain in the first month . . . And ye shall know that I am in the midst of Israel.[23]

Christ will return in the first Nisan following his decimation of the northern army. (More about this later)

Day of Both Advents

In the scriptures, the first day of the month is to be understood unless a certain day of the month is specified, because the Hebrew word for month means new moon. On their lunar calendar, the new moon is the first of the month.

Nevertheless, we are not given any latitude as to which day Christ is to come to Israel. Look at Ezekiel 29, verses 17 and 21. After Ezekiel had established the month and day in verse 17 by saying, "In the **first month, in the first day of the month**, the word of the LORD came unto me," the Lord made a very important statement in verse 21:

> **In that day, will I cause the horn of the house of Israel to bud forth**, and I will give thee the opening of the mouth in the midst of them; and they shall know that I am the LORD.

This could not have been much clearer or we would've figured out God's timetable too soon. It's pure "silver."[24] The search is exciting, isn't it?

It is not difficult to understand, yet it is a little harder to recognize than "his due season" in Deuteronomy 11:14 because there are three verses between the two statements.

A horn represents a king, as in Revelation 17:12, which says that "the ten horns which thou sawest are ten kings." The king of the house of Israel is Jesus Christ.[25] This first month and first day is Nisan 1, for Ezekiel spoke of the Passover being on the 14th of the first month in chapter 45, verse 21. The Passover is in Nisan.

Christ will return on Nisan 1, the beginning of the Jewish regnal year. Each king's reign was counted as beginning on the first of Nisan after his accession. The days before Nisan 1 were counted to his predecessor.

Our Lord is returning to rule as King of kings and Lord of lords as both the regnal and the sacred year begin. Good timing—no other time of year could possibly be so appropriate.

Events at the Temple

Christ will return as he left, to the mount of Olives (Acts 1:12) then the "Lord, whom ye seek, shall suddenly come to his temple."[26]

What will happen there the day he arrives? On this, Scripture does not leave much up to conjecture. It plainly tells us,

> Thus saith the Lord GOD; **In the first month, in the first day** of the month, thou shalt take a young bullock without blemish, and **cleanse the sanctuary**: And the priest shall take of the blood of the sin-offering, and put it upon the posts of the house, and upon the four corners of the settle of the altar, and upon the posts of the gate of the inner court.[27]

It looks like our Lord Jesus Christ, God incarnate, will return on the new moon of Nisan 1 in a sabbatic year, the first year of that greater Sabbath, the millennial Day of the Lord.

Year of Jesus' Birth

Jesus was born on the Jewish Tishri 1 in A.H. 4039, which is our B.C. 5, before the death of Herod the Great, who died near the eclipse of March 13, B.C. 4.

Joseph and Mary probably traveled to Bethlehem on Friday, finding a place to bed down in the stable that night. At

6 P.M. the Jewish Sabbath began. Jesus was born that night. How fitting that he be born on the Sabbath. He is Lord of the Sabbath.[28]

The Jewish date was Tishri 1, 3757, the Jewish New Year (beginning of the civil year) and the Feast of Trumpets. Trumpets were blown because it was the beginning of the month and the Feast of Trumpets. It was the anniversary of that sabbatic Feast of Trumpets when God rested from his creation labors and this *kosmos* began to operate. The Lord marked that day well.

Trumpet peals heralded the birth of our Saviour in Judah, as they will his coronation, which will also be on the Feast of Trumpets.

The Roman year in which our Saviour was born was AUC 749. On our calendar, **Jesus was probably born just before midnight on September 8, B.C. 5.**

Chapter 7

Day of the Cross

Was Jesus actually crucified on Friday?

Good Friday is kept in our churches every year. Yet why do some great Bible teachers think the crucifixion took place on Wednesday?

I had to find out the truth for myself. Either he was crucified on Wednesday or he was crucified on Friday.

My research was thorough. I read everything I could find, periodicals, books, even rare books and old brittle handwritten manuscripts with cream centers and yellowed halos, very hard to read because an "s" is sometimes "ƒ."

Year of the Crucifixion

There is no general agreement on the correct date of the Crucifixion, day or year. However, 30 A.D. is accepted as the correct year more often than any other.

Two Old Testament prophecies point to 30 A.D., Daniel 9:24-26 and Ezekiel 4:6,7. In Daniel, the "Seventy weeks" (*shabuim*) are literally "seventy sevens" or 490 years (70 x 7). After 483 years, but **before Jerusalem was destroyed**, the Messiah was to be "cut off" (karath, killed).

Those 483 years began with "the commandment to restore and to build Jerusalem." The Lord said,

> Cyrus, He is my shepherd, and shall perform
> all my pleasure: even saying to Jerusalem,
> Thou shalt be built: and to the temple, Thy
> foundation shall be laid . . . he shall build my
> city, and he shall let go my captives.[1]

Joseph ben Mattathias, the famous Jewish historian known to the world as Flavius Josephus, recorded that Cyrus gave permission to rebuild Jerusalem. He wrote,

In the first year of the reign of Cyrus, which was the 70th from the day that our people were removed out of their own land into Babylon . . . he gave them leave to go back to their own country, and **to rebuild their city Jerusalem,** and the temple of God.[2]

Ezra 1:1,2 also shows that this commandment was given in the first year of Cyrus. That year was A.H. 3589, our B.C. 454 (Ptolemy's chronology errs by 82 years[3]).

According to Jewish inclusive reckoning, the 483rd year was A.H. 4071 (29 A.D.). Since Messiah was to be killed "after" the 483 years, 30 A.D. fits perfectly. In 29 A.D., the Jewish Nisan 14 fell on April 18, a Monday, which rules that year out, so **30 A.D. is the first possible year.**

The prophecy in Ezekiel 4:6,7 bridges the 40 year gap between the Crucifixion in 30 A.D. and the destruction of Jerusalem in 70 A.D. The Lord told Ezekiel,

Thou shalt bear the iniquity of the house of Judah forty days; I have appointed thee each day for a year. Therefore, thou shalt set thy face toward the siege of Jerusalem, and thine arm shall be uncovered, and thou shalt prophesy against it.

The year 30 A.D. not only fits Daniel's and Ezekiel's prophecies but fits the known facts of the life of our Saviour. Jesus was born on Tishri 1 in A.H. 4039 (probably our September 8, B.C. 5). He was baptized when he "began to be about thirty years of age,"[4] in A.H. 4068 (26 A.D.). Therefore, he began his public ministry near his birthday. This tallies well with the probability that there were leaves on the fig tree furnishing shade when Nathanael sat under it.[5]

On the first Passover of his ministry, the Jews told Jesus that the temple was 46 years in building.[6] According to Josephus, it was begun in the 18th year of Herod's reign.[7] This was A.H. 4042 (B.C. 20/19[8]). Thus the first Passover was that of A.H. 4069 (27 A.D.), one half year after Jesus began his ministry.

There are four Passovers listed in John, in 2:23, 5:1, 6:4 and 12:1. Three are plainly said to be Passovers and the unnamed feast in 5:1 had to be a Passover for when Jesus was in Samaria, he said, "There are yet four months, and then cometh harvest."[9]

The harvest begins with the Feast of Firstfruits on Nisan 16. Therefore the feast in 5:1 when the Jews gathered at Jerusalem was the Passover.[10] Since the Crucifixion was at the time of the fourth Passover, it took place in A.H. 4072 or 30 A.D.

Other facts confirm this date. John 18:21 says, "It is not lawful for us to put any man to death." The power of capital punishment was taken away from the Jews 40 years before the temple was destroyed in 70 A.D. If Christ had been tried by them before 30 A.D., they could have put him to death themselves. Therefore, for this reason also, **his crucifixion could not have been earlier than 30 A.D.**[11]

John the Baptist began his ministry the year of Jesus' baptism. That was "in the fifteenth year of the reign of Tiberius Caesar."[12] The date from which to reckon the fifteenth year of Tiberius is January 16, 12 A.D., when he began to co-reign with Augustus. He was practically the sole monarch over Syria and Palestine from then on. Augustus concerned himself with other parts of the Empire.[13] Following the Jewish custom of figuring years by inclusive reckoning, the fifteenth year was 26 A.D.

Everything dovetails perfectly. Adding another three and one half years for his ministry, we see that Jesus was crucified in 30 A.D. when he was thirty-three and one half years old. This is widely accepted.

Day of the Crucifixion

A few people have thought that Jesus was crucified on Wednesday, others picked Thursday, but most settled on Friday, now called Good Friday. Which is correct?

Here is where we must lay aside all preconceived opinions and examine the scripture evidence with the utmost care, letting it speak for itself.

Some have thought that the Gospel of John disagreed with the other gospels. This is faulty thinking. God does not make mistakes. It is up to us to figure out how to reconcile the accounts, for they are all four correct down to the smallest detail. Some descriptions that seem to differ are only because Jesus performed so many more miracles than are recorded.

Otherwise, the whole world could not contain the books written about him. The gospel writers sometimes described similar but entirely different occurences.

The first thing we have to do is orient ourselves to the Jewish day. This is where the usual mistakes are made. Their days begin at sunset or 6:00 P.M. **The night portion precedes the daylight portion**. The scriptures are consistent, and Genesis 1:5 sets this for the entire Bible, saying, "And the evening and the morning were the first day." **For each date, first we have to account for 12 hours of night then the following 12 hours of day.**[14]

If we forget and think in terms of our days, it is possible to drop a whole day from our calculations. For instance, Leviticus 23:5,6 says, "In the fourteenth day of the first month at evening is the Lord's passover. And on the fifteenth day of the same month is the feast of unleavened bread." It is easy to think that they sacrificed the Passover at the end of the fourteenth day and that the following daylight was the fifteenth, but this is wrong.

They actually sacrificed the Passover in the evening as Nisan 14 commenced. The following daylight portion was still Nisan 14, the Feast of the Passover, not Nisan 15. Keep this in mind as we carefully trace Jesus' steps through Passion Week.

> Jesus, six days before the passover, came to Bethany . . . they made him a supper . . . On the next day many people . . . took branches of palm trees, and went forth to meet him.[15]

Jesus traveled from Jericho on Friday, arriving in Bethany just after sunset, when the Saturday Sabbath began, just as Mary and Joseph did when they traveled to Bethlehem on Friday when Jesus was born. In Bethany, the food for supper would have been prepared during the day as usual on the preparation day preceding the Sabbath.

Since the Passover was Nisan 14, six days before that was Nisan 8, Saturday. Jesus arrived in Bethany after the night portion of Nisan 8 had just begun and stayed there during the following daylight portion, resting on the Sabbath.

On the next day, Sunday, Nisan 9, he rode into Jerusalem seated on a donkey. People "Took branches of palm trees, and went forth to meet him."[16] Therefore, this day came to be called Palm Sunday. This too is generally accepted.

On Palm Sunday, he was presented to the people as king and was rejected by most. He knew the terrible consequences of their decision and lamented,

> If thou hadst known, even thou, at least in this thy day, the things which belong unto thy peace! But now they are hidden from thine eyes.[17]

When "the eventide was come,"[18] it was Monday, Nisan 10. "And on the morrow, when they were come from Bethany,"[19] it was still Nisan 10. It was not the next day, but the morning of that same day, the evening and the morning making one day.[20]

Monday was when he cursed the fig tree and cleansed the temple. Because of his rejection as king the day before, the last tribes of the fig tree nation were to wither away and finally be dispersed 40 years later in 70 A.D.

In a more far-reaching application, Israel will feel the effects of The Curse as this age ends. (More about this later.)

"And when even was come, he went out of the city. And in the morning, as they passed by, they saw the fig tree dried up . . . And they came again to Jerusalem . . . in the temple."[21] This evening and morning was Tuesday, Nisan 11, when he gave the Olivet Discourse after leaving the temple.[22]

After the Olivet Discourse, Luke said, "And in the day time he was teaching in the temple; and at night he went out, and abode in the mount that is called the mount of Olives. And **all** the people came early in the morning to him in the temple [type of Rapture II, as the Day of the Lord begins], for to hear him."[23] That night and morning was Nisan 12, Wednesday.

On the night of Nisan 12, Mary of Bethany anointed Jesus' head with precious ointment. He said, "She . . . is come aforehand to anoint my body to the burying."[24] That was her last chance. The next night, he was taken prisoner.

> After two days [Nisan 12 and 13] was the feast of the passover [Nisan 14], and of unleavened bread: and the chief priests and the scribes sought how they might take him by craft, and put him to death. But they said, **Not on the feast day** [i.e., not on Nisan 14, Passover], lest there be an uproar of the people.[25]

Since they said, "Not on the feast day," **the Crucifixion was not on the Feast of the Passover, Friday, Nisan 14**. It is clear that **the Passover was still future during the trials**. "They . . . went not into the judgment hall . . . that they might eat the passover."[26]

After the Last Supper, when Judas went out, "some of them thought, because Judas had the bag, that Jesus had said unto him, Buy those things that we have need of against the feast."[27] This shows that at that time, the Passover Feast was still future. Also, **all buying had to be done on the day of preparation**, the day before the Passover.

There is no room for doubt. The Scripture plainly says, "Now **before the feast of the passover**, when Jesus knew that his hour was come that he should depart out of this world unto the Father . . . supper being ended, the devil having now put into the heart of Judas Iscariot . . . to betray him . . . He, then, having received the sop, went immediately out; and it was night [the beginning of Jewish days]."[28] The Crucifixion was not on the Passover, but before the Passover, and remember that the night preceded the day. There is still daylight to come before this day is over.

Thursday, Nisan 13, actually was the day of the Crucifixion. It began with the Last Supper and ended with Jesus' death. It was "the first [*prote*, before, prior] day of unleavened bread, **when they killed the passover**,"[29] "And **it was the preparation of the passover**,"[30] the day when the lambs were slain in the afternoon at the temple.

When Mark said that it was the first (or prior) day of unleavened bread, he also quickly said that it was the day when they killed the passover so we would not misunderstand him. He meant that it was Nisan 13, not Nisan 14.

When they came out of Egypt, the Lord instructed them, saying, "In the first month, on the fourteenth day of the month at even, ye shall eat unleavened bread, until the one and twentieth day of the month at even."[31] So, it would be easy to err and think Mark was talking about Nisan 14.

However, it was the Jewish custom to conduct the "*Bediqath Hametz*," the search for leaven, on the afternoon of Nisan 12. Every householder searched the house with a candle, looking for leaven. When every particle was thrown out, the next day, Nisan 13, had to be a day of unleavened bread. This is why some writings of the first few centuries afterward mentioned eight days of unleavened bread instead of seven. The Orthodox Jews still keep Passover eight days. When Pilate brought Jesus out before the people,

> **it was the preparation of the passover** [Nisan 13], and about the sixth hour [Roman time, our 9:00 A.M.]: and he saith unto the Jews, Behold your King: But they cried out, Away with him, away with him, crucify him ... **Then delivered he him therefore unto them to be crucified.**[32]

Jesus died shortly after 3:00 P.M. While it was still Nisan 13, the preparation of the Passover, the legs of the thieves were broken. They died, then a spear pierced Jesus' side spilling his blood for the remission of our sins. For "without shedding of blood is no remission."[33] If his blood had not poured out, we would have been without a Saviour.

John explained why they were in a hurry and broke the legs of the thieves.

> The Jews therefore, because **it was the preparation** [Nisan 13], that the bodies should not remain upon the cross on the sabbath day, (for that sabbath day was an high day,) besought Pilate that their legs might be broken, and that they might be taken away.[34]

The next day was a Sabbath, a special high day, the Feast of the Passover. It was called a Sabbath because Exodus 12:16 prohibited all work on that day. The word sabbath means cessation or rest.

Christ himself is "our passover."[35] He was crucified as the morning sacrifices were being offered at the temple, and died at the same time the passover lambs were being slain, "between the two evenings,"[36] between 3:00 and 5:00 P.M., "at the going down of the sun."[37] The going down of the sun portrayed Christ, the "Sun of righteousness,"[38] when he "descended first into the lower parts of the earth."[39]

The Three Days and Three Nights

From his death until his resurrection, Christ spent "three days and three nights in the heart of the earth."[40]

This did not mean the physical body, but the soul and spirit. At noon, Christ told the thief, "To day shalt thou be with me in paradise."[41] Before Nisan 13 ended, both descended into the lower parts of the Earth, to Paradise.

Those three days and nights were Thursday (day), Friday (night then day), Saturday (night then day) and Sunday (night). Everything fits perfectly. Nothing is strained to fit.

When speaking of the temple of his body, Jesus said, "Destroy this temple, and in three days I will raise it up."[42] Since he died on Thursday, and was resurrected on Sunday, the three days were Friday, Saturday and Sunday. The two men on the road to Emmaus said on Sunday, "The chief priests and our rulers . . . have crucified him. . . . today is the third day since these things were done."[43]

I believe **the Crucifixion was on Thursday, Nisan 13**, but the burial was on the Feast of the Passover, Nisan 14. It was after 6:00 P.M. for Mark 15:42,43,46 says,

> And now when the even was come, because it
> was the preparation, that is, the day before the
> sabbath, Joseph of Arimathaea . . . laid him in
> a sepulchre.

There were two preparation days. Nisan 13 was the preparation of the Passover and Nisan 14 was the preparation of the Saturday Sabbath. That is why Mark had to explain which preparation day he meant.

"Now the next day [Saturday], that followed the day of the preparation, the chief priests and Pharisees came together unto Pilate" and asked that the sepulchre be made sure until the third day, lest his disciples steal him away and say that he has risen. "So they went, and made the sepulchre sure, sealing the stone, and setting a watch."[44]

The burial day, the Saturday Sabbath and the day of resurrection were three successive days with no extra day between the burial day and the Saturday Sabbath. Luke said,

> Joseph . . . begged the body of Jesus . . . laid
> it in a sepulchre. . . . that day was the pre-
> paration, and the sabbath drew on. And the
> women also, which came with him from
> Galilee, followed after, and beheld the sepul-
> chre, and how his body was laid. And they

returned, and prepared spices and ointments; and rested the sabbath day **according to the commandment** [therefore this Sabbath was Saturday]. Now upon the first day of the week [Sunday], very early in the morning, they came unto the sepulchre, bringing the spices . . . And they found the stone rolled away from the sepulchre.[45]

The day of the Passover, which was called a Sabbath, was followed by the Saturday Sabbath. This is one reason why Matthew 28:1 literally says, "In the end of the sabbaths, as it began to dawn toward the first day of the week, came Mary Magdalene and the other Mary to see the sepulchre." There could not have been a day between those Sabbaths or they could have taken the spices to the tomb before Sunday.

Three of the women bought more spices after 6:00 P.M. when the Jewish Sunday began. "And when the sabbath was past, Mary Magdalene, and Mary the mother of James, and Salome, had bought sweet spices, that they might come and anoint him . . . the first day of the week, they came unto the sepulchre at the rising of the sun . . . the stone was rolled away . . . entering . . . they saw a young man . . . he saith unto them, Be not affrighted: Ye seek Jesus of Nazareth, which was crucified: he is risen; he is not here."[46]

Jesus, the only begotten son of God, was **crucified on Nisan 13, our Thursday, April 6, 30 A.D.** This date was preserved by the Montanists, who observed a memorial every year on April 6.[47] **All four of the gospel accounts harmonize.** Why has this been so hard to see?

Thus, Jesus arose during the night of Nisan 16, our Sunday, April 9. Nehemiah, whose name means "conduct of the Lord," pictured the Resurrection when he said, "I came to Jerusalem, and was there three days. And I arose in the night, I and some few men with me."[48] The few who arose with Nehemiah tie in also. Matthew 27:52,53 says, "And the graves were opened; and many bodies of the saints which slept arose, And came out of the graves after his resurrection, and went into the holy city, and appeared unto many."

Some think the Crucifixion was Nisan 14, which according to Jewish Calendar laws only falls on Monday, Wednesday, Friday or Saturday. The Catholic Church insists on Friday, April 7, 30 A.D. They missed by only one day.

If the Crucifixion was on Nisan 13 (and it was, for i was not on the feast day, Nisan 14), according to Jewish calendar laws, it can only fall on Sunday, Tuesday, Thursday or Friday. This eliminates a Wednesday crucifixion.

Not everyone believes that Christ was crucified on either Wednesday or Friday. Seyffarth, Thurman, Aldrich and Westcott picked a Thursday date. Africanus, Bengel, Gresswell and Rusk thought **it was on Thursday, April 6, 30 A.D.**, and I agree with them.

Remember April 6. You will be surprised to find out when it will reappear in God's Timetable.

Extrabiblical Evidence of Jesus

Jesus' life is a historical fact. Secular historians of those early days mentioned Christ. Pliny wrote of Christian trials and mentioned that people worshiped Jesus "as a god."[49]

Tacitus mentioned the Christians persecuted by Nero and said, "Christus, from whom the name had its origin, suffered the extreme penalty during the reign of Tiberius at the hand of one of our procurators, Pontius Pilatus."[50]

Suetonius mentioned Rome expelling Jews because of disorders "instigated because of Chrestus."[51]

Josephus wrote of the "stoning of James, the brother of Jesus, called the Christ" and recorded these facts:

> There was about this time Jesus, a wise man, if it be lawful to call him a man, for he was a doer of wonderful works. **He was Christ**. Pilate, at the suggestion of the principal men among us, condemned him to the cross. **He appeared to his followers alive again the third day**."[52]

In the Talmud and the Midrash, Jewish writers tried to discredit Jesus, but did not deny his existence, his teaching and healing people or his execution. They excommunicated him because he mocked at the words of the wise. It seems that they were not as wise as they thought they were.

These Jewish writers thought Jesus a heretic, a deceiver, and a teacher of apostasy. They said that he was a revolutionary put to death by Pontius Pilate when 33, that he was born out of wedlock . . . **His mother was called Miriam, and was a dresser of women's hair** . . . She is also said to have been descended from princes and rulers, and to have played the harlot with a carpenter.

Because of Jesus' claim that he was both God and the son of man and would go up to heaven, they countered with this:

> If a man say to thee 'I am a God,' he is a liar; if [he says,'I am] the son of man,' in the end people will laugh at him; if [he says] 'I will go up to heaven,' he saith, but shall not perform it.

Most important to me is the evidence of the Jewish writers that Jesus was killed on the day before Passover (Pesah Eve), which in 30 A.D. was on Thursday, April 6:

> **On the eve of Pesah they hung Jeshu** [the Nazarene]. And the crier went forth before him **forty days** (saying), '[Jeshu the Nazarene] goeth forth to be stoned, because he hath practiced magic and deceived and led astray Israel. Any one who knoweth aught in his favour, let him come and declare concerning him. And they found naught in his favour. And **they hung him on the eve of Pesah.**[53]

Jesus died on Passover eve, Thursday, April 6, 30 A.D. The 40 day period before they planned to stone him is a forerunner of the 40 year period prior to the catastrophe when stones will fall like hail on unbelievers at the end of this age.

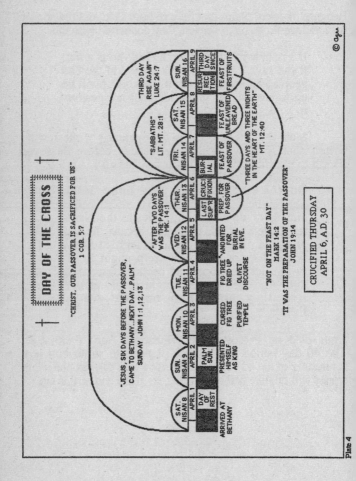

DAY OF THE CROSS

✝ ✝

"CHRIST, OUR PASSOVER IS SACRIFICED FOR US"
1 COR. 5:7

"JESUS, SIX DAYS BEFORE THE PASSOVER,
CAME TO BETHANY...NEXT DAY..."PALM"
SUNDAY JOHN 1:1,12,13

"AFTER TWO DAYS
WAS THE PASSOVER"
MK. 14:1

"SABBATHS"
LIT. MT. 28:1

"THIRD DAY
RISE AGAIN"
LUKE 24:7

SAT. NISAN 8	SUN. NISAN 9	MON. NISAN 10	TUE. NISAN 11	WED. NISAN 12	THUR. NISAN 13	FRI. NISAN 14	SAT. NISAN 15	SUN. NISAN 16
APRIL 1	APRIL 2	APRIL 3	APRIL 4	APRIL 5	APRIL 6	APRIL 7	APRIL 8	APRIL 9
DAY OF REST	PALM SUN.				LAST CRUCI- SUP'R FIXION	BUR- IAL		RESUR- RECTION	THIRD DAY SINCE

ARRIVED AT BETHANY

PRESENTED HIMSELF AS KING

CURSED FIG TREE

PURIFIED TEMPLE

FIG TREE DRIED UP

OLIVET DISCOURSE

ANOINTED FOR BURIAL IN EVE.

PREP. FOR PASSOVER

FEAST OF PASSOVER

FEAST OF UNLEAVENED BREAD

FEAST OF FIRSTFRUITS

"THREE DAYS AND THREE NIGHTS
IN THE HEART OF THE EARTH"
MT. 12:40

"NOT ON THE FEAST DAY"
MARK 14:2

"IT WAS THE PREPARATION OF THE PASSOVER"
JOHN 19:14

CRUCIFIED THURSDAY
APRIL 6, A.D. 30

© agm

Plate 4

Chapter 8

Sign of the End of the Age

Key of Knowledge

Did you miss the sign of Christ's coming and the end of the Age? This sign is an essential clue. In fact, it is the key that unlocks God's hidden treasures concerning time. Until it appeared, certain secrets buried in Scripture remained veiled to our eyes. The Sign of the End of the Age is crucial to our understanding of God's timetable of coming events.

In the last age, they missed their signs. Psalms 74:9 says, "We see not our signs: there is no more any prophet: neither is there among us any that knoweth how long." God is consistent. If they had signs, we will also have signs. We do not want to miss ours. We must watch and search carefully.

Fig Tree Parable Identifies the Sign

The disciples questioned Jesus as he was sitting on the Mount of Olives. "Tell us," they said, "when shall these things be? and **what shall be the sign of thy coming and of the end of the** world [*aionos*, **age**]?"

He answered with a parable that now reveals what the Sign of the End of the Age is. This parable is the cornerstone upon which God's chronology of end-time events is built:

> Now learn a parable of the fig tree; When his branch is yet tender, **and putteth forth leaves**, ye know that summer is nigh: So likewise ye, when ye shall see all these things, know that it is near, even at the doors.[2]

In the Old Testament, the fig tree represented Israel.[3] This branch of the fig tree is the modern nation of Israel because the Greek word *klados*, branch, means scion, a young

93

shoot broken off for grafting. Therefore, this is the young nation of Israel grafted onto her old rootstock.

No new scion begins to grow immediately. The graft must take before the sap can run. Technically, Israel could not grow leaves the day she declared her Independence. First, she must establish how much territory the new graft covers.

The Greek word *apalos*, tender, soft and full of sap, is used to indicate youth. After some time goes by, but before hardened with age, a new graft begins to swell with sap. In other words, after some time had elapsed, but while still a young nation, Israel began to flourish. She could not develop this prosperity until the initial fighting to exist was over, her boundaries were established, and the new graft had taken.

According to the parable, the branch was to put forth leaves while still young. Developing leaves is growing, enlarging the space occupied. The first time the modern established nation of Israel expanded her territory and kept it was during the spectacular **Six-day War of 1967**.

She ended it with over four times her original territory. She grew four good sized leaves, the Golan Heights, Gaza Strip, Sinai Peninsula and West Bank, including eastern Jerusalem and the temple area. Didn't you wonder about its significance when Israel took possession of the temple area?

Jerusalem was to be "trodden down of the Gentiles, until the times of the Gentiles be fulfilled [the times of the Gentiles ended when Israel took all of Jerusalem]. And there shall be signs in the sun . . . moon . . . stars; and upon the earth distress of nations . . . Men's hearts failing them for fear . . . looking after those things which are coming . . . then shall they see the Son of man coming . . . when these things **begin** to come to pass [i.e., when the times of the Gentiles are fulfilled], then look up, and lift up your heads; for **your redemption draweth nigh**" (Luke 21:24-28). **Israel's possession of Jerusalem means the Rapture is near**.

Israel fought in 1956, but relinquished the Sinai and Gaza Strip, hoping UN Emergency Forces in both would keep the peace. Therefore, the fig tree parable was not fulfilled until 1967. Modern Israel had not put forth any durable leaves until the Six-day War. She was then a teenager, nineteen years old.

What else did Jesus say in the parable? "When his branch is yet tender, and putteth forth leaves, ye know that summer is nigh." Has it occurred to you that when Israel grew, it was almost summer? This alone should tell you it was the sign. The Six-day War began June 5 and summer began June 21. The facts fit the parable with the kind of pin point accuracy that only an omniscient God can accomplish.

As he continued the parable, Jesus said, "So likewise ye, when ye shall see all these things, know that it is near." "All these things" includes putting forth leaves. Therefore, the establishment of Israel as a nation in 1948 was **not** the sign.

When Jesus said, "it is near," what did he mean by "it"? Luke's account makes it clear that "it" referred to the time when this age ends and the kingdom of Christ begins. Luke said, "So likewise ye, when ye see these things come to pass, know ye that the kingdom of God is nigh at hand."[4]

You know now why watching was so important. The Six-day War, when Israel took all of Jerusalem, was the sign of Christ's coming and the end of the age. If you recognize it, God's timetable of end-time events will fall into place for you.

The Last Generation and the End of the Age

Immediately following the parable, Jesus said, "Verily I say unto you, this generation shall not pass, till all these things be fulfilled." Therefore, the generation born in 1967 will see everything previously mentioned in Matthew 24 fulfilled, including seeing "the sign of the Son of man."[5]

When Israel came out of Egypt and wandered in the wilderness while one generation died, a Biblical generation was obviously demonstrated to be 40 years. The Lord said,

> According to the days of thy coming out of the land of Egypt [40 years] will I shew unto him marvellous [pala, extraordinary, hidden, difficult] things.[6]

This promise means we can find these hidden things during the last 40 years of this age. Now the Lord will show us. The time is right for many secrets to be unfolded. He said, "Call unto me, and I will answer thee, and shew thee great and mighty things, which thou knowest not" (Jeremiah 33:3).

The Six-day War in the Jewish 5727 plus 40 years is 5767 (our 2007). **The last day of 5767 is the end of the age because Christ is to return on Nisan 1 seven months afterward.** Since 5768 is a leap year, there are seven months between the last day of 5767 and Nisan 5768, thus dropping the end of the age into its slot in time. When Elul 29, 5767 (September 12, 2007) ends, this age will have run its tortured collision course to "the consummation" of Daniel 9:27 and "the end" mentioned in Ezekiel 7:2-7:

> An end, **the end** is come upon the four corners of the land. Now is the end [of this age] come upon thee, and I will send **mine anger** upon thee, and will **judge** thee according to thy ways, and will recompense upon thee all thine abominations . . . An evil, an only [*echad*, certain, other, alike] evil [like that which hit Sodom and Gomorrah], behold, is come . . . **the day of trouble** is near.

Notice the key words: "the end," "mine anger," "judge" and "day of trouble." Immediately after the end of this age, the Lord will sit in judgment and pour out his wrath on unbelievers on the day of trouble.

It will fall on the Feast of Trumpets."What will ye do in the solemn day, and **in the day of the feast of the LORD**? For, lo, they are gone because of destruction . . . **The days of recompence are come**; Israel shall know it: **the prophet** [the False Prophet of Israel] **is a fool, the spiritual man** [the Beast of Rome] **is mad**" (Hosea 9:5-7).

Day of the Lord

God's rest begins on the anniversary of the day God rested. The sabbatical Millennium, the Day of the Lord, starts on the Feast of Trumpets, just as that sabbath when God rested from his creation labors was on the Feast of Trumpets.

As soon as you add 40 years to the Sign of the End of the Age in 5727, and determine that this age must end no later than the last day of 5767 (Elul 29, our September 12, 2007), you have aligned God's timetable with our calendar.

The Millennium begins the next day, Tishri 1, 5768. Several things lock this date into place: (1) the catastrophe on the Feast of Trumpets, (2) the 2,300 days between the Feast of Weeks, when the Tribulation begins, and the end of the shortened Tribulation, and (3) the seven Jewish months between the day of catastrophe and the return of Christ on Nisan 1. From this point on, everything is logically predictable and falls nto place easily. It is not hard to see that recognizing the Sign of the End of the Age is truly the key of knowledge.

Tishri 1, 5768, is a day of many names. It is Jesus' birthday, Coronation Day, the Jewish New Year, the Feast of Trumpets, the day of the trumpet and alarm, the day of God's Wrath, the day of darkness, the time of Jacob's trouble, a day of judgment, etc.

So much will happen this day, good in heaven and bad on Earth, that it will take two chapters later on just to describe what takes place. Much of the Bible is devoted to the prophecies concerning the events of this one particular day, often referred to as "**that day**" in Scripture.

John referred to Passover, 30 A.D. when he said, "that sabbath day was an high day" (John 19:31). I think this Feast of Trumpets at the beginning of the Millennium will be the highest of all high days, a day to remember forever and ever.

The date on our calendar is **Thursday, September 13, 2007, a dark day, anniversary of another dark September 13**, long ago when God said, "Let there be light: and there was light." When he again commands that there be light as this age ends, the dark smoky heavens will roll aside like a scroll and men will see Christ sitting on his throne. This Sign of the Son of Man will jump start hearts.

The Day the Tribulation Begins

According to Daniel 8:14, the worst part of the Tribulation, or the Seventieth Week of Daniel,[7] will last 2,300 days. Daniel asked, "How long shall be the vision concerning the daily sacrifice." This represents the first half of the Tribulation, when the Beast in Rome and the False Prophet of Israel sign a seven year covenant of peace that allows the Jewish people to begin sacrificing in the newly erected temple in Jerusalem.

Then Daniel continued, "and the transgression of desolation, to give both the sanctuary and the host to be trodden under foot?" This represents the last part of the Tribulation.

The transgression of desolation takes place in the middle when an idol is placed in the temple. This act of desecration abruptly stops daily sacrificing for the rest of the Tribulation. So together, the time when they can sacrifice plus the time when they can't, represent the shortened Tribulation.

Next, Daniel was told how long this period would last. "Unto **two thousand and three hundred days**; then shall the sanctuary be cleansed."

Matthew 24:15-22 shows that the last half of the Tribulation is when the time is shortened.

> When ye therefore shall see the abomination of desolation [an image] spoken of by Daniel the prophet, stand in the holy place [in the temple] ... Then let them which be in Judaea flee ... For then shall be great tribulation, such as was not since the beginning of the world to this time, no, nor ever shall be. And except those days should be shortened, there should no flesh be saved: but for the elect's sake those days shall be shortened.

Matthew told us that the Tribulation would be shortened. Daniel gave the number of days it would last, 2,300 days.

Using Jewish inclusive reckoning, where the first date is counted as number one, count backward 2,300 days from Tishri 1. You will find that **the Tribulation week of years begins on the Feast of Weeks.**

Can you think of a better time? Isn't that the most logical time you can think of for it to start if you were drawing up the plans? God works logically, and he gave us the brains to understand his logic, but we do need the indwelling Holy Spirit to help us figure it all out.

This feast is on Sivan 6, 5761 (our Monday, May 28, 2001). It is Pentecost, which is also called the Feast of Weeks, as in Deuteronomy 16:9,10:

> Seven weeks shalt thou number unto thee: begin to number the seven weeks from such time as thou beginnest to put the sickle to the corn. And thou shalt keep **the feast of weeks** unto the LORD thy God.

The Feast of Weeks is the most appropriate time for the beginning of the Seventieth Week of Daniel. This refers to the vision Gabriel gave Daniel concerning 70 weeks of years (70 x 7 = 490) remaining to Israel.[8] The final week is the seven year Tribulation. (More about the seventieth week in chapter 12.)

Chapter 9

Modern Parallels

_____

God has planned well. Knowing the end from the beginning, he was able to plant subtle clues throughout the Bible that we failed to recognize until now. Many other things in Israel's history have their echo today. Parallels, types, and similitudes help us understand the prophecies of the latter days of this age. Secrets are hidden in Biblical history.

But oh that God would speak, and . . . shew thee **the secrets of wisdom**, that they **are double to that which is!**[1]

Jeremiah told people there would be another Exodus. He recorded, "The days come, saith the LORD, that they shall no more say, The LORD liveth, which brought up the children of Israel out of the land of Egypt; But, the LORD liveth, which brought up and which led the seed of the house of Israel out of **the north country**, and from all countries whither I had driven them; and they shall dwell in their own land."[2]

Although the gathering will not be completed until after Christ returns, it has begun. Part of the house of Israel is now dwelling in their own land, many of whom came from the north country, Russia. Their ship, The Exodus, was well named for this migration parallels those early days.

Zephaniah 2:1-3 foretold that the Jews would gather in Israel before the Day of Wrath, therefore before Christ returns.

[Gather] together, O nation not desired; **Before** the decree [_choq_, law, set appointed time] bring forth . . . **before** the day of the LORD'S anger come upon you. Seek ye the LORD . . . it may be ye shall be hid [Rapture II is that same day] in the day of the LORD'S anger.

99

We should be alert to how history fit into the prophetic picture of the past and watch current developments. Job said,

> [Enquire] . . . of the former age, and prepare thyself to the search of their fathers . . . because **our days upon earth are a shadow**: Shall not **they teach thee**, and tell thee, and utter words out of their heart.[3]

Once you find out that former things recorded in Scripture were shadows of things to come, Israel's dry old history suddenly becomes an absorbing study.

God Mapped out the Year of Main Events

One of the strangest things in all of this is the realization that God singled out six blocks of years, totaled them up and saw to it that they were listed in Scripture to mark the year of the most important coming events of our time.

Each block is in the four hundreds; and there are no others, except for the 434 that is added to 49 to make the 483 years in Daniel 9.

(1) 400 from the casting out of Ishmael to the Exodus[4]
(2) 430 from Abram's call to the Exodus[5]
(3) 450 from the division of Canaan to king Saul, the period of the judges[6]
(4) 480 from the Exodus to the time construction began on the temple[7]
(5) 483 from the time the commandment was given to rebuild Jerusalem to just before the Crucifixion[8]
(6) 490 from the commandment to rebuild Jerusalem to the Second Advent, excluding the church era in the gap between the 69th and 70th week of years.[9]

The correlation between circumstances in the last age and those in this age are not difficult to see. For instance: God told Abraham "That his seed would sojourn in a strange land; and that they [Egyptians] should bring them into bondage, and entreat them evil four hundred years. And the nation to whom they shall be in bondage will I judge, said God: and after that shall they come forth, and serve me in this place."[10]

In the last age, the Israelites were oppressed by Egyptians 400 years, starting when Ishmael was cast out, then began their Exodus to the promised land. In this age, they were oppressed 400 years while the Ottoman Turks held the land. Then, they again began an exodus to the promised land.

The Ottoman Turks took over Jerusalem in the Jewish 5278, our 1517 A.D., on their drive into Egypt. Both Palestine and Egypt became Ottoman provinces at that time.

After the early days of Ottoman rule, Palestine in general deteriorated under their maladministration. Both Arab and Jew in the land suffered terrible poverty.

Even the Jews who were out of the land were oppressed. They were so hated, persecuted and killed that there finally arose a Zionist movement, first led by Theodor Herzl then by Chaim Weizmann, with dreams of going back to the land and establishing a national homeland for the Jews.

Theodor Herzl, a journalist, was raised in Budapest. Inflamed by the unfairness to an innocent Jew in the Dreyfus Affair, he wrote his popular book *Der Judenstaat*, The Jewish State, published in 1896. He told of the Jew's longing for a return to Palestine and organized an international Zionist movement to create a homeland there secured by law. The First Zionist Congress was in Basel, Switzerland, in 1897.

Herzl's dream included a voluntary exodus to a Jewish state. He was not to see his dream fulfilled, for he died in 1904, when 44 years old. However, the Zionists started a successful program of buying up as much land as possible in Palestine. A great number of Jews began settling on it.

The same year that the Ottomans took Jerusalem, Martin Luther tacked his ninety-five theses to the church door in Wittenberg, Germany. That was 5278, our October 31, 1517, the beginning of the Protestant Reformation.

On the 400th anniversary of this event, the tide began to change for the Jews. On October 31, 1917, the British Lord, General Edmund Allenby, took Beersheba and began his drive toward Jerusalem. By November 2, the Balfour Declaration was signed, giving the Zionists great hope.

To gain Jewish support and because Chaim Weizmann, a chemist, discovered how to make synthetic cordite, an explosive, for them, Britain granted his request that his people be allowed to reestablish a homeland in Palestine.

This Balfour declaration stated in part: "His Majesty's Government view with favor the establishment in Palestine of a National Home for the Jewish people, and will use their best endeavors to facilitate the achievement of that object."

On December 8, the Turks were seized with panic and left Jerusalem without a shot being fired. They left behind a letter of surrender which was brought to the Christian General Allenby as he and his officers were in his tent praying. He had dropped propaganda leaflets signed Lord Allenby. Because of an old prophecy, the Turks thought they would lose the city when a man of Allah delivered it, so they fled.

The year 1917 was marked by the number seven. The maximum number of solar and lunar eclipses in one year is seven. The seventh appeared just as General Allenby marched into Jerusalem.[11] He officially took possession on December 11. The people received him with joy as a liberator.

As the First World War ended, the modern exodus to Palestine began. The League of Nations gave Great Britain mandate over Palestine in 1922. Immigration was greatly speeded up by the terrible persecution of the Jews by the Nazis and Communists, and on the day the British withdrew their mandate, tiny Israel bravely declared her Independence to avoid having her land partitioned as had been approved by the United Nations General Assembly November 29, 1947.

She became a nation **Iyar 5, 5708** (Friday, May 14, 1948) with 872,000 people. As the British Mandate ended, David Ben-Gurion read aloud the Declaration of Independence, announcing the establishment of the State of Israel.

It was obvious suicide. Saudi Arabian contingents, Egypt, Jordan, Syria, Lebanon, and **Iraq** pounced on her to squash out her life. She was badly outnumbered. But, Israel fooled the world; her time had come. She fought desperately and with God's help stayed firmly grafted into her old rootstock. God's angelic hosts must have fought for her.

Chief Rabbi Isar Yehuda Unterman said that the war was not an ordinary thing, but a chapter to attach to the Bible.[12] The Lord had not forgotten his people. Israel, "thou art an holy people unto the LORD thy God: the LORD thy God hath chosen thee to be a special people unto himself, above all people that are upon the face of the earth" (Deuteronomy 7:6).

From the Jewish 5278 (our 1517) to 5708 (our 1948) is 430 years. Both 400 and 430 year periods marked very important milestones in the modern history of the Israelites.

The second parallel is obvious. In the last age, God called one man, a gentile named Abram, out of idolatry in Babylonia, then after 430 years, brought the Israelites out of Egypt where they had been bitterly oppressed. In this age, God again called one man, a gentile named Martin Luther, out of idolatry in what Luther himself called **"Babylon."**[13] Then after 430 years, God brought the Israelites out of nations where they had been bitterly oppressed. These parallels are too obvious to have happened by chance.

These first two parallels establish the mathematics to be continued for the entire series. The base year is the Jewish 5278. The total of each succeeding block of years is to be added to 5278, not to the sum of 5278 and the previous block.

(1) 5278 plus 400 equals 5678 (our 1917/1918)
(2) 5278 plus 430 equals 5708 (our 1947/1948)
(3) 5278 plus 450 equals 5728 (our 1967/1968)
(4) 5278 plus 480 equals 5758 (our 1997/1998)
(5) 5278 plus 483 equals 5761 (our 2000/2001)
(6) 5278 plus 490 equals 5768 (our 2007/2008)

Remember that Jewish civil years start in our September or October, on Tishri 1, the Jewish New Year. They span parts of two of our years. To be exact, computations must be made using the Jewish Calendar.

We have a new series: 5678, 5708, 5728, 5758, 5761, and 5768. Do important things happen in these years?

Yes! The list is impressive. It's exciting to think that long ago God arranged this for us to find in our days. Truly, the Bible is especially written for us. I doubt that any one before us has recognized these parallels.

In 5678 (1917), the modern exodus began. In 5708 (1948), Israel declared her Independence. The year 5728 began on the Jewish New Year in 1967, soon after the Sign of the End of the Age appeared. It marked the beginning of the last 40 years of probation, which are a countdown to the return of Christ. The year 5758 **(1998) is, I believe, the year of the Rapture**. The year 5761 (2001) is when the Tribulation begins. The year 5768 (2007/2008) is the year of both Christ's coronation and a little season later, his return to Earth.

No man could have planned this. Only God, who had his complete timetable in mind, could have known how to draw these parallels. Truly, Scripture is God breathed.

In the last age, Samuel anointed Saul king over Israel at the end of the 450 year period of the judges. An "evil spirit from God was upon Saul" (1 Samuel 16:23). He ruled 40 years and had his kingdom taken away from him because he disobeyed God's injunctions.[14] He killed himself by falling on his own sword after a battle with the Philistines in the valley of Jezreel, also known as the valley of Megiddo.[15] David, a type of Christ, then ascended the throne.

In this age, after the 450 years, we have another 40 years of probation. Near the end, the Satan indwelt false prophet, king of Israel, will be deposed when Satan's own home, which is called the Sword of the Lord, strikes the Earth (also pictured for us by Haman being hung on his own gallows). Then, Jesus, the "son of David,"[16] will become king and Armageddon will be fought in the valley of Megiddo.

In the 480th year after the children of Israel were come out of the land of Egypt[17] in the last age, Solomon, the son of David, began to build the first temple.

The parallel in our days is easy to see. In the 480th year, Jesus Christ, the son of David, will raise up the church, the "temple of God,"[18] when the Rapture occurs. The Jews will then also begin to build the literal temple in Jerusalem.

In Daniel's prophecy concerning the 483 years [(7 x 7) + (62 x 7)], there were to be "troublous times,"[19] suggesting the Tribulation. It begins in the 483rd year, seven years before Christ returns in the 490th year, by the end of which the seventy *shabuim* (sevens, or 70 x 7) will be fulfilled and the "most Holy" anointed King of kings and Lord of lords.[20]

This is why Sarah, who represented the free Jerusalem[21] had to wait until she was 90 years old to give birth to Isaac, the son of promise.[22] There will be 90 years between the liberation of Jerusalem in the Jewish 5678 (1917) and the return of Christ as promised in 5768 (2008).

"This is the word of promise, the Lord said, at this time will I come, and Sarah shall have a son."[23] More prophetic than has been commonly realized, this precious promise applies to both advents of Jesus Christ, though in different ways. The "Lord said, at this time will I come," and the Lord Jesus was born on Isaac's birthday. It also applies to the Second Advent because free Jerusalem will be 90 years old when the Lord Jesus Christ, the son of promise, comes.

Since the "Lord said, at this time will **I come**," it is proof that "God was in Christ, reconciling the world unto himself" as 2 Corinthians 5:19 plainly states.

So all six blocks of years mark important events in our days, some of the most important events ever to take place. Three are history; three are future. God knew that half would be past by the time we could figure these parallels out. He also knew that we would be reassured that if three had happened on schedule, he would bring the other three to pass on time.

It was 400 years before Jerusalem was liberated, and 430 years before Israel became a nation. At the 450 year mark, the last 40 years of probation began. Christ will return in the 40th year. Like Solomon, the son of David, Christ will be married the day he is crowned.[24] As Isaac was married when 40, Christ will be married in the 40th year.[25]

The Sign of the End of the Age was in 5727. That year plus 40 is the end of the age. The 40 years of probation started in 5728 and extend through the return of our Lord seven months after the end of the age.

The Rapture should take place in the 480th year, the Tribulation begin in the 483rd year, and our Lord Jesus Christ return in the 490th year.

Other correlations can be found. Thirty is the number of maturity. Just 30 years after Jerusalem was liberated from the Turks in 5678, Israel matured and declared her Independence in 5708. Thirty years after the 40 years of probation began in 5728, I believe the church will mature and be taken to heaven in the Rapture, in 5758 (1998).

Jesus was 33 when crucified, maximum tribulation for him. Thirty-three years after the 40 years of probation began in 5728 is 5761 (2001), the year the Tribulation begins.

In 30 A.D., on Pentecost Sunday, 50 days after the resurrection of Christ on the Feast of Firstfruits, the church was born on Earth. Fifty years after Israel's national resurrection in 5708 is 5758 (1998), which is, I believe, the birth of the church into heaven. I believe both births of the church take place on a Pentecost Sunday, the Lord's Day. Remember the **two** loaves that were to be waved on Pentecost 50 days after the wave-sheaf on the Feast of Firstfruits?[26]

These correlations are all so good, their discovery demonstrates that all along the will of God has been to show the last generation when these things will take place.

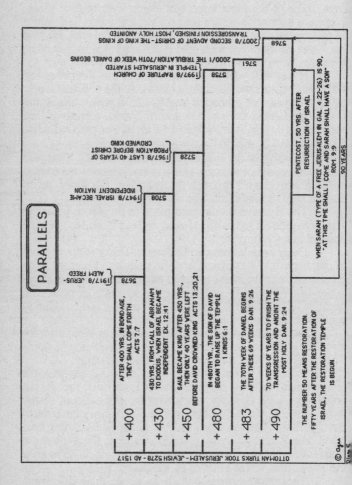

PARALLELS

OTTOMAN TURKS TOOK JERUSALEM - JEWISH 5278 - AD 1517

+ 400 — AFTER 400 YRS. IN BONDAGE, THEY SHALL COME FORTH ACTS 7:7

+ 430 — 430 YRS. FROM CALL OF ABRAHAM TO EXODUS, WHEN ISRAEL BECAME INDEPENDENT EX. 12:41

+ 450 — SAUL BECAME KING AFTER 450 YRS., THEN ONLY 40 YEARS WERE LEFT BEFORE DAVID CROWNED KING ACTS 13:20,21

+ 480 — IN 480TH YR., THE SON OF DAVID BEGAN TO RAISE UP THE TEMPLE 1 KINGS 6:1

+ 483 — THE 70TH WEEK OF DANIEL BEGINS AFTER THESE 69 WEEKS DAN. 9:26

+ 490 — 70 WEEKS OF YEARS TO FINISH THE TRANSGRESSION AND ANOINT THE MOST HOLY DAN. 9:24

THE NUMBER 50 MEANS RESTORATION. FIFTY YEARS AFTER THE RESTORATION OF ISRAEL, THE RESTORATION TEMPLE IS BEGUN.

1917/8 JERUS-ALEM FREED
5678

1947/8 ISRAEL BECAME INDEPENDENT NATION
5708

1967/8 LAST 40 YEARS OF PROBATION BEFORE CHRIST CROWNED KING
5728

1997/8 RAPTURE OF CHURCH
TEMPLE IN JERUSALEM STARTED
5758

2000/1 THE TRIBULATION/70TH WEEK OF DANIEL BEGINS
5761

2007/8 SECOND ADVENT OF CHRIST - THE KING OF KINGS
TRANSGRESSION FINISHED, MOST HOLY ANOINTED
5768

PENTECOST, 50 YRS. AFTER RESURRECTION OF ISRAEL

WHEN SARAH (TYPE OF A FREE JERUSALEM IN GAL. 4:22-26) IS 90, "AT THIS TIME SHALL I COME AND SARAH SHALL HAVE A SON" ROM. 9:9

90 YEARS

© Ogah
Plate 5

"The righteous perisheth, and no man layeth it to heart: and
merciful men are taken away, none considering that the righteous
is taken away from the evil to come." Isaiah 57:1

Chapter 10

The Prize

Contrary to contemporary thought, I believe God
planned for us to be able to figure out when the Rapture would
occur as soon as the Sign of the End of the Age appeared.
This sign was the Six-day War. That was the first time the
established nation of Israel put forth leaves that didn't fall off.

Jesus warned the churches, "If . . . thou shalt not
watch, I will come on thee [the churches] as a thief, and thou
shalt not know what hour I will come upon thee."[1] Therefore,
if we do watch, we can know when the bridegroom will come
to take his virgin (i.e., blameless) bride to his father's house.

Pretribulation

Today, there are more Gentiles than Jews in the
church. "Esaias saith, There shall be a root [i.e., God] of
Jesse, and he [Jesus, both God and man, a Jew descended
from Jesse through David] that shall rise to reign over the
Gentiles, in him shall the Gentiles trust."[2] Therefore the
Gentile Enoch makes a good type of the church.

Just as Enoch was taken to heaven before the flood
judgment,[3] I believe the Rapture of the church must precede
the Tribulation judgment. Christ told the Philadelphian church,

> behold, I have set before thee an open door [a
> symbol of the Rapture] . . . I have loved thee.
> Because thou hast kept the word of my
> patience, I also will keep thee **from** the hour of
> temptation [*peirasmou*, adversity, trouble,
> **trial** (i.e., the time of Jacob's trouble, the
> Tribulation)], which shall come upon **all the
> world**, to **try** [*peirasai*] them that dwell
> upon the earth. Behold, I come **quickly**.[4]

When does Christ come quickly? At the Second Advent, every eye will see him coming. That might take some time. He will come in like manner as he ascended. Acts 1:9 says that "while they beheld, he was taken up; and a cloud received him out of their sight." They saw him being taken up. He didn't just instantly disappear. As we will see later, there will be seven Jewish months between the time they see him "**coming** in the clouds of heaven [the Sign of the Son of Man],"[5] and his touchdown on Mount Olivet on Nisan 1.

He does come quickly at the Rapture. To the church at Ephesus, the Lord said to "repent, and do the first works; or else I will come unto thee **quickly**, and will remove thy candlestick." To the church at Pergamos, he said, "Repent; or else I will come unto thee **quickly**." To the church at Philadelphia, he said, "Behold, I come **quickly**: hold that fast which thou hast, that no man take thy crown."

Crowns are given after the Rapture. Continuing, Jesus promised the Philadelphian church, "Him that overcometh will I make a pillar in the temple of my God, and he shall go no more out: and I will write upon him the name of my God, and the name of the city of my God, which is **new Jerusalem**." We go to the heavenly New Jerusalem at the Rapture.

Thus it is easy to see from Revelation 3:10 and the surrounding verses that this time of trouble that we are to be kept from is the Tribulation. The open door represents the Rapture in Revelation 4:1. The heavenly New Jerusalem is our destination, and crowns are presented soon after we arrive.

We pray in the Lord's prayer, "lead us not into temptation [*peirasmon*, trouble], but deliver [*rhuomai*, haul from danger, rescue] us from evil." The greatest trial, temptation, and evil will all be present during the Tribulation.

It will not be easy living here when the Beast and the False Prophet rule, the Mark of the Beast will be required to be able to buy or sell, those who take the Mark of the Beast will be forever lost, and believers will be hunted and put to death. The catastrophe at the end is no fun either.

In Matthew 26:41, the Lord said, "Watch and pray, that ye **enter not** into temptation [*peirasmon*, trial, adversity, trouble]." This could easily apply in our days. Are we to watch and pray that we go in the Rapture and enter not into the terrible Tribulation?

Even the Old Testament hints at the Rapture occasionally. Psalms 94:13 speaks of giving "rest **from the days** of adversity, until the pit be digged for the wicked." The days of adversity immediately preceding the digging of the pit (at the time of Jacob's trouble) are those of the Tribulation.

The order of events can be seen in Paul's letter to the Thessalonians. "That day [Day of the Lord] shall not come, except there come a falling away [*apostasia*, defection from a state, separation (as in divorce); from the root *aphistemi*, to withdraw oneself, desert a station in life, remove, go away, absent oneself from, depart; i.e., **the Rapture**] **first**, and the man of sin be revealed, the son of perdition."[6]

He apostasia means "the departure" and was so translated in early versions, including The Geneva Bible, Tyndale's translation, Cranmer's version, the Great Bible, Breecher's Bible, Beza's translation and the Coverdale Bible.

The False Prophet (man of sin and son of perdition) can be recognized when he and the Roman Beast sign the peace treaty. Therefore, the departure (Rapture) has to take place **before** he signs that treaty on the Feast of Weeks at the beginning of the Seventieth Week of Daniel, the Tribulation.

Marriage customs of Jesus' day help us understand the steps that must be followed concerning Christ and the church. According to Unger's Bible Dictionary, in those days, the bride and groom were betrothed after the groom left his father's house, journeyed to the bride's house, paid the purchase price and returned to his father's house to prepare a place for her. About a year later, the bridegroom would come for the bride, take her to his father's house, consummate the marriage, and celebrate the wedding feast seven days.

The correlation is good. Jesus left his Father's house, came to Earth, paid the purchase price, and returned to his Father's house to prepare a place for us. Later, he will come at the Rapture and take his Bride to his Father's heavenly house.

After that, the Marriage of the Lamb and the Marriage Supper of the Lamb will take place in the seventh month in the seventh year of the Seventieth Week of Daniel at the beginning of the seventh 1,000 year day. Seven months later, we will all take a trip. God sure does things in sevens.

Jesus said, "In my Father's house are many mansions . . . I go to prepare a place for you. And if I go and prepare a place for you, I will come again, and receive you unto myself; that where I am, there ye may be also."[7]

The "Lord himself shall descend from heaven with a shout," said Paul, describing the Rapture, "with the voice of the archangel, and with **the trump** [singular] of God." This is the **first trump**. There are two, one at the Rapture, the other at the Translation of the Tribulation Saints (Rapture II).

Numbers 10:4 is a shadow of what will happen at the Rapture: "And if they blow but with **one trumpet**, then the princes, which are heads of the thousands of Israel [i.e., the 24 elders of Revelation 5:4, twelve princes of the twelve tribes of Israel, representing the Old Testament Saints, and twelve apostles, also Israelites, representing the Church Saints], shall gather themselves unto thee."

Continuing his description of the Rapture, Paul said, "and the dead in Christ [including the princes, apostles and the groups they head up] shall rise first. Then we which are alive and remain shall be **caught up together with them in the clouds**, to meet the Lord in the air: and so shall we ever be with the Lord. Wherefore comfort one another with these words."[8]

As the shortened Tribulation ends and the Day of the Lord begins, it will be the **Day of Wrath, a day of darkness** and the time of Jacob's trouble. There will be no comfort on Earth that day. Only in heaven will there be peace and light. We are not part of the day of darkness on Earth because **Rapture I comes before the Tribulation**. Paul said,

> But ye, brethren, are **not in darkness** that
> that day [Day of the Lord] should overtake you
> as a thief. . . . we are not of the night, nor of
> darkness. . . . let us watch and be sober. . . .
> putting on the breastplate of faith and love; and
> for an helmet, **the hope of salvation**
> [*soteria*, **rescue**, i.e., the Rapture]. For **God
> hath not appointed us to wrath**, but to
> obtain salvation by our Lord Jesus Christ.
> Who died for us, that, whether we wake or
> sleep, we should live together with him.
> Wherefore comfort yourselves together.[9]

At the end of both passages, Paul said that we would be with the Lord and to comfort each other, because they refer to the same thing, the Rapture. We have the hope of being rescued and taken to heaven before the Tribulation begins.

The Rapture is that blessed hope. Paul said that "we should live soberly, righteously, and godly, in this present world; Looking for that **blessed hope**, and the glorious appearing of the great God and our Saviour Jesus Christ."[10] (Jesus Christ is both "God and our Saviour.")

Job said, "**He shall** deliver [*natsal*, **snatch away**] **thee** in six troubles [suggesting the Rapture in year 6,000]: yea, in seven [suggesting the seven year Tribulation] **there shall no evil touch thee** [how would that be possible on Earth in such an evil time?] . . . **Thou shalt be hid** [how? where?] from the scourge of the tongue [the False Prophet speaking as Satan when in charge of world government] neither shalt thou be afraid of destruction [at the end of the shortened Tribulation] . . . thou shalt know that **thy tabernacle shall be in peace** [there is no peace on Earth at the end of the shortened Tribulation, a northern army and her allies will attack Israel]; and thou shalt visit **thy habitation** [in heaven], and shalt not sin [no sin in heaven]."[11]

When the Rapture takes place, we will visit our heavenly habitation. During the seven year Tribulation, no evil will touch us. This would be practically impossible if we were on Earth at that time. This is an evil world, and it will be far worse during the Tribulation years.

We are to be suddenly plucked out of this present age. Galatians 1:4 mentions **Jesus Christ**, "**Who gave himself for our sins, that he might deliver** [*exeletai*, **pluck out, rescue, extricate**] **us from this present evil world** (*aionos*, **age**)."

John Wrote as if the Rapture was Happening

John stood as if at the exact point in time when the Rapture occurs as he wrote "THE Revelation of Jesus Christ." The very name tells it. The Revelation is the *apokalupsis*, appearing or **coming**. Christ will appear **first** when he **comes** for believers at the Rapture.

First Peter 1:7 uses the same word when referring to the Rapture. Peter spoke of an inheritance reserved in heaven for us, and then said, "That the trial of your faith . . . might be found unto praise and honour and glory at the appearing [*apokalupsei*] of Jesus Christ."

John wrote Revelation from the vantage point of the Rapture. We can also see this in the last chapter. Verses 14 and 20 say, "Blessed are they that do his commandments, that they may have right to the tree of life [as

111

in the message to the churches in 2:7], and may enter in through the gates [at the Rapture] into the city [New Jerusalem]. . . . He which testifieth these things saith, Surely I come quickly." Jesus comes quickly at the Rapture. So Revelation begins and ends with the Rapture.

The third verse of Revelation **sets the scene**, as in a play. It says, "**Blessed** is he that readeth, and they that hear the words of this prophecy, and keep those things which are written therein [including overcoming and having written upon him the name of the heavenly New Jerusalem as in 2:7]: for **the time is at hand**." What time is at hand?

The time of blessing is the Rapture, the blessed hope. After that is the Tribulation, a time of trial, not blessing. The fourth verse says the message is from "**him which is [at the Rapture]**, and which was [at the First Advent], and which is to come [at the Second Advent]."

As the Rapture takes place, these mortals must put on immortality. To picture this, John, "that disciple whom Jesus loved,"[12] stood on the isle of Patmos (which means "mortal") in the Icarian Sea, a section of the Aegean Sea, and became in the spirit as **he acted out the Rapture** of the Philadelphian church whom Jesus "loved." I believe he acted it out on the Lord's Day to show us that it would happen on Sunday just as the day of Pentecost was on Sunday in the year 30 A.D.

On Resurrection Sunday in 30 A.D., Christ ascended to his Father, then returned and appeared to members of the Church.[13] Didn't this picture the Sunday Rapture? Won't he return and appear to members of the Church on our Resurrection Sunday?

As you read Revelation, chapter 1, starting with verse ten, put yourself in John's place. He wrote as if the Rapture was happening right then. What he saw and heard represents the glorious things we will see and hear as we experience the Rapture.

He began, "I was [*egenomen*, literally, I became, began to be] in the Spirit on the Lord's day, and heard behind me a great voice, as of a trumpet." This is the first "trump of God," the one heard at the Rapture when the princes of Israel are gathered.

The voice said, "I am Alpha and Omega, the first and the last [i.e., Jehovah of the Old Testament and Jesus Christ of the New Testament]. As John turned, the Lord was revealed to him as if the Rapture had just taken place. He said,

> I turned to see the voice that spake with me.
> And being turned, I saw seven golden candle-
> sticks; And in the midst of the seven candle-
> sticks one like unto the Son of man . . . his
> hairs were white . . . his eyes were as a flame
> of fire . . . he had in his right hand seven stars.

Scripture interprets this symbolism for us in verse twenty. "The seven stars are the angels of the seven churches: and the seven candlesticks which thou sawest are the seven churches."

The saints of the seven church eras are at that time represented as being with the Lord. Symbolically, the resurrection has just taken place and they are now "as the angels,"[14] who do not die. He just that moment snatched them up.

The seven stars represent all the overcomers of all the church eras, for seven means complete. When the Rapture takes place, all seven will have come into being. They already exist today. The Rapture is near. The Lord commanded John,

> Write the things which thou hast seen, and the
> things which are [at the time of the Rapture],
> and the things which shall be hereafter.[15]

The usual interpretation is that "the things which thou hast seen" refer to the vision of Christ he has just seen, the "things which are" are the seven Churches, and "the things which shall be hereafter" are Tribulation events.

Where is the Rapture in this interpretation? I blindly accepted this interpretation for many years, but now I see that though close, it does not hit the target dead center.

True, the things hereafter refer to the Tribulation. But, think the rest through again. Work backwards. What comes before the Tribulation? the Rapture. Then is it unreasonable to expect the "things which are" to be things that take place at the Rapture? Next, figure out what precedes the Rapture. The Churches. Right? Put it to the test and see if it fits. This interpretation opens up some hidden secrets we have missed.

As proof that this is correct, right after the Lord explained the meaning of the seven stars and the seven candlesticks in the next verse, John proceeded to do exactly what he was instructed to do.

He immediately began writing the messages to the churches. These were, **from the vantage point of the**

Rapture, already past, the "things which thou hast seen." From that point on, events are presented as close to their proper order as possible, considering that several things happen at the same time, with the exception of some obviously parenthetical passages and the final sign off which reverts to the time of the Rapture.

The scenes of the Rapture are the "things which are." Besides what he had already written concerning the Rapture, John wrote more about it just as soon as he finished the messages to the churches. After that, he wrote of the Tribulation. This reveals the **correct chronological order:** first the church eras, next the Rapture, then the events in heaven after the Rapture, after that the Tribulation. The Millennium and the return of Christ follow the Tribulation.

After recording the Lord's messages to the seven church eras, John wrote chapters four and five. In these, he described the Rapture and the heavenly scene that followed it.

"After this I looked, and, behold, a door was opened in heaven." This door is the same as "the gates of righteousness . . . This gate of the Lord, into which the righteous shall enter"[16] as the translation takes place.

He's picking up the narrative of the Rapture again to tell us what happens next. "The first voice which I heard was as it were of a trumpet talking with me"[17] ("the trump of God"[18]). It is the voice of Christ, the same voice he heard in the first chapter, when he said, "**I am Alpha and Omega, the first and the last.**"[19] He is both Jehovah of the Old Testament and Jesus Christ of the new, God in Christ reconciling the world unto himself.

Christ said, "Come up hither, and I will shew thee things which must be **hereafter [after the Rapture].**[20] And immediately I was in the spirit: and, behold, a throne [surrounded by an emerald rainbow] was set in heaven." John became in the spirit and was called to heaven, showing what will happen to us at the Rapture.

The one sitting on the throne looked "like a jasper **and** a sardine stone." The jasper and sardine, or sardius, were the first and last stones set in the breastplate of the high priest. In other words, he is "the First **and** the Last," Jehovah of the Old Testament **and** Christ of the New Testament.

Before the throne were seven [which means complete and perfect] lamps of fire, "which are the seven Spirits of God [representing the complete and perfect essence of the

Godhead]." In the midst and around the throne were four living creatures saying, "Holy, holy, holy, **Lord God Almighty**, which was [the Lord God Almighty was in Christ at the First Advent], and is [is now in him at the Rapture], and is to come [will be in him at the Second Advent]."

Around that throne were 24 lesser thrones. The elders who sat on them had on their heads crowns of gold, which they cast before the throne, saying, "Thou art worthy, O Lord, to receive glory and honour and power: for thou hast created all things, and for thy pleasure they are and were created."

The Lord held in his right hand a seven sealed book, the Book of the Purchase of Earth. **No man** in heaven or on Earth or under the Earth was able to open it. Then **Jesus Christ [proving he was not just a mere man or he could not have opened it, either]**, as a Lamb that had been slain, was also seen "in the midst of the throne [i.e., present with God]." **He also had the seven Spirits of God** [the essence of God], and was worthy to open it. "And he came and took the book out of the right hand of him that sat upon the throne."

The four living creatures and the 24 elders fell down before the Lamb, who is also the Lion [the king] of the tribe of Judah, the Root of Jesse, both **the Root** [Jehovah] **and offspring of David** [Jesus].

> And they sang a new song, saying, Thou art worthy to take the book, and to open the seals thereof: for thou wast slain, and hast redeemed us to God by thy blood out of every kindred, and tongue, and people, and nation; And hast made us unto our God kings and priests: and we shall reign on [*epi*, on or over] the earth.[21]

These elders represent all the redeemed. Otherwise, they could not be out of every kindred, and tongue, and people, and nation. There are more than 24 nations on Earth.

Twelve is the complete heavenly number. Those on the thrones are the leaders of their groups. Twelve of these are the heads of the 12 tribes of Israel, representing the Old Testament Saints. The others are the 12 apostles, representing the Church Saints. Jesus told the apostles, "Verily I say unto you, That ye which have followed me, in the regeneration when the Son of man shall sit in the throne of his glory, ye also shall sit upon twelve thrones, judging the twelve tribes of Israel."[22]

The 24 elders represent all the redeemed in heaven at the time of the Rapture: and **they are in heaven BEFORE the Tribulation**, before the seals are broken on the seven sealed book. When the first is broken, the Tribulation begins. (When the last is severed, the asteroid will impact Earth.)

Luke warned," take heed to yourselves, lest at any time your hearts be overcharged with surfeiting, and drunkenness, and cares of this life, and so that day come upon you unawares. For as a snare shall it come on all them that dwell on the face of the whole earth. **Watch** ye therefore, and pray always, that ye may be accounted worthy to **escape** [*ekpheugo*, to vanish from, i.e., to vanish at the Rapture to keep us from] all these things that shall come to pass, and to stand before the Son of man."[23] Because of the Rapture, we can escape the worst that is to happen since man was put on Earth. This is our "**blessed hope**" (Titus 2:13).

Pentecost, Firstfruits of Wheat Harvest

Since John told us that he became in the spirit on the Lord's day, we know that the Rapture will happen on Sunday. Chances are very good that it will be on Pentecost.

On Pentecost Sunday in 30 A.D., the church was born on Earth. At the Rapture, it will be born into heaven. There are two births of the church. It would be just like God to plan for the second to take place on the anniversary of the first. It would be logical if the Pentecostal period began and ended on Pentecost, and God works logically.

When that early Pentecost Sunday arrived in 30 A.D., God (the Holy Spirit) descended to the church to indwell it. On Rapture Sunday, God (Christ, both man and God) will again descend to the Church. The correlation is excellent.

When the disciples spoke on the former Pentecost, "every man heard them speak in his own language."[24] When the Rapture occurs, every participant, no matter what his mother tongue, will understand Christ's command to "Come up hither." Just as before, the miracle will be in the hearing.

Pentecost was the "feast of harvest"[25] when "the firstfruits of wheat harvest"[26] were to be brought into the house of the Lord. The Rapture is when believers, called both "a kind of firstfruits"[27] and "wheat,"[28] will be brought into the heavenly house of the Lord. To picture this for us, the Lord instructed Israel to "bring out of your habitations **two** wave-loaves" as firstfruits on Pentecost.[29] Since each of the loaves was made up of many separate grains of wheat ground into flour, they each perfectly represent groups of believers.

It has been thought that these two loaves represented gentiles and Jews, for both groups of believers make up the church. However, since each loaf is made up of many separate grains of wheat flour and can include both gentiles and Jews, it seems that the first loaf that was to be waved represented the first birth of the church, when 120 left their dwellings and assembled in the upper room in Jerusalem. Even the fact that it was an upper room is significant; it typified heaven.

I believe the second loaf that was to be waved represented the second birth of the church. Between now and the beginning of the Tribulation in 2001, believers will also leave their habitations and assemble in another upper room, this time in the heavenly New Jerusalem, for the Lord "builds **His upper room in the heavens**" (Amos 9:6, Berkeley Version). Hebrews 12 refers to the heavenly Jerusalem:

> For ye are not come unto the mount that might be touched, and that burned with fire [Sinai], nor unto . . . darkness [the day of darkness is at the end of the shortened Tribulation] . . . But ye are come unto mount Sion [Zion], and unto the city of the living God, the **heavenly Jerusalem**, and to an innumerable company of angels, To the general assembly and church of the firstborn, which are written in heaven, and to God the Judge of all, and to the spirits of just men made perfect. And to Jesus . . . **See that ye refuse not him that speaketh** [when from the heavens he says, "Come up hither"]. For if **they escaped not** who refused him that spake on earth, much more shall **not we escape** [flee away, **vanish**, i.e., be Raptured], if we turn away from him that speaketh from heaven.[30]

Before we get into the first part of this passage, let's look again at that last part. It means, don't refuse Jesus Christ when he shouts, "Come up hither." If you do, you will not escape in Rapture I. You will have to stay here and endure the terrible Tribulation. He has given you an early way out. Be sure you take it. Rapture I will take place before The Wicked one is revealed when he signs the seven year covenant. Rapture II, when "the fulness of the Gentiles be come in" (Romans 11:25), will happen at the end of the age just before the Wrath of God hits Earth and all Israel is born in a day.

> The righteous perisheth [*abad*, wanders away, **escapes**, i.e., the Rapture], and no man layeth it to heart: and merciful men are **taken away**, none considering that **the righteous is taken away from the evil** [the Tribulation] **to come** (Isaiah 57:1).

> God is faithful, who will not suffer you to be tempted above that ye are able; but will with the temptation [*peirasmo*, trial, proving, adversity, affliction, i.e., the Tribulation] **also** make **a way to escape** [*ekbasin*, **go up out of**, i.e., Rapture II], that ye may be able to bear it (I Corinthians 10:13).

In our scripture from Hebrews 12, why were the earthly Mt. Sinai and the heavenly Mt. Sion mentioned in the same passage of Scripture? First, to reinforce the fact that we are not going to be present at the end of the Tribulation, when there will be fire and darkness as there was at Sinai. Second, it was, I believe, to give us a clue that the Rapture will occur in Sivan. It is almost like saying that though it occurs at the same time of year, we are not coming to Sinai, but to the heavenly New Jerusalem.

Moses said, "In the third month, when the children of Israel were gone forth out of the land of Egypt, the same day came they into the wilderness of Sinai."[31] The third month is Sivan, the month of Pentecost. Jewish tradition says **the first trumpet sounded on Pentecost** and the Ten Commandments were given that day. Exodus, chapters 19-24, shows that he was at Sinai on Sivan 6 and the first trumpet did sound in early Sivan. They arrived at Sinai on the first day of Sivan because *chodesh*, "month," means new moon, the first of the month on their lunar calendar. In Scripture, if another day of the month was meant, the number of the day was included.

God gave the Ten Commandments three times. First, orally, next on two tables of stone that Moses furiously threw down and broke (as two other stones would later be thrown down and broken) because the Israelites made a golden calf, then on two replacement stones. "And he wrote on the tables [the replacements], according to the first writing, the ten commandments, which the LORD spake unto you in the mount out of the midst of the fire in the day of the assembly."[32]

That day of the assembly was probably on Sivan 6, Pentecost, this is the **first trumpet** of Scripture, and it was blown by a heavenly being. The Rapture will be "the assembly of the saints" of Psalm 89:7 and the "general assembly" of Hebrews 12:23. At the Rapture, we will hear the first "trump of God" and the Lord's call and go up unto God as Moses went up unto God at Sinai. However, instead of going up on Mt. Sinai, we will go up to the heavenly Mt. Zion.

Pentecost was the day the Israelites were to bring "the firstfruits of fruit of all trees . . . unto the house of the Lord: **Also the firstborn of our sons.**"[33]

Men are "trees of righteousness, the planting of the LORD."[34] We are "a kind of firstfruits of his creatures."[35] Therefore, the Rapture should be when these firstfruits are to be brought into the heavenly house of the Lord.

> **Also** in the day of the firstfruits [Pentecost], when ye bring a **new** meat-offering unto the LORD, after your weeks be out [Pentecost is seven weeks plus one day after the Feast of Firstfruits], ye shall have an holy convocation [an assembly].[36]

Therefore we can tie these events together symbolically, but it is not necessary to go that far. We are told plainly that **the firstborn of sons are to be brought into the house of the Lord on Pentecost. That prefigures the Rapture when the first trump is blown.**

The phrase, "after your weeks be out," is a shadow of things to come. In 30, A.D., Pentecost was the 50th day after Christ's resurrection. The Rapture seems to be 50 years after Israel's national resurrection, seven weeks of years plus one.

People like Edgar C. Whisenant, who wrote *88 REASONS Why The Rapture Will Be In 1988*, and Dr. Charles R. Taylor, who wrote *Watch 1988! The Year of*

Climax, probably missed the Rapture by about ten years. Both thought it would be on the Feast of Trumpets in 1988.

I expect Rapture I on Pentecost in 1998 and Rapture II on the Feast of Trumpets in 2007 just as the Wrath of God is about to explode in furious rebukes upon this planet. Search the scriptures to see if these things are so. Maybe you can escape the Tribulation that is coming to try the whole world.

Paul hinted that a door would be opened to him on Pentecost. He said, "I will tarry at Ephesus until Pentecost. For a great [*megale*, used of space and its dimensions, prepared on a grand scale, exceedingly high and spacious] door and effectual [*energes*, efficient, powerfully working] is opened unto me.[37]

"Door" is the symbol of a Rapture as in Revelation 4:1 where "a door was opened in heaven." As the Rapture is about to take place, an exceedingly high spacious and powerfully working door will open in heaven. I believe it will open on Pentecost.

In the fig tree parable in Matthew 24:33, "doors" are mentioned."So likewise ye, when ye shall see all these things, know that it is near, even at the **doors** [plural]."

Now that the Sign of the End of the Age has appeared, know that the kingdom of God is near, even at the doors. The two translations (Rapture I and Rapture II) are the doors by which we can get quick entry into the kingdom of God. The doors will open so we can escape, for great terror is in store for those left behind; all knees will be weak as water. So, when you see the Sign of the End of the Age, know that both translations are near.

Paul acted out the Rapture on Pentecost when he said that he went "bound in the spirit unto Jerusalem" on Pentecost.[38] This will also be true at the Rapture. I believe we will go bound in the spirit, the Holy Spirit, unto New Jerusalem on Pentecost. It is the Holy Spirit that seals us until the day of redemption.

The Secret of the Stairs

Song of Solomon, 2:8-14, gives some excellent date clues for the Rapture. Solomon was a son of David, a good type of Christ, who is the Son of David. This is my favorite passage of Scripture. It is a beautiful picture to keep in mind.

The Secret of the Stairs

The voice of my beloved! behold, he cometh leaping upon the mountains, skipping upon the hills . . . My beloved spake, and said unto me, Rise up, my love, my fair one, and come away. For, lo, the winter is past, the rain is over and gone; The flowers appear on the earth; the time of the singing of birds is come, and the voice of the turtle is heard in our land; The fig tree putteth forth her green figs, and the vines with the tender grape give a good smell. Arise, my love, my fair one, and come away. O my dove, that art in the clefts of the rock, in the secret *places* of the stairs.

The word "places" is not in the original. This is the secret of the stairs. "Rise up," it says, "my love, my fair one, [the Bride] and come away [the Rapture]. For, lo, the winter is past [it is spring], the rain is over and gone [the latter rain of Nisan, our March 28 through April 26, is over]; The flowers appear on the Earth [April showers bring May flowers, so it is May, and May 31, 1998 is Pentecost]; the time of the singing of birds is come [spring, when we will sing "a new song" as we fly like birds up to heaven[39]], and the voice of the turtle [*tor*, turtledove, a migratory bird that returns suddenly in the spring and is a symbol of the Spirit of God or the Spirit of Christ; see Romans 8:9] is heard in our land; The fig tree [Israel] putteth forth her green figs [the fruit of Israel is not quite ripe], and the vines with the tender grape give a good smell [it is the time of the firstripe grapes, i.e., Sivan].

"Arise, my love, my fair one and come away [the Rapture]. O my dove [one sealed with the Spirit of God until the day of Redemption], that art in the clefts of the rock [i.e., in Christ, for "that Rock was Christ"[40]], in the secret of the stairs."[41]

The Rapture is the secret of the stairs. Like Jacob's ladder, the top of the stairs reaches to heaven, angels ascend and descend on it and the Lord stands above it. We will go up then through a great door in heaven to stand before Christ.

Just look at the exciting date clues our loving God has given us. It is not dreary winter, but beautiful spring, and after the latter rain, every sprig is coming to life with lush foliage.

Spring is appropriate for the Rapture is a time of resurrection. The green figs enable us to place the Rapture between the end of the latter rain (April 26) and when the early figs ripen, in some years the end of May, in others early June. Pentecost is Sivan 6 (May 31 in 1998) after the rains are over and there are birds, green figs and May flowers. The Lord's timing is perfect. A beautiful spring day makes us want to fly when we hear the voice of the turtledove, i.e., the Lord, for the Lord himself shall descend with a shout.

As you study Scripture, you will find other parallels. For instance, after leaving Egypt on the Passover in the first month, when Moses sent them to spy out the promised land, it was the "time of the firstripe grapes. So **they went up**" (shadow of the Rapture), "and searched the land."[42] The Septuagint says it was "the days of **spring**, the forerunners of the grape." In Israel, grapes begin to ripen in Sivan, so we will go up to search our promised land in the Jewish month of Sivan.

Three Dates Possible

The first birth of the Church was on the Jewish Sivan 6, Pentecost Sunday, May 28, 30 A.D. If the Rapture is on Pentecost Sunday, there are only three possible days on which it could occur. The Rapture must take place before the Tribulation begins in 2001. Between now and then, Sivan 6, the day of Pentecost, falls on Sunday just three times: June 7, 1992; June 4, 1995 and May 31, 1998. Take your choice.

Jesus taught in parables so the wicked would not understand. Just as he told one to show when the age ends, he told a parable to show us when the Rapture would happen.

He began by saying, "A certain man had a fig tree planted in his vineyard," The certain man represents himself, and the fig tree is Israel. In Hosea 9:10, the Lord said, "I saw your fathers as the firstripe in the fig tree at her first time: but they went to Baalpeor, and separated themselves unto that shame."

Continuing the parable, Jesus said, "And he came and sought fruit thereon, and found none." Christ will come on Pentecost when green figs should be on the fig tree, gather his saints and look for fruit on the fig tree nation, Israel. The nation will be there, having been grafted onto her old rootstock, but nationally, they will not have accepted him yet.

"Behold," he explained, "these three years [the Jewish 5758, 5759 and 5760], I come seeking fruit on this fig tree, and find none: cut it down," he ordered; "why cumbereth it the ground? And he answering said unto him, Lord, let it alone this year also, till I shall dig about it, and dung it: And if it bear fruit, well: and if not, then after that [after Pentecost 5761, when the Tribulation begins] thou shalt cut it down."[43]

During the Tribulation, Israel will feel the ax blade chipping at her trunk. If Christ did not help in her darkest hour at the end, she would certainly fall. The number of days even have to be shortened or no flesh would be saved. Humankind would suffer the fate of the mammoths and dinosaurs.

The four years mentioned in the parable are the four that precede the Tribulation. According to Jewish reckoning, where the first year is counted, they are 5758, 5759, 5760 and 5761 (our 1998, 1999, 2000 and 2001). If the Rapture takes place on Pentecost in 1998 and the Tribulation begins on Pentecost in 2001, the parable fits perfectly. This would place **the Rapture on Sivan 6, 5758, which is our May 31, 1998**, the last possible date on which it could happen on a Pentecost Sunday before the Tribulation begins in 2001.

Pentecost is also called the Feast of Weeks. That is an exceptionally good name for the day the clock will begin to tick off the seven years of the Tribulation, the Seventieth Week of Daniel, Monday, May 28 (the same date Pentecost fell on in 30 A.D.), in the first year of the 21st century, 2001.

"Pentecost" means 50. Why did the first birth of the church come on Pentecost, 50 days after the resurrection of the Son of God? Christ ascended on the 40th day. Why did the Holy Spirit wait **another ten days** before descending on the Church? Was it because the resurrection of the Church would come 50 years after the resurrection of the nation of Israel? The Lord called Israel "my son."[44]

Israel declared her Independence in 1948. Since the Ascension was on the 40th day, add forty years to 1948 and you will get 1988, when many expected the Rapture. Then because the Spirit of God waited another ten days before descending on the Church, add **another ten years.** You will again arrive at 1998. A correlation is possible.

Israel went up to Jerusalem to celebrate Pentecost on the 50th day. Is the Rapture when the Church Saints go up to the heavenly New Jerusalem to celebrate in the 50th year? The Old Testament Saints are there now, but they await the gathering of all the saints to be changed. They are to be made perfect with us." And these all [Old Testament Saints], [having obtained a good report through faith, received not the promise: God having provided some better thing for us, that they without us should not be made perfect."[45]

Some think Old Testament Saints will be resurrected 1,335 days after the idol is put in the Temple. I believe they will join us at the Rapture and return when we return with Christ. Then, on day 1,335, Daniel will stand in his lot in Israel when the land is divided by lot among the 12 tribes.

In the Septuagint, Psalms 23 (24 in KJV) is "A Psalm for David on the **first day of the week**," and verses 3-7 suggest the Rapture: "Who shall **go up** to the mountain of the Lord, and who shall stand in his holy place? He that is innocent in his hands and pure in his heart . . . Lift up your gates, ye princes [the elders], and be ye lifted up, ye everlasting doors [symbol of the Rapture]." This reinforces the idea that Old Testament saints (Saturday sabbath keepers) will be present and that the trip to the place Christ is preparing for us will be on the first day of the week, Sunday.

I believe the birth of the church on Earth prefigured the birth of the church into heaven. Believers [wheat] are harvested on Pentecost.

1st birth . . . 50 days after Resurrection of Christ . . . Pentecost Sunday
2nd birth . . . 50 years after Resurrection of Israel. . . . Pentecost Sunday

Days of Noah

The Rapture is as the days of Noah (Noe in Greek). "But as the days of Noe were, so shall also the coming of the Son of man be. For as in the days that were **before the flood** they were eating and drinking, marrying and giving in marriage, until the day that Noe entered into the ark, And knew not until the flood came, and took them all away; so shall also the coming of the Son of man be. Then shall two be in the field; the one shall be taken, and the other left. . . . Watch therefore: for ye [the disciples of Jesus prior to Pentecost] know not what hour your Lord doth come."[46]

Enoch was translated "before the flood." He understood when the flood was coming for he named his son Methuselah, which means "when he is dead, it will be sent." (According to the apocryphal Book of Jasher, he knew when he would be taken up.) Later, Noah was taken up in the Ark. He knew when it would be for man had been given 120 years.

Today, the wise can understand. The foolish virgins and unbelievers do not know the day or the hour, but if we watch, we can even know the hour. Revelation 3:3 says, "If therefore thou shalt not watch, I will come on thee as a thief, and thou shalt not know what hour I will come upon thee."

In the parable of the ten virgins we are probably told the hour; "at **midnight** there was a cry made [as the voice of the archangel in I Thessalonians 4:16], Behold, the bridegroom [Christ, Mark 2:19] cometh; **go ye out to meet him**" (Matthew 25:6). If the Lord came at midnight and followed the time zones around the globe, it would only take one day to gather the Bride, May 31, anywhere on Earth.

"Noah was 600 years old when the flood of waters was upon the earth."[47] Do you realize that **Pentecost, 1998, is in year 6,000 since Adam was driven out of Eden**, year 6,000 of the Great Week of the Mortality of Man? Didn't Noah's 600 years prefigure these 6,000 years?

Six is the number of man, created on the sixth day. So it would be perfect if the Rapture was on the sixth day of the Jewish month in the sixth millennial day of heaven. Man was placed on the Earth in the sixth day to be tested, and will, I believe, be **promoted into heaven in year 6,000** of the Great Week of the Mortality of Man if he passes the test.

There are other correlations. Noah went up into the ark, the Lord shut him in (door is a symbol of the Rapture), "And it came to pass after seven days, that the waters of the flood were upon the earth"[48] to destroy the wicked. This ties in with the latter days. As in the days of Noah, the Rapture is going up before the seven year Tribulation, at the end of which the wicked are to be destroyed.

Do you think the Rapture will happen on Pentecost, Sivan 6, 5758 (our May 31, 1998) in year 6,000 since Adam left Eden? Do you think it will take place at midnight? If so, be ready as May 31 **begins**. The Jewish Sivan 6 begins at 6:00 P.M. on our May 30th. It seems possible that the Rapture might take place as soon as Sivan 6 and May 31 coincide.

In the morning, I wonder how many Laodiceans will go to church not suspecting anything, only to find that their pastor and most of the congregation are gone. Do you think there won't be crying and shedding of tears as they realize what has taken place? Will any church be unaffected by this?

The Prize

Paul called the Rapture "the prize." He said,

> I count all things but loss . . . that I may win Christ, And be found in him . . . That I may know him, and the power of his resurrection . . . If by any means I might attain unto the resurrection of the dead [the Rapture]. Not as though I had already attained, either were already perfect: but I follow after, if that I may apprehend that for which also I am apprehended of Christ Jesus. Brethren, I count not myself to have apprehended: but this one thing I do . . . I press toward the mark for the prize of the **high calling** of God in Christ Jesus.[49]

The Greek words *ano kleseos*, translated "high calling," mean upward invitation. I believe that his upward invitation of God in Christ Jesus is the Rapture, the prize we want to win. Paul wrote Timothy, saying,

> Know ye not that they which run in a race run all, but one receiveth the prize? So run, that ye may obtain, And every man that striveth for the mastery is temperate in all things. Now they do it to obtain a corruptible crown; but we an incorruptible. I therefore so run, not as uncertainly; so fight I, not as one that beateth the air: But I keep under my body, and bring it into subjection: lest that by any means, when I have preached to others, I myself should be a castaway.[50]

The word *adokimos*, translated "castaway," means disqualified. Paul does not want to be disqualified from the race. He wants to run well and win the prize. We know that he did. Just before he died, he said, "I have fought a good fight, I have finished my course, I have kept the faith: Henceforth there is laid up for me a crown of righteousness.[51]

If we do as well, we will get a crown of righteousness after we win the Rapture, the prize of the upward invitation of God in Christ Jesus, and hear the shout, "Come up hither."

"I am the true vine, and my Father is the husbandman. Every branch in me that beareth not fruit he taketh away." John 15:1,2

Chapter 11

Foolish Virgins

Salt Can Be Cast Out

Is it possible to be a castaway who is spewed out of Christ's mouth at the Rapture and left behind?

If you think not, then how do you explain the salt being cast out? Jesus told believers,

Ye are the salt of the earth, but if the salt have lost his savour, wherewith shall it be salted? it is thenceforth good for nothing, but to be cast out, and to be trodden under foot of men.[1]

The Vine Can Be Pruned

I [Jesus] am the true vine, and my Father is the husbandman. Every branch **in me** [in Christ] that beareth not fruit **he taketh away.**[2]

This is glossed over by many, but it is important. Every branch in Christ, and therefore a believer, that does not have the fruit of the Spirit is pruned from the vine at some time.

The "fruit of the Spirit is love [*agape*, God's love], joy, peace, longsuffering, gentleness, goodness, faith, Meekness, temperance."[3]

Thou Shalt Not Make Clean Riddance

Israel's instructions for the day of Pentecost were explicit. They were told, "When ye reap the harvest of your land, thou shalt **not make clean riddance of the corners of thy field.**"[4] If the Rapture harvest is reaped on Pentecost, this is strong reason to think that some could be left behind.

I believe Christ is coming as a thief at the time of the firstripe grapes.[5] Scripture says, "If thieves came to thee, if robbers by night . . . would not have stolen till they had enough? If the grape-gatherers came to thee, would they not **leave some grapes**?"[6]

Israel was instructed, "When thou cuttest down thine harvest in thy field, and hast **forgot a sheaf in the field, thou shalt not go again to fetch it** . . . When thou beatest thine olive tree, **thou shalt not go over the boughs again** . . . **When thou gatherest the grapes of thy vineyard, thou shalt not glean it afterward**."[7]

Was God setting a precedent? Do these verses suggest that believers can be cast out to be trodden upon during the Tribulation? Jesus said,

> All that the Father giveth me shall come to me; and him that cometh to me I will in no wise cast out [believers cannot be lost]. . . . this is the Father's will . . . of all which he hath given me I should lose nothing, but should raise it [those left behind?] up **again** [repetition, i.e., Rapture II] **at the last day** [as the age ends].[8]

This statement is why so few Christians worry about being cast out. But, if there is a last day, there also must be a first day. What about the first day? The first day is the first trump, the day of Rapture I. "And if they blow but with one trumpet, then the princes, which are heads of the thousands of Israel, shall gather themselves unto thee."[9]

In Revelation 4:4, the twelve princes of Israel are seen in heaven as "elders" immediately after the Rapture. Twelve is the complete heavenly number. These twelve represent the Old Testament Saints. The Church saints are there too, represented by the twelve apostles, who are also Israelite "elders."

The last day is the last trump, the day the Tribulation Saints are raised up at Rapture II. Isn't it possible that some might be cast out the first day but cannot be cast out the last day? On the last day, **all** believers will be called from heaven and Earth to the assembly at the Judgment Seat of Christ.

Do you want to be sure of gaining entrance to heaven at the first trumpet call so you do not have to go through the terrors of the terrible Tribulation? Then Listen to Peter as he addresses those who are **already believers**, the brethren.

[Add] to your faith virtue; and to virtue, knowledge; And to knowledge, self-control; and to
self-control, patience; and to patience, godliness; And to godliness, brotherly kindness;
And to brotherly kindness, love. For if these
things be in you, and abound, they make you
that ye shall neither be barren nor unfruitful in
the knowledge of our Lord Jesus Christ. But,
he that lacketh these things is blind
[like the Laodiceans] **and cannot see afar
off** [heaven], and hath forgotten that he was
purged from his old sins. . . . brethren [be-
lievers], give diligence to make your **calling
and election** sure; for if ye do these things,
ye shall never fall . . . **an entrance** [*eisodos*,
entering through a door, i.e., the Rapture]
shall be ministered unto you abundantly
into the everlasting kingdom of our Lord
and Saviour, Jesus Christ.[10]

Calling and election are both mentioned. We must
make sure that we are not only called, but elected. We are
called to run in the race, but must also be elected to office.

Old sins are already covered by the blood of Christ
when we first believe, but what about new sins? Why did
Jesus wash Peter's feet? Jesus said, "If I wash thee not, thou
hast no part with me" (John 13:8). Our new sins must also be
brought under the blood. How do we get our new sins
forgiven too?

John made it very plain when he said, "If we confess
[*homologeo*, acknowledge] our sins, he is faithful and just to
forgive us our sins, and to cleanse us from all unrighteousness.[11] We have to confess our sins **to God**, and he will
forgive them. Then we are back in fellowship with him and
filled with his Holy Spirit. If we confess our known sins,
God will at the same time forgive all our sins, for we can sin
without realizing it.

Along with Paul, "I pray, that your love may abound
yet more and more in knowledge and in all judgment; That ye
may approve things that are excellent; that ye may be sincere
and without offence till the day of Christ [day of the Rapture];
Being filled with the fruits of righteousness, which are by
Jesus Christ, unto the glory and praise of God."[12]

The Partial Rapture Theory

Had you thought that Christians could not be left behind when the church is translated to heaven? The closer we get to Rapture I, the more vital it is for us to know the truth. If some can be left behind, we need to know what to do to participate in the first translation. Otherwise, we might have to endure the horrors of the Tribulation.

Those who believe in a partial Rapture say that Biblical exhortations to be faithful, to be ready for Christ's coming and to lead Spirit-filled lives suggest that the Rapture is a reward. They think that only the faithful will be caught up on that day.

The opposite view is that translation is a part of salvation by grace, that the church is the Body of Christ and cannot be divided, and that when Jesus takes his body to heaven, he will not leave a finger behind.

Adherents of the latter forget that the Body of Christ is already divided; Christ "is the head of the body, the church,"[13] and is already in heaven. Their proof would not stand up in court. When a baby is being born, its body does not appear all at once. Its head appears first, then its shoulders. Soon, the rest of the body follows. It would not be incongruous, therefore, if Jesus, the head, was born into heaven first. Next come the shoulders and chest with two arms, Old Testament saints and overcomers of the church. The lower torso, Tribulation saints, with its two legs, new converts and the remainder of the church, follow relatively quickly.

True, God will deal with Israel during the Tribulation, it is the Seventieth Week of Daniel, but the church age is also to be prolonged until the Day of the Lord begins. **Both the Age of the Jews and the Age of the Church will be extended**. A great multitude will be translated out of **all nations** at the end of the Tribulation. The remainder of the church could be among them or martyred because of their faith.

Blindness "in part is happened to Israel, until the fulness of the Gentiles be come in [Rapture II at the end of the age]. And so all Israel shall be saved [the remnant will be born in a day, the very day of Rapture II]" (Romans 11:25,26).

We are all saved by grace, no matter which translation we take part in, Rapture I or Rapture II. Paul said, "For by grace are ye saved through faith: and that not of yourselves: it is the gift of God: Not of works,lest any man should boast."[14]

True believers are all sealed by the Holy Spirit until the day of redemption[15] whether we go to heaven before the Tribulation begins or just before the wrath of God hits.

Proponents of the view that all true Christians will be included in the Rapture claim Romans 8:1 as proof that none can be left behind. It says that there is now "no condemnation [*katakrima,* damnatory sentence] to them which are in Christ Jesus."

However, those left behind would not be damned, only chastised, as the Laodiceans.[16] Whether carnal or spiritual at the present time, all believers would be caught up to heaven by the last day. None can be lost. True believers have eternal security. Yet, we know that chastisement is the norm for Christians who misbehave because we will never suffer condemnation later on. "Whom the Lord loveth he chasteneth, and scourgeth every son whom he receiveth."[17]

The House is to be Broken up

In referring to the Rapture, Jesus first compared it to the days of Noah, then he told the disciples,

> **Watch** therefore for ye know not what hour your Lord doth come. But **know this**, that if the goodman of the house had known in what watch the thief would come, he would have watched, and would not have suffered his house to be broken up. . . .be ye also ready.[18]

He said, "Know this." Here is something important for the church to know. The house is the church. Hebrews 3:6 speaks of Christ and adds "whose house are we." The thief is the Lord.[19] Then the church is "to be broken up." The Lord will come and take away all the best things in the house as a thief would do. And like any burglar, it looks like he will leave behind all those things of little worth.

Parable of Wise and Evil Servants

Jesus continued, giving a parable of a faithful and wise servant contrasted with an evil servant. Both are believers. The evil servant is still a servant. He believes in the Lord, but he says, "My lord delayeth his coming." The wise servant does not say this. Instead, he gives them meat in due season.

> But and if that **evil servant** shall say in his heart, **My lord** delayeth his coming [the Lord will come as planned]; And shall begin to smite his fellowservants, and to eat and drink with the drunken; The lord of that servant shall come in a **day** when he looketh not for him, and in an **hour** that he is not aware of, And shall **cut him asunder, and appoint him his portion with the hypocrites**: there shall be weeping and gnashing of teeth.[20]

This makes it clear that the evil servant will not know the day or hour of the Lord's return. What about the good servant?

The word "hypocrites" here means pretenders. The evil servant is a real believer, not a pretender, but he will be cut off and appointed a portion with the pretenders. He will be so unhappy that he will cry bitterly over what he has lost because it was within easy reach, yet he let it slip from his grasp.

Luke is clear that the servant is a believer. He adds that if the servant lives like an unbeliever, he will be cut off and appointed his portion with the unbelievers:

> Who then is **that faithful and wise steward**, whom his lord shall make ruler over his household, **to give them their portion of meat in due season** [the time of the end]? Blessed is that servant, whom his lord when he cometh shall find so doing. Of a truth I say unto you, that he will make him ruler over all that he hath. But and if **that servant** say in his heart, **My lord** delayeth his coming; and shall begin to beat the menservants . . . and to be drunken; The lord of that servant will come in a **day** when he looketh not for him, and at an **hour** when he is not aware [**the wise servant can know both the day and hour of the Rapture, but the evil servant will not know either**], and will **cut him in sunder, and will appoint him his portion with the unbelievers**.[21]

The one cut in sunder is a believer. Yet, he will have to go through the Tribulation with the pretenders and unbelievers. We can't say we weren't warned. It will be a sad day if we have to say, "I almost made it."

When John saw Christ at the Rapture, Christ "had in his right hand seven stars: and out of his mouth went a sharp twoedged sword."[22] This is not the Second Advent, after which Armageddon will be fought. Why is a sword necessary when he comes for the Church unless it is to cut off the evil servants? The message to the church of Pergamos says,

> These things saith he which hath the sharp **sword with two edges** . . . So hast thou also them that hold the doctrine of the Nicolaitanes [elevation of priests over laity], which thing I hate [all believers are priests, Revelation 1:6]. Repent; or else I will come unto thee quickly [at the Rapture], and will fight against them [that hold the doctrine of the Nicolaitanes] with the **sword** of my mouth. He that hath an ear, let him hear **what the Spirit saith unto the churches.**[23]

In the parable of the talents, Jesus also spoke of a servant [believer] weeping. "And cast ye the unprofitable servant into outer [*exoteros*, exterior, outside of doors] darkness: there shall be weeping and gnashing of teeth."[24] Are the doors the servant will be outside of those of the Rapture?

Parable of the Wedding Garment

When Christ takes his Bride, the evil servant will be left behind because he will not have on a wedding garment. To take part in the Marriage of the Lamb, we must be clothed with fine linen, clean and white. The "fine linen is the righteousnesses of saints."[25] Jesus illustrated this necessity in a parable:

> When the king came in to see the guests, he saw there a man which had not on a wedding garment: And he saith unto him, Friend [someone he knows, not a stranger], how camest thou in hither not having a wedding garment? And he was speechless. Then said

133

the king to the servants, Bind him hand and foot, and take him away, and cast him into outer [*exoteros*, exterior, out of doors, i.e., out of the Rapture door] darkness: there shall be weeping and gnashing of teeth.[26]

Why was he speechless? He was in total shock because he thought he belonged there, that no believer could be cast outside the doors that the righteous shall enter when Christ says, "Come up hither." He was trusting in that. He did not know that he was wretched, miserable, poor, blind and naked like the Laodiceans. No wonder he wept so bitterly.

How would you feel to be left behind to maybe be a martyr during the Tribulation? Regret would envelope you like a flame. You would think, "Oh what have I done? and for what?" Nothing here could be worth that.

Jesus demonstrated a progressive intimacy in the book of John. First he called believers servants, then friends and later brethren. The one without a wedding garment was only called "friend." That may be significant. I would rather be classed brethren. Jesus said that many

shall come from the east and west [at the Rapture], and shall sit down with Abraham, and Isaac, and Jacob [Old Testament Saints, who come with Christ at the Rapture], in the kingdom of heaven. But the children of the kingdom shall be cast out into outer darkness: there shall be weeping and gnashing of teeth.[27]

Keep your Garments

White goes where the light is. We will have to weep outside heaven's door in the darkness if we do not have on a white wedding garment. We are the Bride of Christ. When Christ comes at the Rapture to take his Bride, we should be dressed in white and ready. Will he wait if we are not ?

If you have white garments, you can lose them. Jesus said, "Behold, I come as a thief. Blessed is he that watcheth, and keepeth his garments, lest he walk naked, [like the Laodiceans[28]] and they see his shame."[29] Why would we have to watch and keep our garments unless we were in danger of losing them? The Lord knows chastisement works.

It yieldeth the peaceable fruit of righteousness unto them which are exercised thereby. Therefore lift up the hands which hang down, and the feeble knees; And make straight paths for your feet, lest that which is lame be turned out of the way; but let it rather be healed. Follow peace with all men, and holiness, without which **no man** shall see the Lord.[30]

Though the Tribulation saints have at one time worn "the garment spotted by the flesh,"[31] they will have "washed their robes, and made them white in the blood of the Lamb"[32] by the time they make their grand entrance into heaven's door when Rapture II takes place after the age ends.

It is possible to defile your garments, but to those who "have not defiled their garments," Jesus said, "They shall walk with me in white: for they are worthy. He that overcometh, the same shall be clothed in white raiment."[33]

The Laodiceans

At the Rapture, those wearing white robes will participate. The Laodiceans will not have white garments, so may be left behind. Christ warned, **"I counsel thee** [we'd better take heed] **to buy of me gold** [symbol of deity] **tried in the fire** [pure], **that thou mayest be rich; and white raiment, that thou mayest be clothed."**[34]

They are Christians for they have to be in Christ before they can be spewed out of his mouth. "I know thy works," he says, "that thou art neither cold nor hot, I will spue thee out of my mouth."[35] Jesus did not mince his words. *Emesai* means vomit. He literally said, "I will vomit thee out of my mouth."

These immature Christians are not working parts of the Body of Christ. They are still in the stomach, unassimilated. Therefore, like food that is still in the stomach, they can be vomited out and left behind when the translation takes place.

Laodicean means "people of judgment," an apt term for those who are not judged worthy of translation when the first trumpet sounds at the Rapture. It looks like they will be left behind for chastisement, but **they cannot be lost**.

Addressing them, Jesus said, "To him that overcometh will I grant to sit with me in my throne."[36] They will just get there at a later time with the other Tribulation saints. It looks like these two legs of the Body of Christ will be born into the kingdom of heaven when the door opens at the last trump.

The Philadelphians represent those who are taken to heaven before the Tribulation, at the first trump. They are to be awarded certain crowns.[37]

Even though left behind, the Laodiceans are classed as sons of God. The Lord loves them and wants them to walk with him in "white raiment."[38] Hebrews 12:8 says, "If ye be without chastisement, whereof all are partakers, then are ye bastards, and not sons." However, the Laodiceans are chastened. Jesus said to them, "As many as I love, I rebuke and chasten: be zealous therefore, and repent."[39]

Only after they repent and open the door of their hearts to Christ, will they be taken through the door of translation to heaven to sit with him in his throne. When they repent and confess their sins to God, they will be forgiven and be filled with the Holy Spirit. Jesus said, "I will come in to him."

Wise and Foolish Virgins

Immediately after speaking of the servant who would be appointed his portion with the hypocrites, Jesus said, "Then," which is the Greek *tote*, meaning at the same time. So we can assume that he was speaking of the time of the Rapture. He then gave us the parable of the ten virgins.

> Then shall the kingdom of heaven be likened unto ten virgins, which took their lamps, and went forth to meet the bridegroom. And five of them were wise, and five were foolish. They that were foolish took their lamps, and took no oil with them: But the wise took oil in their vessels with their lamps. While the bridegroom tarried, they all slumbered and slept. And at midnight there was a cry made, Behold, the bridegroom cometh; go ye out to meet him. Then all those virgins arose, and trimmed their lamps. And the foolish said unto the wise, Give us of your oil; for our lamps are gone out. But the wise answered, saying, Not so; lest there be not enough for us and you: but go ye rather to them that sell, and buy for yourselves. And while they went to buy, the

136

bridegroom came; and **they that were ready went in with him to the marriage**: and the door [which opens in heaven at the Rapture[40]] was shut [like the door of the Ark]. Afterward came also the other virgins, saying, Lord, Lord, open to us. But he answered and said, Verily I say unto you, I know you not.[41]

Christ is the bridegroom coming for his bride, the church. The oil represents the indwelling Holy Spirit.

The King James Version says, "Our lamps are gone out," but the Greek literally says, "Our lamps are going out." The Greek word *sbennuntai* means are being quenched, going out, being extinguished.

Another form of the same word, *sbennute*, is found in 1 Thessalonians 5:19. It says, "Quench not the Spirit." In the parable, the blazing oil of the Holy Spirit was being quenched. Yet we are commanded to quench not the Spirit. Why? Is the parable to show us why we should not quench the Holy Spirit? Is it a timely warning to believers? After all, Paul wrote his letter to the Thessalonian "brethren," i.e., believers.

Many top-notch teachers think the virgins represent the professing church. They think the wise are true believers and the foolish mere professors who are not genuinely regenerated and indwelt by the Holy Spirit.

However, since *sbennuntai* means "are going out," the lamps of the foolish virgins had some oil in them. At first, they were lit. The problem was in not having along an extra supply in another vessel.

I believe that all ten virgins represent Christians. They are all virgins. The moment we truly believe in Christ, our sins are forgiven and we become pure undefiled virgins whose lamps are filled with the blazing oil of the Spirit of Christ.

Paul said, "Do all things without murmurings and disputings: That ye may be blameless and harmless, the sons of God [by adoption[42]], without rebuke, in the midst of a crooked and perverse nation, among whom ye shine as lights in the world."[43]

We are to live so as to be blameless and not deserve rebuke. We should not be lukewarm like the Laodiceans for the Lord rebuked them. Our lights should shine brightly, not be on the verge of going out. We would not like to be foolish virgins and be left behind at the first trumpet call. There are too many disadvantages in trying for the last trumpet, like being a martyr, for instance.

We will go with time to spare and visit our habitation They will either be martyrs or make it by the skin of their teeth just before God's wrath is poured out on the Earth. Some will forfeit rewards, yet be saved so as by fire—as fire is falling.

The earnest of the Spirit that seals us until the day of redemption is enough oil to ensure that we are never lost, but it may not be enough to guarantee us the prize, the Rapture Scripture says, "Let no man rob you of your prize."[44]

We should not quench the Holy Spirit. Instead, we should confess our sins, stay in fellowship, be filled with the Spirit and by so doing win the prize.

After the Rapture, the other virgins said, "Lord, Lord open to us. But he answered and said, Verily I say unto you, I know you not."[45] He did not say that he never knew them only that he does not know them at the present time. I believe this is the moment when they are vomited out of his mouth He is disgusted with them.

This is as the days of Noah. When the door of the Ark was closed, he did not open it again until those days of tribulation were over. "Jesus said, "Not every one that saith unto me, Lord, Lord, shall enter into the kingdom of heaven but he that doeth the will of my Father which is in heaven."[46]

That is the key, doing the Lord's will. "And this is his commandment. That we should believe on the name of his Son Jesus Christ, and love [*agapomen*] one another."[47] This agape love is God's love, flowing through us to others.

Then we should have agape love. How do we get it? Be filled with the Spirit, for "the fruit of the Spirit is love [*agape*]."[48] "God is love [*agape*]."[49] This is one of his attributes, like sovereignty, righteousness, justice, omnipotence, omniscience, and omnipresence.

"If we love [*agapomen*] one another, God dwelleth in us, and his love [*agape*] is perfected in us."[50] "Wherefore be ye not unwise, but understanding what the will of the Lord is And be not drunk with wine, wherein is excess; but **be filled with the Spirit**."[51] When we are filled with the Spirit, we have fellowship with God. When we sin, we grieve his Spirit and are out of fellowship with our righteous God. We are to

grieve not the holy Spirit of God, whereby ye
are sealed unto the day of redemption. Let all

bitterness, and wrath, and anger, and clamour, and evil speaking, be put away from you, with all malice: And be ye kind one to another, tenderhearted, forgiving one another, even as God for Christ's sake hath forgiven you.[52]

If we say that we have fellowship with him, and walk in darkness, we lie, and do not the truth: But if we walk in the light, as he is in the light, we have fellowship one with another, and **the blood of Jesus Christ his Son cleanseth us from all sin**. If we say that we have no sin, we deceive ourselves, and the truth is not in us. **If we confess our sins, he is faithful and just to forgive us our sins**, and to cleanse us from all unrighteousness.[53]

We must try to walk in righteousness, and when we sin, we must confess that sin to God to be filled with his Holy Spirit and be in fellowship again. Remember, Jesus dramatized this when he washed Peter's feet. Peter said, "Thou shalt never wash my feet." Jesus answered with a stern warning, "If I wash thee not, thou hast **no part** with me."[54]

Those who have quenched the Spirit, whose lives are no different than nonbelievers, who have not confessed their sins and gotten back into fellowship with God may be taking an awful chance of being chastised during the Tribulation. Yet, they will be taken later to be with the Lord. No one will be left out on the "last day." Our Lord Jesus Christ declared,

No man can come to me, except the Father which hath sent me draw him [by means of the oil of the Holy Spirit]: and I will raise him up at the last day."[55]

Paul warned, "Let him that thinketh he standeth take heed lest he fall."[56]

Many are Called but Few are Chosen

Over 500 years before Jesus was born, Ahasuerus was king of Persia. His kingdom extended from India to Ethiopia.

On the seventh day of a sumptuous feast in his palace, he sent for his queen, but Vashti refused to come. In his anger, he divorced her. After that, he had a group of fair young virgins brought to his palace. He chose one that pleased him, Esther, from among them and made her his queen.[57] (Notice that **he did not choose all the virgins**.) Later, he remembered Vashti.

This pictures what will happen when Christ chooses his bride. When the seventh millennium of time should be about to dawn, the Lord will send for his queen (the Rapture in year 6,000). Israel will refuse to come, so instead, he will call the virgins, wise and foolish, from which to choose his bride.

Only the wise are ready and go with their bridegroom. At the end of the shortened Tribulation, he will remember Israel when she blows the trumpets of alarm in her darkest hour, the "time of Jacob's trouble."

Describing the Marriage of the Lamb in a parable, Jesus said,

> The kingdom of heaven is like unto a certain king, [God] which made a marriage for his son, [Jesus] And sent forth his servants to call them that were bidden to the wedding: and they would not come. . . . Then saith he to his servants, The wedding is ready, but they which were bidden [Israel] were not worthy [because they have not accepted their Messiah]. Go ye therefore into the highways, and as many as ye shall find, bid to the marriage. So those servants . . . gathered together all as many as they found, both bad [like the foolish virgins] and good [like the wise virgins] . . . And when the king came in to see the guests, he saw there a man which had not on a wedding garment: And he saith unto him, **Friend**, how camest thou in hither not having a wedding garment? And he was speechless. Then said the king . . . take him away, and cast him into outer darkness: there shall be weeping and gnashing of teeth. For **many** [Israel, plus both wise and foolish virgins] **are called**, **but few** [the wise virgins] **are chosen**.[58]

Few, only those wearing white wedding garments, are chosen. Like Esther, we must be both called and chosen. The "fine linen is the righteousnesses of saints."[59] Those garments should not be spotted by the flesh, but washed in the blood of the Lamb.

> Christ . . . gave himself for it; That he might sanctify and cleanse it with the washing of water by the word. That he might present it to himself a glorious **church, not having spot**, or wrinkle, or any such thing; but that **it should be holy and without blemish.**[60]

Those foolish virgins who are left behind at the Rapture should immediately ask for the Holy Spirit. They will need him badly during the Tribulation.

> Which of you shall have a **friend**, and shall go unto him at midnight [the bridegroom came at midnight in the parable of the ten virgins], and say unto him, Friend, lend me three loaves . . . he . . . shall answer and say, Trouble me not: **the door is now shut** [like the door at the Rapture], and my children are with me in bed; I cannot rise and give thee. I say unto you, Though he will not rise and give him, because he is his friend, yet because of his importunity he will rise and give him as many as he needeth. And I say unto you, Ask, and it shall be given you . . . If ye then, being evil, know how to give good gifts unto your children: how much more shall your heavenly Father **give the Holy Spirit to them that ask him?**[61]

Ye shall have Tribulation Ten Days

The Lord sent a message to the early church under persecution that also could apply to the church during the Tribulation. He said,

> Fear none of those things which thou shalt suffer: behold, the devil shall cast some of you

into prison, that ye may be tried; and ye **shall have tribulation ten days**: be thou faithful unto death, and I will give thee a crown of life. He that hath an ear, let him hear what the Spirit saith unto the churches.[62]

These ten days could symbolically represent ten years. Days stand for years in Genesis 6:3: man's "days shall be an hundred and twenty years." Also, in Ezekiel 4:6: "I have appointed thee each day for a year."

There are ten years between the Rapture in the Jewish 5758 and the Translation of the Tribulation Saints as the first day of 5768 begins. No wonder ten is the complete earthly number. According to Jewish reckoning, the ten years of tribulation for the Church would be 5758, 5759, 5760, 5761, 5762, 5763, 5764, 5765, 5766, and 5767. (These are our 1998, 1999, 2000, 2001, 2002, 2003, 2004, 2005, 2006 and 2007.) This is another reason to think that the Rapture will take place in 1998.

It looks like some of the Church will have tribulation ten years. This message was to the church in Smyrna, which means bitterness. If a Christian does get left behind, he will weep with bitterness for he could have gone the first time. Those with Christ are "called, and chosen, and faithful."[63]

In Exodus 19:10-17, Moses was instructed to have the people wash their clothes. Then "**when the trumpet soundeth long, they shall come up to the mount**. . . . And Moses brought forth the people out of the camp **to meet with God**." This probably took place on Pentecost as I believe the Rapture will. It shows we must have clean garments, not ones spotted by the flesh. When the Tribulation saints finally are seen in heaven, they "have washed their robes, and made them white in the blood of the Lamb" (Revelation 7:14). We must confess our sins to God, as in I John 1:9, so we can be counted clean and worthy to stand before him. Otherwise, we may have ten years of tribulation.

Lockup

The ten years are the Lord's lockup. In old-fashioned typesetting, metal type is painstakingly set in rows and then locked into place in a wooden block. By mentioning ten days of tribulation, he locked the Rapture into its place in time.

Chapter 12

The Seventieth Week of Daniel

The beginning of the Seventieth Week of Daniel[1] is that watershed of history after which things go downhill until the Lord returns. It arrives amid fanfare as a covenant of peace is signed by Roman and Israeli leaders, the two evil statesmen of the new world order. The torch of hope for world peace is lit.

When Daniel prayed, Gabriel was sent to help him understand. In the prophecy he was given, "Seventy weeks" (*shabuim*, sevens, 70 x 7 = 490), seventy weeks of years, were to be counted from the commandment to restore and build Jerusalem until Christ is anointed and everlasting right-eousness brought in. According to the noted Bible chrono-loger, Martin Anstey, Cyrus gave the command to rebuild Jerusalem and the temple in B.C. 454.[2] Of Cyrus, the Lord said in Isaiah 45:28, "He is my shepherd, and shall perform all my pleasure: even saying to **Jerusalem, Thou shalt be built**; and to the temple, Thy foundation shall be laid."

The prophecy in Daniel 9 was divided into seven sevens (49 years), sixty-two sevens (434 years) and the final seven. There was a gap between those 483 years (they ended at the Crucifixion) and the 70th week of years. The Church Age is running in that space. The Seventieth Week of Daniel will run concurrently with the Tribulation, a seven year trial "upon all the world," when extensions of three ages, Gentiles, Jews, and the Church, will run together. This is "**judgment**." "A wise man's heart discerneth both **time** and **judgment**."

The 70 years of Babylonian captivity were a type of this 70th week. There will arise another proud king of Baby-lon who will build the city, set up an image and command all to worship it or be killed.

As suggested by Nebuchadnezzar being given the mind of a beast for seven years,[3] beasts will rule during the Tribulation, first the Roman Beast, then the False Prophet.

A tribulum is a flail used in threshing by hand to separate wheat from chaff. During the Tribulation, the Lord "will thoroughly purge his floor, and gather his wheat into the garner; but he will burn up the chaff with unquenchable fire."[4]

This seven years will be a time of escalating tension, trials and trouble. Evil leaders, war against the saints, famine, pestilence and death will stomp misery on all humanity. It will start out with the flaming hope of enduring world peace, but that will be quickly extinguished as men abruptly realize that they have been duped by the greatest snake oil con artist of all time, the smooth talking Satan indwelt Israeli False Prophet.

The Dragon, Beast and False Prophet

There is a progressive revelation in Scripture of the dragon, the red dragon, the Beast and the False Prophet. All are operative during the Tribulation judgment at this age's end.

In Daniel 2, Nebuchadnezzar dreamed of a great image representing world governments. Later on, he set up a huge golden image **threescore** cubits tall **and six** cubits wide in the province of Babylon and commanded people to come to the dedication and worship it or be cast into a fiery furnace.[5] These will have their parallel in the middle of the Tribulation when another image representing world government will be worshiped, and many will receive the mark of the beast, "Six hundred **three score and six**,"[6] an intensification of the threescore and six of Nebuchadnezzar's image.

There are three Babylons. Babel had a numerical system based on the 6, hence our 60 minutes to the hour. False religion rode upon Egypt, but the idolatrous Mystery Religion of Babylon began at the Tower of Babel with Nimrod, Semiramis and Tammuz. It is one of Satan's counterfeit religions. The 66 points to Babylon in Nebuchadnezzar's day and the same Mystery Religion. The 666 indicates a final Babylon with its Mystery Religion in our near future. The study of the former helps us understand the latter.

In Nebuchadnezzar's dream, the head of gold represented Babylon, the chest and arms of silver stood for Media-Persia, the belly and thighs of brass pictured Greece and the legs of iron symbolized Rome. God formed Italy in the shape of a leg and foot so we would not fail to make this connection. As in the dream, a stone like an upper millstone will thresh those kingdoms and break them all in pieces "like the chaff of the **summer** threshingfloors."[7] The stone will fall on the Feast of Trumpets, Tishri 1, 5768, in the summer.

God gave Nebuchadnezzar power, glory, and dominion over **all men, wild beasts and birds** of the air. In it's parallel during the Tribulation, world government will rule over **all men**, **wild beasts** (Revelation 13), even unclean hateful **birds**, i.e., demon possessed men (Revelation 18:2).

Daniel's dream in his 7th chapter expands this picture. He saw four beasts coming up out of the sea (nations[8]). The first was like a lion (symbol of Babylon), the second like a bear (Media-Persia) and the third like a leopard (Greece).

Verse 23: "The fourth **beast** [**world government, led first by the Beast of Rome** and later by the Israeli False Prophet], strong and terrible, shall be the fourth kingdom upon earth, which shall be diverse from all kingdoms, and **shall devour the whole earth**, and shall tread it down, and break it in pieces ["and parted my land," Joel 3:2]." Verse 19's "and stamped the residue with his feet," ties it in with the feet of Nebuchadnezzar's image, which portray a revived Roman empire in our days.[9]

The "ten horns **out of this kingdom** [these ten nations are not the whole world government, just **part** of it, ten members of it] are ten kings that shall arise [the European Economic Community (EEC) rising before the Rapture]: and another [the False Prophet of Israel] shall rise after them [and after the Rapture]; and he shall be diverse from the first [not European], and he shall subdue three kings" (verse 24).

The Common Market (EEC), started with The Treaty of **Rome**. It was signed in March, 1957, to work toward a free flow of goods and services and a customs union.

In 1958, the EEC began operations with six member nations: Italy, Belgium, France, Luxembourg, Netherlands and West Germany. In 1979, Greece became the tenth to join (ratified in 1981). Spain and Portugal joined in 1986. Austria has applied. She would make thirteen. The present members are Italy, West Germany, France, Belgium, Netherlands, Luxembourg, Ireland, Denmark, Britain, Greece, Spain and Portugal. On July 17, 1979, the first EEC parliament was formed. All barriers to free movement of capital and people as well as to free trade are to be removed in 1992. On October 25, 1990, the EEC summit in **Rome** voted in a timetable that would bring a single European currency into use by 2000. A majority of people also want to elect a president of Europe.

If the ten horns represent the EEC, it will first have thirteen members including the ten kings. Then, God will use the False Prophet to pluck up three, leaving ten during the Tribulation. The Lord explained why they are to be severed. He said, "Three shepherds also I cut off in one month; and my soul lothed them, and their soul also abhorred me."[10]

Daniel 7:8 says, "I considered the horns [kings] . . . there came up among them another little horn [the False Prophet], before whom there were three of the first" (*qadmay*, from root *qadam*, to precede in time, **preceding**) horns plucked up by the roots." The Confraternity Version is clear: "three of the **previous** horns were torn away."

The fourth kingdom of Daniel 7 is the iron legs empire of the image in Nebuchadnezzar's dream, the old Roman Empire with eastern and western divisions. Today, the empire of the feet and toes is different. The feet are part iron (Rome) and part clay (soil of other nations) united by an ecclesiastical Roman empire. During the Tribulation, the empire will be both ecclesiastical and political. A portion of this empire, the ten toes, **part iron (Rome) and part clay (soil of other nations**) are allied in the EEC. These ten kings have "one mind [as in the EEC], and shall give their power and strength [military might] unto **the beast** [of Revelation 13:4, the Roman leader of world government]."[11]

In Revelation 12:3,4, we see another seven headed beast, "a great red dragon having seven heads and ten horns, and seven crowns upon his heads. And his tail drew the third part of the stars of heaven, and did cast them to the earth."

In verse 7, "there was war in heaven . . . the dragon fought and his angels . . . And the great dragon was cast out, that old serpent, called the Devil, and Satan [also Leviathan] . . . he was cast out into the earth, and his angels."

These two puzzle pieces interlock. Therefore, the tail of the seven headed great red dragon that represents world government is the dragon, also called the serpent, Satan.

In Revelation 17:9 (Confraternity), "The seven heads are seven mountains [kingdoms] . . . **and** they are seven kings." Just as both Nebuchadnezzar and his kingdom were called the head of gold, these symbols represent both the kingdoms and their kings. Some prophecies also have more than one fulfillment, one near and one far off in the future.

The red dragon symbolizes world kingdoms, and there are seven. Satanic counterfeit religions ride every one, so they are all brushed with Satan's color. A portion of the final one has ten kings, who may have already received their crowns in our days, plus the tail of the dragon, which is Satan himself indwelling the False Prophet from Midtribulation to its end.

We see the same beast in Revelation 17. It too has "seven heads and ten horns," and is a scarlet coloured beast, showing that the seven world empires are infused with Satanism. Upon this beast rides a harlot church called "MYSTERY, BABYLON THE GREAT, THE MOTHER OF HARLOTS [false religions] AND ABOMINATIONS OF THE EARTH."

Gliding to the final king, we see the "beast [Satan] that was [in Judas], and is not [in man now], even he is the eighth [the great red dragon's tail], and is of the seven [Satan works in all seven world governments and indwells the False Prophet in the seventh], and goeth into perdition. And the ten horns which thou sawest are ten kings, which have received no kingdom as yet: but receive power as kings one hour with the beast."[12] The last hour of a 1,000 year day is the last 41 2/3 years of this age, so the ten kings could be in power now.

When Greece became tenth to join the EEC in 1979, ten kings were in place within the hour, and the ten final kings "shall make war with the Lamb, and the Lamb shall overcome them: for he is KING OF KINGS AND LORD OF LORDS."[13]

The unnamed but dreadful, terrible and exceedingly strong beast in Daniel 7:7,23 must be a **great red dragon** [world government] "with teeth of iron [Rome] and claws of brass [Greece] **that will devour the whole world.**"

The first head was Egypt. Ezekiel 32:2 says of Pharaoh, "Thou art like a young lion [Babylon] of the nations, and thou art as a whale [*tannim*, **dragon**] **in the seas** [nations] . . . and troubledst the waters [nations] with thy feet [as the feet of Nebuchadnezzar's image, i.e., our days]."

The iron [Rome] and brass [Greece] represent the Beast and False Prophet. The Beast of Revelation 13:4-10 is a Roman "prince."[14] The Grecian Empire was divided into four parts after the death of Alexander: Thrace, Greece, Egypt and Syria. Therefore, the False Prophet could be a Syrian Jew.[15]

John said, "I saw three unclean spirits . . . come out of the mouth of the dragon [Satan], and out of the mouth of the beast [Roman leader of world government in the first half of the Tribulation], and out of the mouth of the false prophet [Israeli leader of the world church and government in the last part]. For they are the spirits of devils, working miracles, which go forth unto the kings . . . of the **whole world**, to gather them to the battle of that great day of God Almighty."[16]

Once we know that **the red dragon with seven heads is world government** and that Satan, who works in it coloring it red, is the dragon who is also the serpent, Revelation 13 is easier to understand. Literally he, the dragon, "stood upon the sand of the sea, and saw a beast [the red dragon, world government] rise up out of the sea [nations[17]], having seven heads [Egypt, Assyria, Babylon, Media-Persia, Greece, Rome and the revived Roman empire] and ten horns . . . the beast which I saw was like unto a leopard [Greece], and his feet were as the feet of a bear [Media-Persia], and his mouth as the mouth of a lion [Babylon]: and the dragon gave him [the mouth speaking from Babylon] his [Satan's] power, and his [Satan's] seat [throne], and great authority."

"And I saw one of his heads [the sixth] **as it were** [symbolic language] wounded to death: and his deadly wound was healed [as the Roman Empire died, world power continued in the ecclesiastical empire, from which the leader of the world government of the Tribulation may come]: and all the world wondered after the beast [world government]. And . . . worshipped the dragon [Satan] which gave power unto the beast: and they worshipped the beast, saying, Who is like unto the beast? [it's Roman leader[18]] **who is able to make war with him**? . . . power was given unto him to continue forty and two months. And he opened his mouth in blasphemy against God . . . and them that dwell in heaven [the Rapture is past, and he did not go]. And it was given unto him to make war with the saints [calling them heretics as in the dark ages?] . . . and power was given him **over all . . . nations**."

The wild beast of Revelation 13:11-18 is the Satan indwelt False Prophet. "I beheld another beast coming up out of the earth [Israel]; and he had two horns [two sources of power] like a lamb [Jesus has two, he is man and God], and he spake as a dragon [Satan]. And he exerciseth all the power of the first beast before him [probably because of the Beast's incapacitating wound, the False Prophet takes over as head of the world government and the world church], and causeth the earth and them which dwell therein to worship the first beast, whose deadly wound was healed: and . . . deceiveth them that dwell on the earth . . . saying . . . make an image to the beast [the former leader], which **had** [literal language] **the wound by a sword** [the sword was not mentioned when referring to world government], and did live. And he had power to give life unto the image . . . and cause that as many as would not

148

worship the image of the beast should be killed. And he causeth all . . . to receive a mark . . . that no man might buy or sell, save he that had the mark, or the name of the beast, or the number of his name [666] . . . it is the number of a man [the False Prophet, leader over all nations].

Thus two evil men wield Satan's vicious power for seven years. The first will emerge out of the nations, not necessarily Rome, but will have headquarters in the city of seven hills, Rome (as in Revelation 17) then in Babylon (as in Revelation 18). The second will spring up in Israel. They are the Beast and the False Prophet of Revelation 10:20. The Beast will move to new headquarters in Babylon. The "profane wicked prince of Israel,"[19] the "idol shepherd,"[20] will also end up in Babylon. He "is a proud man, neither keepeth at home."[21] According to Jeremiah 50:12, Babylon will be the "hindermost [last] of the nations," i.e., the final seat of world government in this age, the seventh head of the red dragon, the revived Roman empire with headquarters in Babylon.

After the Pretribulation Rapture, the False Prophet will "come in peaceably."[22] Four years afterward, by Jewish inclusive reckoning, the Roman Beast will receive the crown mentioned in Revelation 6:2 as leader of the world government. The "secrets of wisdom . . . are double to that which is,"[23] and the "fourth year of Jehoiakim . . . king of Judah . . . was the first year of Nebuchadrezzar king of Babylon."[24]

Both will sign a seven year covenant of peace on the Feast of Weeks, Sivan 6, 5761 (May 28, 2001). This act will reveal their identities. The covenant will give the Jews the right to resume sacrificing in their rebuilt Temple and guarantee peace if they give allegiance to the world government.

When Satan is cast down to Earth, he will enter the False Prophet and take over as leader of world government. He will "obtain the kingdom by flatteries."[25] Both beasts are still on the scene when Christ returns.[26] The first wears the crown for three and a half years,[27] then the second takes command. Both are bad; "the prophet [False Prophet] is a fool; the spiritual man [Roman Beast] is mad" (Hosea 9:7).

The Ancient and Honorable Head

The counterfeit Mystery Religion of Babylon moved to Rome when Attalus III willed Pergamos, where "Satan's seat" was in Revelation 2:13, to Rome, where "the dragon gave him [the Beast] his power, and his [Satan's] seat [throne] . . . And they worshipped the beast." The harlot church of Revelation 17 is a city of "seven mountains [Rome], drunken with the blood of . . . martyrs [so-called heretics?] of Jesus," that "great city, which **reigneth over the kings** of the earth."[28]

The seventh **head** of the red dragon [world government] is an older man heaped with honors with headquarters first in Rome, then in Babylon. The **tail** of the red dragon is a young man. The wicked won't live out half his days,[29] and he is the ultimate wicked one. He comes in his own name, is accepted by many as messiah, but is the idol shepherd, the False Prophet, the priest-king of Israel.

The Lord will "cut off from Israel head and tail . . . in one day. **The ancient and honourable, he is the head; and the prophet that teacheth lies, he is the tail.**"[30]

At the end of the age, "the curse . . . shall enter into the house of the thief [False Prophet, a priest-king who steals what is not his], and into the house of him that **sweareth falsely by my name**" (Zechariah 5:3,4). Are these the False Prophet and the Beast? The second beast of Revelation 13 exercises **all** the power of the first, so are both priest-kings?

As the Tribulation commences on the Feast of Weeks, Jesus will open the first seal on the Book of Purchase of Earth. It's his by right of creation and by right of redemption.

As the "ancient and honourable" Beast rides forth on a white horse (symbol of a prince of peace), he will have a bow but no arrows (he directs the world army shots but does not own the armaments). Why? all nations have some armaments.

Given his crown as a prince of peace, he will go forth to conquer the world. He is the Roman "prince that shall come,"[31] whose people destroyed Jerusalem and the Temple in 70 A.D. under the leadership of Titus. His great prophesied authority would be fulfilled if he is a Roman champion of world peace who is also elected head of world government.

The Roman Empire was a combined ecclesiastical and civil government. Caesar was worshiped as the Pontifex Maximus, a pagan title for the high priest of Babylon. If this empire is to be revived, it should culminate in a combined ecclesiastical and civil world government. It seems possible since the ancient and honourable is the head, and the red dragon's final head represents world government in this age.

Maybe the False Prophet's grand slam proposal of how to bring about peace will be to elect this ancient and honorable man leader of world government. Then his emerging out of the nations, yet heading a Roman empire, people worshiping him, his own lack of armaments, and the "who is able to make war with him?" would all make sense.

The False Prophet could then take over the office and become the supreme priest-king of both the ecclesiastical and civil governments of the world. Isn't this what Satan wants? The harlot of Babylon is to be destroyed because, "**all nations** have drunk of the wine of the wrath of her fornication, and the kings of the earth have committed fornication [**joined, become one**] **with her.**" Matthew 7:15 warns, "Beware of **false prophets, which come to you in sheep's clothing**, but inwardly they are ravening wolves."

Comparing the symbols of Revelation 13:2 with Daniel 7:4-6 shows that he will be like Alexander the Great of Greece (the leopard), Cyrus of Media-Persia (the bear), Nebuchadnezzar of Babylon (the lion) and of course Rome. He will conquer quickly, as Alexander did, and make Babylon capitol of the world, as Nebuchadnezzar did and as Alexander planned. He will assist the restoration of the Temple in Jerusalem as Cyrus did and will speak as Nebuchadnezzar from Babylon for he has a "mouth as the mouth of a lion."[32] Like the lion, he will be a king of beasts, and like Nebuchadnezzar, a "king of kings"[33] with a beast's mind for seven years. He may move to Babylon at the end of a year. After twelve months, Nebuchadnezzar said, "Is not this great Babylon, that I have built for the house of the kingdom by the might of my power, and for the honour of my majesty?"[34]

Babylon will be a mart of nations. There may be international fairs with nations setting up booths. As the world capitol, she will be headquarters of the world government, the world church, and maybe a world market and the world bank.

Thought to have solved the world's problems, the Beast will be worshiped by those whose names are not written in the Book of Life. He will war against the saints because they will not worship him, just as early Christians were killed when they would not repeat, "Caesar is Lord."

The headquarters of the world church will be moved to Babylon in the land of Shinar (Iraq), and be set there upon her own base, where the tower of Babel stood.[35] In Revelation 17, we see the harlot church in Rome, "that great city built on "seven mountains," which "reigneth over the kings of the earth." The harlot's name is "MYSTERY, BABYLON THE

GREAT, THE MOTHER OF HARLOTS [false religions who join with another god] AND ABOMINATIONS [idols] OF THE EARTH." She's "drunken with the blood of the saints, and . . . of the martyrs of Jesus" like the Beast.

Revelation 18 describes the same harlot after she has been moved to the literal city of Babylon. Her headquarters in Rome will be burned for the "ten horns [EEC?] . . . shall hate the whore [because those who do not worship the image of the Beast are killed?] . . . and burn her with fire."

The literal Babylon will be destroyed with a rock. A "mighty angel took up a stone like a great millstone, and cast it into the sea, saying, Thus with violence shall that great city Babylon be thrown down, and shall be found no more."[36]

When Christ breaks the second seal on the Book of Purchase of Earth in Revelation 6, a red horse appears. Red is Satan's color. Satanic power and a great sword will be given to his rider, the Roman Beast who rides the white horse. Peace is removed from the Earth by a world army under the leadership of the Beast. The covenant will not preserve peace in the world.

Opening the third seal reveals a black horse with the same rider as the first two horses. There will be a prolonged drought during the entire reign of the Beast as leader of the world government, three and one half years. God's two witnesses will "have power to shut heaven, that it rain not."[37] Widespread famine will result in many deaths.

The Tail of the Great Red Dragon

The False Prophet will be revealed as soon as the Rapture takes place. The Holy Spirit prevents his coming to power before that. Second Thessalonians 2:3-8 shows that the Rapture comes first, "And then [tote, at the same time] shall that Wicked [the False Prophet] be revealed, whom the Lord [Christ] shall consume with the spirit of his mouth [God]."

Since the fourth year of the king of Israel was the first year of the king of Babylon,[38] the Rapture probably will occur four Jewish years before the Tribulation. Then the fourth year of the False Prophet would be the first of the Beast.

In 1998, the 480th year since the Ottoman Turks took Jerusalem, I believe two temples will be raised up. One is figurative, the Church. It will be caught up to heaven. The other is literal. Construction will begin on the restoration temple in Jerusalem. As in the days of Darius, it should take four years by Jewish inclusive reckoning to complete.[39]

The False Prophet will think he will be accepted as the Messiah if he builds the temple. Satan said he "will be like the most High,"[40] and Christ will rebuild the temple again at the beginning of the Millennium.

Zechariah 6:11-13 probably symbolizes raising both the figurative and literal temples:

> [Make] crowns, and set them upon the head of Joshua [Jesus in Greek] . . . Behold the man [Jesus Christ] whose name is The BRANCH [branch of God] . . . he shall build the temple of the LORD [the figurative]: Even he shall build the temple of the LORD [the literal]; and he shall bear the glory, and shall sit and rule upon his throne; and **he shall be a priest upon his throne: and the counsel of peace shall be between them both.**

Satan will try to imitate as much of this as possible when he sets up the False Prophet as the powerful priest-king of Israel.

Like Judas, the False Prophet steals. He says, "my hand hath found as a nest the riches of the people."[41] But, after 2,300 days of the Tribulation, the Lord will cast down The Curse, a stone, upon literal Babylon, "and it shall enter into the house of the thief [False Prophet], and into the house of **him that sweareth falsely by my name** [the Beast]: and it shall remain in the midst of his house, and shall consume it with the timber thereof and the stones thereof."[42] **Judgment must begin at the house of God.**[43]

In Revelation 6, when Christ opens the fourth seal, "behold a pale horse: and his name that sat on him was Death [the False Prophet], and Hell [Satan] followed with him. And power was given unto them over the fourth part of the earth, to kill with sword, and with hunger, and with death, and with the beasts [kings] of the earth [world government's army]."[44]

This fourth of the Earth includes Israel for the False Prophet will war against Christians in God's land. Since the Bible considers Jerusalem the center of the Earth, this quarter probably centers on Israel and includes both Spain and most of India. All of Europe would be within its boundaries.

The False Prophet will say that they will not see the sword, neither have famine. He will also promise them assured peace.[45] But the Lord says, "The prophets prophesy lies in my name: I sent them not . . . yet they say, Sword and famine shall not be in this land; By sword and famine shall those prophets be consumed."[46]

> Because ye have said, We have made a cove-
> nant with death [the False Prophet], and with
> hell [Satan] are we at agreement . . . your
> covenant with death shall be disannulled, and
> your agreement with hell shall not stand; when
> the overflowing scourge [tsunami, or tidal
> wave] shall pass through, then ye shall be
> trodden down by it.[47]

The False Prophet "is a proud man [exhibiting Satan's pride], neither keepeth at home [he will move to Babylon], who enlargeth his desire as hell [Satan], and is as death, and . . . gathereth unto him all nations [heads up world government] . . . Woe to him that increaseth that which is not his [who steals] . . . and to him [Satan] that ladeth himself with thick clay! [indwelling the False Prophet's body, which like Adam's is made from the elements of clay]."[48]

Satan has been the arch deceiver ever since the Garden of Eden. Therefore, it is no surprise that this man will do great signs and wonders to deceive those living on Earth.

Of course, Satan will "confess not that Jesus Christ is come in the flesh. This is the deceiver [Satan] and the antichrist [the False Prophet]."[49] He is anti, against, Christ. This Satan possessed man is against Christ as no other man in all of time could ever be, but he is a pretender, a liar, and a deceiver. He will do or say whatever suits his purposes.

There are many antichrists. The Beast blasphemes God and swears falsely by God's name, but the False Prophet is The Antichrist. The conflict is between God and Satan, Jesus (the God man) and the False Prophet (the Satan man), Christ and Antichrist.

He is The Liar and The Antichrist. First John 2:22 says, "Who is a liar [Satan, Genesis 3:4] but he that denieth that Jesus is the Christ? He is antichrist, that denieth the Father and the Son." In this, Satan is an outrageous liar because he knows the Father and the Son, yet will sit "in the temple of

God shewing himself that he is God." And according to II Thessalonians 2:4,11, many will believe The Lie.

From the time that he is Satan possessed, the False Prophet will minister three and one half years just as Jesus did. Since Jesus was 30 years old when he began his ministry, maybe the False Prophet will be 30 when he becomes leader of all nations and live 33 1/2 years as Jesus did. He will not live out half his days,[50] and Satan said, "I will be like the most High."[51] Alexander the Great died when he was 33 years old after conquering the known world in about three years time. It could be more than just coincidence.

The False Prophet, called the idol shepherd, is thought to be of the tribe of Dan. Dan does not have 12,000 sealed in Revelation 7, and was associated with idolatry. When Jacob lay on his death bed, he gathered his twelve sons together to tell them what would befall them in the last days. He said, "Dan shall be a serpent [Satan] by the way, an adder in the path, that biteth the horse heels [the white horse of Revelation 6], so that his rider [the Beast] shall fall backward."[52] It looks like Satan will cause the incident that incapacitates the Beast when the False Prophet obtains the kingdom.

Revelation 13's beast out of the sea applies first to the seventh world government then to its final leader. Verse 14 makes a very positive statement, the beast "had the wound by a sword and did live." The language is figurative, "as it were wounded," when applied to the world government and seems very literal when applied to its leader. The sword is not mentioned when the reference is to the world government. It is only mentioned when the reference is to the leader.

Daniel 11:21-23 declares that the "vile person [the False Prophet], to whom they shall not give the honour of the kingdom . . . shall come in peaceably, and obtain the kingdom by flatteries [*chalaqlaqqoth*, smoothnesses, i.e., smooth talk]. And with the arms of a flood shall they be overflown from before him, and shall be **broken; yea, also the prince of the covenant** [the Beast]. And after the league made with him he shall work deceitfully: for he shall come up, and shall become strong with a small people."

In the middle of the Tribulation, after the famine brought on because it will not rain during the days of Elijah's prophecy, the False Prophet will ride forth on a pale horse. "And he ["another little horn" of Daniel 7:5] shall speak great words against [**anti**] the most High [**Christ**], and shall wear out the saints of the most High, and think to change times and laws: and they shall be given into his hand until a time [one year] and times [two years] and the dividing of time [one half year]."[53] He will war against the saints these three and one half years.[54]

I believe this horn is the False Prophet. Daniel said, "I beheld then because of the voice of the great words which **the horn** spake: I beheld even till **the beast** was slain, and his body destroyed, and given to the burning flame."[55] In the parallel passage in Revelation 19:20, they are identified as the Beast and the False Prophet: "And **the beast** was taken, and with him **the false prophet** . . . both were cast alive into a lake of fire." Therefore the False Prophet is this horn.

The smooth talking False Prophet has Satan's eyes. Therefore his "look was more stout than his fellows." Since he will speak as Satan, his mouth "spake very great things."

This man, the second beast of Revelation 13, is more evil than the first beast. In Revelation 13:11, he has two horns." One little horn is the man, the False Prophet. The other is Satan, who indwells him. Daniel described both in chapter eight. Verses 23-25 portray the little horn that is the False Prophet. Man cannot stop him, but God will.

> [When] the transgressors are come to the full, a king of fierce countenance, and understanding dark sentences [*chiydah*, knotty hidden things], shall stand up. And his power shall be mighty, but not by his own power [by Satan's]: and he shall destroy wonderfully, and shall prosper, and practise, and shall destroy the mighty [the three kings] and the holy people [the saints]. And through his policy also he shall cause craft [*mirmah*, deceit] to prosper . . . he shall magnify himself in his heart, and by peace shall destroy many: he shall also stand up against the Prince of princes [Jesus Christ]; but he shall be broken without hand."

Verses 9-12 refer to the other little horn, Satan. This little horn comes from the heavenlies. Some consider this passage the most difficult Scripture to interpret, but it is not hard if you compare it with Revelation 12:3-9. Daniel said,

And out of one of them [the four winds of heaven] came forth a little horn [Satan], which waxed exceeding great . . . even to the host of heaven; and it cast down some of the host and of the stars to the ground, and stamped upon them [one third of the angels fell[56]]. Yea, he magnified himself even to the prince of the host [he will fight against Michael the archangel[57]] and by him the daily sacrifice was taken away [because he causes an image to be placed in the Temple and the False Prophet to sit in the Temple claiming to be God], and the place of his sanctuary was cast down [Satan's home in the heavenlies will be cast down to the earth on day 2,300 of the Tribulation].

The False Prophet is that "man of sin . . . the son of perdition; Who opposeth and exalteth himself above all that is called God, or that is worshiped; so that he as God sitteth in the temple of God, shewing himself that he is God . . . that Wicked . . . whose coming is after the working of Satan with all power and signs and lying wonders."[58] That last part ties in with the description of the second beast of Revelation 13.

Since Satan goes into perdition, the son of perdition is the one indwelt by Satan. Only two men are called sons of perdition, Judas and the False Prophet, both of whom Satan enters into. Though in a different body each time, Satan comes twice in a human body, simulating the two advents of Christ.

The wicked one will come up with evil devices, including the image, to destroy the poor with **lying** words.[59] He will bless the covetous. He will not seek after God, but will have a mouth full of cursing, **deceit and fraud**.[60] The Lord called him a foolish idol shepherd: "I will raise up a shepherd in the land, which shall not visit those that be cut off, neither shall seek the young one, nor heal that that is broken, nor feed that that standeth still: but he shall eat the flesh of the fat . . . Woe to the idol shepherd that leaveth the flock!"[61] The "palaces shall be forsaken."[62] He will move to Babylon in the desert. "Wherefore if they shall say unto you, Behold, he is in the **desert**: go not forth" (Matthew 24:26).

And the king shall do according to his will; and he shall exalt himself, and magnify himself above every god, and shall speak marvellous things against the God of gods, and shall prosper till the indignation [the catastrophe that will blast through the crust of the earth at the end of this age] be accomplished. . . . Neither shall he regard the God of his fathers [the Jews], nor the desire of women [Jesus, whom they wanted to bear], nor regard any god: for he shall magnify himself above all. But in his estate shall he honour [with images, gold, silver and precious stones] the God of forces [the leader of world government, commander of all the armed forces of the world] . . . and **he . . . shall divide the land** for gain."[63]

This is at least part of what Daniel 7:23 means when it says he "shall devour the whole earth . . . and break it in pieces." He should not divide God's land. It will bring judgment. The Lord said that he will gather all nations in the valley of Jehoshaphat, and will plead with them there for his people and for his heritage Israel, whom they have scattered among the nations, and **parted his land.**[64]

Judas was a treasurer and a thief. He held the bag and bought food and necessities for the apostles.[65] The other son of perdition is also a "treasurer"[66] and a thief. It seems that he will have control over the world bank (which has existed since December 27, 1945 and which will probably utilize a new generation of computers now being developed). He will say,

By the strength of my hand I have done it, and by my wisdom . . . and I have removed the bounds [national boundaries] of the people, and have robbed their treasures . . . And my hand hath found as a nest the riches of the people [in the world bank]: and as one gathereth eggs that are left [because the saints will not take the Mark of the Beast], have I gathered all the earth; and there was none that moved the wing, or opened the mouth, or peeped.[67]

What can they do? The wicked False Prophet will take over as head of the world government and exercise control over the world bank. He "gathereth unto him all nations, and heapeth unto him all people."[68] He will be commander in chief of all the armies of the world. He will war against the saints. They cannot take the Mark of the Beast, the name of the world government or the number **666** so they can buy or sell or they will be lost forever. **It is the mark of Satan.** He smugly thinks he has the whole world in his neat little trap.

"In the transgression of an evil man there is a snare,"[69] but the Lord always gives man a way out. Look at Psalms 124: "If it had not been the LORD who was on our side, when men rose up against us: Then they had swallowed us up quick, when their wrath was kindled against us . . . Blessed be the LORD, who hath not given us as a prey to their teeth. Our soul is escaped as a bird out of the snare . . . the snare is broken, and we are escaped. Our help is in the name of the LORD, who made heaven and earth."

We need God on our side. We must call on the Lord Jesus Christ to save us. According to John 1:10, "the world was made by him." Acts 4:12 states, "Neither is there salvation in any other: for **there is none other name under heaven given among men, whereby we must be saved.**"

"God is faithful, who will not suffer you to be tempted above that ye are able; but will with the temptation also make a way to escape, that ye may be able to bear it."[70] There is a way out of Satan's trap. Call on Christ and you will find it.

When the devil took Jesus up into a high mountain, showed him all the kingdoms of the world and promised to give them to him if Jesus would only fall down and worship him, he revealed what he would give to his two beasts—all the kingdoms of the world. It is coming true in our days.

In the parable of the great eagle, Babylon [Iraq] is a land of traffic and a city of merchants.[71] She will be built at tremendous cost, probably using funds left in the bank by the saints. Saddam Hussein has already started its restoration. Among several other buildings, Nebuchadnezzar's palace has been rebuilt. All kinds of merchandise will be shipped there. Merchants of the Earth and all that own ships will become rich because of her costliness.[72] But, the "peoples labor only for fire, and nations weary themselves for nought" (Habakkuk 2:13 RSV).

The False Prophet will be there. "Babylon...is become the habitation of devils, and the hold of every foul spirit [including Satan]."[73] One of the beasts will probably say, "I will pull down my barns, and build greater; and there will I bestow all my fruits and my goods."[74]

During the Tribulation, if you want to be rich, just take the Mark of the Beast so you can buy merchandise and sell it to Babylon. You could become temporarily wealthy. But, look out! there is a crash coming. The Lord said,

> I will punish Bel [Satan in the false prophet] in Babylon, and I will bring forth out of his [the False Prophet's] mouth that which he hath swallowed up [Satan]: and the nations shall not flow together any more unto him: Yea, the wall of Babylon shall fall [as the wall of Jericho fell on the seventh day, the wall of Babylon will fall as the seventh millennial day begins]. **My people, go ye out of the midst of her**, and deliver ye every man his soul from the fierce anger of the LORD.[75]

As the wall of Jericho fell, the deserted house of Rahab, the harlot, was dashed to the ground, for it was built upon the wide wall. In its modern parallel, an asteroid, a broken section of Satan's former planet Rahab, will be cast down to the Earth. When this deserted house of Rahab is dashed to the ground, the house of the harlot will be destroyed at Babylon. This is why the Lord said, "I will make mention of Rahab and Babylon to them that know me" (Psalms 87:4). (More about this later.)

After God cursed the ground, Adam had to leave his earthly paradise near the Euphrates River southeast of Babylon. Let this be a warning to those who live near there during the Tribulation. Leave! Get out of there! Escape from that general area before The Curse falls to Earth, destroying Babylon, and forming the volcanic Lake of Fire.

> The merchants . . . made rich by her [Babylon], shall stand afar off for the fear of her torment, weeping and wailing . . . for **in one hour is she made desolate.**[76]

"I am a God, I sit in the seat of God, in the midst of the seas; yet thou art a man, and not God, though thou set thine heart as the heart of God." Ezekiel 28:2

Chapter 13

The Final Crescendo Begins

In contrast to the two evil beasts, two powerful men will begin their ministry on the Feast of Weeks. They will witness for God during the **first half** of the Tribulation.[1] According to Revelation 11:3, they must prophecy three and a half years, and the last half of the Tribulation is shortened.

God's Two Witnesses

One is Elijah. Malachi 4:5,6 says, "Behold, I will send you Elijah the prophet before the coming of the great and dreadful day of the LORD. And he shall turn the heart of the fathers to the children, and the heart of the children to their fathers, lest I come and smite the earth with a curse." The curse smites the Earth as the Day of the Lord begins. Elijah must preach a full three and a half years sometime before that.

The other witness is Moses. Some have thought he was Enoch, but Enoch was a **gentile** who was "translated that he should **not see death**."[2] Both witnesses will be killed and in the past were taken to heaven from the same area (Mt. Nebo is a peak of Mt. Pisgah) to help us connect the two.

Revelation 11:4 has good clues: "These are the two olive trees [**two Jews**, Jeremiah 11:16], and the two candlesticks [believers, Revelation 1:20] standing before the God of the earth." This refers to Zechariah 4:11-14: "These are the two anointed ones, that stand by the Lord of the whole earth."

Christ is the Lord of the whole Earth. "Thy Redeemer the Holy One of Israel; The God of the whole earth shall he be called."[3] When Christ was transfigured, Moses and Elijah appeared with him.[4] These two anointed ones stood by the Lord of the whole Earth, thus identifying the two witnesses.

Colossians aptly means "correction," for in that letter, which he said should also be read by the Laodiceans, Paul gave the Tribulation saints a mysterious message. He said, **"Touching whom ye received commandments: if he come unto you, receive him."**[5] Who gave them the commandments? Enoch? No. Israel received the Ten Commandments by the hand of Moses.

Every clue points to Moses and Elijah. During the Tribulation, God will be dealing a lot with Israel, and both these men are Israelites. Moses probably stands for those saints who will die and be resurrected, Elijah for those who will be translated without first experiencing death.

Just as Moses got Pharaoh's attention when the Israelites were to leave Egypt, these two will command attention for they will have great power. People will be utterly astonished by the things they will do.

Both witnesses will have power to shut heaven, so it will not rain during the days of their prophecy.[6] This parallels a feat accomplished by God through Elijah in the days of the wicked Ahab, eighth king of Israel (type of the False Prophet, another "eighth" king[7] of Israel) and his idolatrous wife, Jezebel (meaning "unmarried," type of the harlot church).

In those days, Elijah prayed that it might not rain, and it didn't rain three and one half years.[8] This will be duplicated during the first half of the Tribulation. The drought will bring on the severe famine described under the third seal.[9]

As in the days of Joseph, seven years of famine will follow seven years of plenty.[10] Joseph took up a fifth of the grain in the good years. The Rapture takes place in the fifth good year (1994, 1995, 1996, 1997, **1998**, 1999, 2000). Be part of this group. You won't want to see how bad the next seven can get (2001, 2002, 2003, 2004, 2005, 2006, **2007**).

In the parable of the wheat and the tares, Christians are called wheat.[11] In Scripture, five means division. Since one fifth of the grain was taken up, maybe the Rapture involves one fifth of the saints. In the wilderness, when the first trumpet sounded, only the princes assembled at the door of the tabernacle of the congregation.[12]

Christ is returning as the latter rain. Therefore, the lack of rain at this time will demonstrate that neither the Beast nor the False Prophet could be the Messiah.

Some will think the False Prophet is the Messiah. Jesus, whose name means Jehovah is salvation, said, "I am come in my Father's name, and ye receive me not: if another shall come in his own name, him ye will receive."[13]

The two witnesses have power to turn the waters to blood, and to smite the Earth with plagues.[14] These things remind us of the plagues God punished Egypt with when Pharaoh would not let the Israelites go. This points directly to Moses, who brought the Israelites out of Egypt.

Egypt's plagues were shadows of what will come when Satan will not open "the house of his prisoners."[15] Isaiah 10:26 in the NASB is very clear. In his indignation, the Lord will lift up his staff "the way *He did* in Egypt."

Day 1,260

The two witnesses are to "prophesy a thousand two hundred and threescore days."[16] I believe the last day of their ministry will be Sunday, Cheshvan 23, 5765 (our November 7, 2004). This will be the exact middle of the Seventieth Week of Daniel, the end of the first beast's reign as head of the world government, a day of bedlam in God's land.

This is the day of the war in heaven, when the "dragon, that old serpent, which is the Devil, and Satan,"[17] plus his demons[18] will be thrown down to the Earth.[19] Satan possessed, the False Prophet will then speak "as a dragon."[20]

The False Prophet will cause the sacrifice and oblation to cease[21] by desecrating the temple. Putting a statue of the Roman Beast in the temple will be instigated by Satan and encouraged by the False Prophet.

As in Nebuchadnezzar's Babylon, a law will be enacted, commanding all to worship the idol or be killed."The throne of iniquity . . . frameth mischief by a law."[22]

The "prophet is a fool [possessed by the fool, Satan], the spiritual man [Pontifex Maximus of the Mystery Religion of Babylon] is mad . . . the prophet is a snare of a fowler in all his ways, and hatred in the house of his God."[23]

Revelation 13:11-18 shows how people are trapped into idolatry so they can conduct business. The False Prophet

> spake as a dragon . . . and causeth the earth
> . . . to worship the first beast . . . And he
> doeth great wonders [*semeia*, signs], so that he
> maketh fire come down from heaven . . . And
> deceiveth them . . . by the means of those
> miracles which he had power to do . . . saying
> to them . . . that they should make an image

> . . . And he had power to give life unto the
> image . . . that the image of the beast should
> both speak, and cause that as many as would
> not worship the image of the beast should be
> killed. And he causeth all . . . to receive a mark
> in their right hand, or in their foreheads: And
> that no man might **buy or sell**, save he that
> had the mark, or the name of the beast, or the
> number of his name . . . it is the number of a
> man . . . Six hundred three score and six.

Buying and selling suggest that the False Prophet is a "treasurer."[24] Since the weight of gold that came to Solomon in one year was 666 talents,[25] 666 points to gold controlled by the king of Israel, the False Prophet (in the world bank?).

Babylon's math system was based on the six, and our universal computer code for international communication is six. Therefore, 666 suggests international, international, international, and Babylon, Babylon, Babylon. When the False Prophet is its leader, the international headquarters of world government will be located at Babylon III on the Euphrates.

Because letters have numerical values in Greek, Teitan (a name for Satan) and Earnist each add up to 666. However, whatever else this number may mean, it means man, man, man, for six is the number of man, created on the sixth day. This will be the ultimate of man playing God, but he will still be a man, though indwelt by Satan. He will say, **"I am a God**, I sit in the seat of God, in the midst of the seas [nations]; **yet thou art a man, and not God**, though thou set thine heart as the heart of God" (Ezekiel 28:2).

> If any man worship the beast and his image,
> and receive his mark in his forehead, or in his
> hand, The same shall drink of the wine of the
> wrath of God, which is poured out without
> mixture into the cup of his indignation: and he
> shall be tormented with fire and brimstone in
> the presence of the holy angels, and in the
> presence of the Lamb: And the smoke of their
> torment ascendeth up for ever and ever, and
> they have no rest day nor night, who worship
> the beast and his image, and whosoever
> receiveth the mark of his name.[26]

Satan will not waste any time trying to get man to worship him. Just as soon as he is cast out of heaven in the middle of the Tribulation, he will cause the False Prophet to commit an act of supreme arrogance, sitting in the temple showing that he is God.

God's two witnesses will refuse to worship him or the image or receive the mark of the beast. Therefore, Satan, the beast that ascends out of the bottomless pit,[27] will kill them. Their bodies will lie on the street in Jerusalem, unburied.[28] On the very brink of tragedy, unbelievers will actually rejoice, but they will be in for a startling surprise.

This is the day that believers in Judea better obey the Bible's instructions to run for their lives, exhibiting their faith by taking nothing with them.[29] When that idol goes in the temple and the False Prophet sits there showing that he is God, they must flee, making no provision for the flesh.

They must believe, trust in and rely on God totally. He has promised that they would be nourished for three and one half years "from the face of the serpent,"[30] and they simply have to believe it and act on it immediately.

The False Prophet will send troops to kill them.[31] They have to be quick and flee like Hell is after them. He is.

Matthew 24:15-22 says,

> When ye . . . see the abomination of desolation . . . stand in the holy place . . . let them which be in Judea flee into the mountains: Let him which is on the housetop not come down to take any thing out of his house: Neither let him which is in the field return back to take his clothes. And woe unto them that are with child, and to them that give suck in those days! But pray ye that your flight be not in the winter, neither on the sabbath day [this would make it harder to make the decision to run]: For then shall be great tribulation, such as was not since the beginning of the world to this time, no, nor ever shall be. And except those days should be shortened, there should no flesh be saved.

Jesus said to pray that your flight be not in the winter or on the Sabbath. That prayer will be answered. This will be Sunday, November 7, neither winter nor the Jewish Saturday sabbath.

The "great tribulation" refers to the last three and one half years. The first half of the seven year Tribulation will not be shortened because Moses and Elijah must prophesy "a thousand two hundred and threescore days."[32]

Since the Bible says to flee to the mountains, many are expected to flee to Petra (Sela, the rock or cliff) in the middle of the Tribulation. Petra is a city carved out of rose sandstone with an entrance through a very narrow easy to defend siq or ravine between two mountains. In some places the two mile slit is so narrow that men have to walk through in single file.

Petra was discovered by Johann Ludwig Burkhardt, a Swiss archaeologist, in 1812. It was an amazing find, beautiful, desolate, well hidden, the ancient capital of Edom in the Wady Musi, southeast of the Dead Sea. Esau's descendants probably built it for Esau went to Mount Seir in Edom. There are amazing temples and tombs carved into the face of the rose-red sandstone. Outside, they are beautifully ornate. Inside each architectural facade are caves in which one could be secure. Besides buildings, there is a road, a High Place and an outdoor Amphitheater. Some people have placed New Testaments inside the buildings for anyone fleeing there to read. I hope the entire Bible and this book will be there also.

Israel will be "given two wings of a great eagle [airplanes?], that she might fly into the wilderness, into **her place**, where she is nourished for a time, and times, and half a time, from the face of the serpent."[33]

The Lord has promised to take care of these Jews for these last three and one half years. He could do it by airdrops from other nations, for after he returns he will judge the nations on the basis of how they treated his brethren.

After Three and One Half Days

There will still be rejoicing over the deaths of the two witnesses when the spirit of life from God will enter into their bodies. After three and one half days, they will stand up on their own feet and ascend to heaven as a great voice from heaven commands, "Come up hither."[34]

Spellbound with shock, their enemies will watch as they ascend. It will be conclusive proof of the mighty power of God and the absolute truthfulness of his word.

Infuriated, the False Prophet will declare all-out war against Christians in a paroxysm of rage. Quickly, his troops will mobilize and follow after those who have fled. They can have a three and a half day head start if they run as soon as the idol is put in the temple.

All hope for a quick victory will vanish as the Earth opens her mouth and swallows up the troops when a major earthquake rocks Jerusalem the same hour the two witnesses ascend. Seven thousand men will die,[35] but the False Prophet will escape. Later, when Christ returns, the False Prophet will be cast into the Lake of Fire.[36]

Not only do the fleeing ones escape getting killed by the Satan indwelt False Prophet, they also escape getting killed by the earthquake.

When the Bible says to run, RUN!

> The highways lie waste, the wayfaring man ceases; the enemy [the False Prophet] has broken the covenant, [that guaranteed peace] he has despised the cities and the witnesses [Moses and Elijah], he regards no man.[37]

> And the dragon was wroth with the woman, and went to make war with the remnant of her seed, which keep the commandments of God, and have the testimony of Jesus Christ.[38]

In those trying days of the Great Tribulation, the last three and one half years, it will be difficult to be a Christian unless one is willing to be martyred. Satan will try to force submission to him and his cohorts. No one will even be allowed to buy or sell unless he gives allegiance to the beast. How would you make a living? or eat?

Today it is easy to be a believer. Many do not realize the urgency of the situation and keep putting off accepting Christ, maybe for lack of interest, certainly not for lack of evidence. They have everything to gain and nothing to lose.

The day will come in which those who seek to save their lives by accepting the False Prophet because of his promise of peace will lose eternal life while those who receive Christ and are killed for their faith will gain eternal life. By peace he shall destroy many.

There is more to man than just his physical body. If a believer, you are "spirit and soul and body."[39] Christ has kindled your dormant spirit to life. From the moment of salvation, although your body can die, your spirit and soul can never die. "If Christ be in you; the body is dead because of sin; but the Spirit is life because of righteousness."[40]

If you haven't done it before, ask him in. Exercise your will. Make a definite decision to accept Christ as your personal Saviour and tell him of your decision. You will receive his Spirit, and his Spirit is life, eternal life. Today is the day. It is too important to put off. Tell someone of your decision. Record the day of your salvation. It is your spiritual birthday, the day you are born into God's family.

The latter half of the Tribulation will be a dreadful time in which to live. Hearts will fail because of fear. Those who accept Christ will be the targets of Satan's vicious rage, and those who side with Satan will have the bowls of God's wrath poured out on them.

The Fifth Seal

Terrible things happen on Earth as each seal breaks. We have seen what will happen as the first four are broken. Both the Beast and the False Prophet will kill Christians, so when the fifth seal separates, the souls of martyrs are seen under the altar. They ask how long till they will be avenged. The answer is that it will not be long, just a little season, probably summer. It is also clear that the war on saints is not yet over. Others will have to die for their faith.[41]

End of the Age

The Day of Preparation for the Feast of Trumpets is the end of this age, the end of the shortened Great Tribulation and the day God's fury will come up in his face when Israel is attacked. September 12, 2007 (Elul 29, 5767) is 2,299 days after the two beasts sign the Covenant of peacc.

A stone from the heavens is already tumbling toward the Earth, unstoppable, lethal, deadly. The "besom of destruction," the terror of terrors, is on its way.

God will roll back the heavens like a scroll; men will see Christ sitting on his throne. This is "the sign of the Son of man in heaven." During the Millennium, The Lord "will destroy in this mountain the face of the covering cast over all people, and the vail that is spread over all nations"[42] so we cannot see God. This is a preview. The Lord described the end of this last day of the age:

> the end is come . . . upon thee, and I will
> send mine anger upon thee, and will judge thee
> [the Judgment Seat of Christ] . . . The morning
> [of the Day of the Lord] is come unto thee . . .
> the time is come, the day of trouble is near [it is
> the following day, which is just about to begin]
> . . . Now will I shortly pour out my fury.[43]

The Feast of Trumpets

As the text continues, the next day has come, the first day of the millennial Day of the Lord. "Behold . . . it is come: the morning is gone forth; the rod [False Prophet] hath blossomed, pride [Satan] hath budded. Violence is risen up into a rod of wickedness: none of them shall remain."[44]

Blow the trumpets! Sound the alarm! Sound the alarm! Israel is being attacked! A gigantic multi-nation army is attacking from the north. Though they will be fully determined to annihilate this tiny nation, once for all, their intent will be frustrated. The Lord will intervene and defend his land. He will stop the demon possessed hordes with a stone just as David slew Goliath, the part-angel, part-man giant, with a stone.

As the sixth seal tears free, great celestial disturbances begin. Dark smoke causes the sun to not give her light, the moon to look as red as blood, and the stars to cease shining.

Immediately, men will plead for the rocks to, "Fall on us, and hide us from the face of him that sitteth on the throne, and from the wrath of the Lamb: For **the great day of his wrath is come**; and who shall be able to stand?"[45]

Against the great northern confederacy, the Lord said,

> I will plead against him with pestilence and
> with blood; and I will rain upon him, and upon
> his bands, and upon the many people that are
> with him, an **overflowing rain** [*shataph
> geshem*, gushing shower, i.e., a tsunami], and
> great hailstones, fire, and brimstone. Thus will
> I magnify myself, and sanctify myself; And I
> will be known in the eyes of many nations

[when they look up and see Christ], and they shall know that I [Christ] am the LORD.[46]

The words translated "overflowing rain" do not mean literal rain. Israel is the "land that is not cleansed, nor rained upon in the **day of indignation.**"[47] This is a gushing tidal wave scouring the land when "a great mountain burning with fire was cast into the sea." [48] The Lord said, "When the **overflowing scourge** shall pass through, then ye shall be trodden down by it."[49] In Luke 21:25, Jesus mentioned "the sea and the waves roaring." This is when they really ROAR.

Habakkuk 3:10-12 shows why there is a tidal wave: "**the overflowing of the water passed by . . . The sun and moon stood still** in their habitation [because the Earth will rock] . . . Thou didst march through the land in **indignation**, thou didst thresh the heathen in anger." He will thresh with both fire and water, for "the heavens and the earth . . . are . . . reserved unto **fire** against the **day of judgment** and perdition of ungodly men" (II Peter 3:7).

This is **Jesus' long day** that will be extended until the battle is won. The stone that will be tossed into Earth will cause this planet to rock, prolonging the day.

A transient tidal wave will also hit Babylon, Iraq: "**The sea is come up upon Babylon**: she is covered with the multitude of the waves thereof. Her cities are a desolation, **a dry land** [normally desert], and a wilderness, a land wherein no man dwelleth."[50] The Lake of Fire will form at Babylon, so she will be dry, then wet, then covered with molten rock.

The oceans will overflow when earth's poles reverse. "**BEHOLD, the LORD maketh the earth empty, and . . . waste, and turneth it upside down**, and scattereth abroad the inhabitants . . . The earth also is defiled . . . **because they have transgressed the laws, changed the ordinance, broken the everlasting covenant. Therefore hath the curse devoured the earth . . . and few men left.**"[51]

Jeremiah 12:12 declares that "the sword of the LORD shall devour from the one end of the land even to the other end of the land: no flesh shall have peace." All hands will be feeble, all knees weak as water, in the day of God's wrath.[52]

"Behold, I shew you a mystery; We shall not all sleep, but we shall all be changed, In a moment, in the twinkling of an eye, at the last trump."
1 Corinthians 15:51,52

Chapter 14

The Last Trump

As this age wanes into nothingness, the silvery blast of trumpets will be heard in God's land. At 6:00 P.M., the Feast of Trumpets will usher in **"that day,"** the first day of the sabbatical Millennium, on the anniversary of the Feast of Trumpets in B.C. 4043 when God rested on the sabbath day.

September 13, B.C. 4043 was that dark day of Genesis 1:3, when God began restoring Earth. September 13, 2007, will be a dark day preceding another restoration of Earth. Thirteen, Satan's number, marks this day, lucky for believers, extremely unlucky for those who rebel against God.

It is Tishri 1, 5768 (Thursday, September 13, 2007), 2,300 days after the Beast and False Prophet sign the covenant of peace on the Feast of Weeks in 5761 (May 28, 2001).

Translation of the Tribulation Saints

In heaven, as the Feast of Trumpets begins, the angels will gather together both the Old Testament Saints and the Church Saints who were taken to heaven when the Rapture took place, probably in 1998.

Christ will "send his angels," said Matthew, "with a great sound of a trumpet, and they shall gather together his elect from the four winds, from one end of heaven to the other."[1]

When Mark described this scene, there was one important difference:

after that tribulation, the sun shall be darkened
. . . And the stars of heaven shall fall . . . then
shall they see the Son of man coming in the
clouds . . . Then shall he send his angels, and
shall gather together his elect from the four

171

winds, from the uttermost part of the **earth** to the uttermost part of heaven."[2]

Here, there is another group mentioned, those gathered from the Earth. It is the Translation of the Tribulation saints (Rapture II). They have to endure 2,299 days of tribulation, but will wing it to heaven just before God's wrath is poured out on Earth.

The Eagles Join the Body of Christ

The Tribulation saints are the high flying eagles. They "that wait upon the LORD shall renew their strength; they shall mount up with wings as eagles; they shall run, and not be weary; and they shall walk, and not faint."[3] They will join the body of Christ, "For wheresoever the carcass [body, i.e., the Body of Christ] is [it's in the heavenly New Jerusalem], there will the eagles be gathered together."[4]

As the Days of Lot

The Rapture of the church saints is as the days of Noah, which means rest. They go up into their heavenly "Ark" to rest prior to a delay of seven revolutions of time before the armies come in like a flood at Armageddon.

This is different. The Translation of the Tribulation Saints, Rapture II, is as the days of Lot. Fire and brimstone will fall from heaven **that same day**.

> [As] it was in the days of Lot . . . the same day that Lot went out of Sodom it rained **fire and brimstone** from heaven, and destroyed them all. **Even thus shall it be in the day when the Son of man is revealed.** . . . [when the Sign of the Son of Man is seen] in that night [the Feast of Trumpets begins at 6:00 P.M.] there shall be two men in one bed; the one shall be taken, and the other shall be left . . . Two men shall be in the field; the one shall be taken . . . Where, Lord? Wheresoever the body [the Body of Christ, the church] is, thither will the eagles be gathered together.[5]

The Last Call

No fire and brimstone falls at Rapture I, the first trump. The Translation of the Tribulation Saints is the last trump, when fire and brimstone do rain down. By then **all** the saved will be in heaven and will be changed at that time.

> Behold, I shew you a mystery [*musterion*, secret]; We shall not all sleep, but we shall **all be changed**, In a moment, in the twinkling of an eye, **at the last trump**: for the trumpet shall sound, and the dead shall be raised incorruptible, and we shall be changed. For this corruptible must put on incorruption, and this mortal must put on immortality.[6]

Israel was told to make two silver trumpets to call the assembly, and there are two translations, or Raptures. Israel was told if "they blow but with one trumpet, then the princes, which are heads of the thousands of Israel, shall gather themselves unto thee." This represents Rapture I, when the elders of Revelation 4 are seated on their thrones. Half of the elders are the heads of the twelve tribes of Israel. The other half are the twelve Jewish apostles.

"And when they shall blow with them [plural], **all** the assembly shall assemble themselves to thee at the door of the tabernacle of the congregation."[7] This represents the gathering in heaven of the whole Body of Christ, including the Church, the Bride of Christ who is snatched away at Rapture I, and those caught up at the Translation of the Tribulation Saints.

The door of the tabernacle of the congregation represents the door we go through when translated. At the Rapture, "a door was opened in heaven." Thus, "door" is a symbol of a Rapture, and Christ is that door by which we enter heaven. He said, "I am the door: by me if any man enter in, he shall be saved, and shall go in and out, and find pasture" (John 10:9).

There are different ranks in the first resurrection. There may be different ranks in Christ's army as well. It seems that he will call the officers (the groups the "elders" of Revelation 4:4 represent) first, then the rest of the troops.

> [In] Christ shall all be made alive. But **every man in his own order** [*tagmati*, rank]:

Christ the firstfruits; afterward they that are
Christ's at his coming.[8]

"There is one body, and one Spirit, even as ye are
called in one hope of your calling; One Lord, one faith, one
baptism, One God and Father of all."[9] Notice that it does not
say one calling. That is because there is more than one calling.
There is one hope but two callings. The Lord was very careful
how he phrased every single word and line of Scripture. This
is proof of its divine origin.

The Last Day

In the end, no believer will be cast out. **All** will be
raised up. The last group will be translated at the last day, as
this age is ending and the Millennium beginning. Jesus said,

> **All** that the Father giveth me shall come to me;
> and him that cometh to me I will in no wise cast
> out. . . . this is the Father's will which hath
> sent me, that of all which he hath given me I
> should lose nothing, but should **raise it up
> again** [a repetition, i.e., Rapture II] **at the
> last day** [as the last great day, the millennial
> Day of the Lord, begins].[10]

The first day is when Rapture I takes place. The last day,
when "all" will finally be changed as the last trump sounds, is
when Rapture II finishes the job. Many are confused about
when the Rapture will occur because there are two Raptures.
I believe the Rapture of the church is in the third
Jewish month, in Sivan, and the Translation of the Tribulation
saints, also called Rapture II, is in the seventh Jewish month,
Tishri. In the days of Hezekiah, the Israelites brought in the
firstfruits and tithes and laid them in piles in the third and
seventh months to picture this for us. We are "a kind of
firstfruits of his creatures."[11] Also, the Raptures are when we
are brought into the Father's house by the might of Jehovah.

> In the third month [Sivan/May] they began to
> lay the foundation of the heaps, and finished
> them in the seventh month [Tishri/September].[12]

174

This is exciting. **It locks in the month of both translations**, one in the third and the other in the seventh Jewish month. In the former, the Lord begins to call his own to heaven. In the latter, the assembly of the saved is completed.

The Feast of Trumpets

Joel gave us a lot of information about events on the first day of the millennial Day of the Lord:

> Blow the **trumpet** in Zion [it is the Feast of Trumpets], sanctify a fast, **call a solemn assembly**: Gather the people, sanctify the congregation, assemble the elders, gather the children . . . **let the bridegroom go forth of his chamber** [*cheder*, private apartment] **and the bride out of her closet** [*chuppah*, chamber]. Let the priests . . . weep . . . and . . . say, Spare thy people, O LORD, and give not thine heritage to reproach, that the heathen should rule over them . . . Then will the LORD be jealous for his land, and pity his people. **Yea, the LORD will answer . . . I will remove far off from you the northern army.**[13]

The only feast day on which the Israelites were to fast was the Day of Atonement on Tishri 10. Therefore, this blowing of the trumpet indicates the preceding Feast of Trumpets on Tishri 1.

An assembly is called on the Feast of Trumpets in the heavenly Zion. The Old Testament Saints are gathered and the elders, the twelve princes of Israel and the twelve apostles,[14] come in and are seated on their thrones. The scene is set. Next, the children are gathered. Who are they?

They are the Tribulation Saints, the last generation, as in I John 2:18. Just as the Israelite children went into the earthly promised land after 40 years, during which most of the older generation died in the wilderness, the Tribulation Saints will go to their heavenly promised land 40 years after the Sign of the End of the Age appeared. This gathering of the children is Rapture II after most of the older generation have died off.

Then, "let the bridegroom [Christ] go forth of his chamber, and the bride [Bride of Christ, the Church Saints] out of her closet." The Bride is already in heaven, but she is still a bride, not a wife. The Marriage of the Lamb has not yet taken place.

Who are the priests that plead, "Spare thy people, O LORD"? This is similar to the time that Queen Esther pleaded for her people with king Ahasuerus. Since Esther is a type of the Bride of Christ and he "hath made us kings and priests unto God and his Father,"[15] the Bride may plead for Israel.

The northern army that attacks Israel as the age ends will be stopped in answer to all pleas. In Revelation 8:3, the prayers of all saints are mentioned just before the seven trumpet judgments hit, tying these passages together.

The Tribulation saints will be pulled out at the last moment before God's wrath causes devastating destruction.

> But take ye heed: [Jesus said] behold, **I have foretold you all things**. But in those days, after that tribulation [at the end of the age], the sun shall be darkened, and the moon shall not give her light, And the stars of heaven shall fall [*esontai ekpiptontes*, shall be falling out], and the powers that are in heaven shall be shaken. And then [*tote*, at the same time] shall they **see the Son of man** coming in the clouds with great power and glory [the Sign of the Son of Man, Matthew 24:30]. And then [*tote*, at the same time] shall he send his angels, and shall **gather together his elect** from the four winds, **from the uttermost part of the earth** to the uttermost part of heaven."[16]

Meteors, fragments either shed from the asteroid as it passes Roche Limit, 10,500 to 11,000 miles out, or from a nuclear hit, will be descending. Revelation 6:13 says it is "as a fig tree casteth her untimely figs, when she is shaken of a mighty wind." Men will call out to the rocks, "Fall on us, and hide us from the face of him that sitteth on the throne, and from the wrath of the Lamb: For the great day of his wrath is come."[17]

At that time, man will look up and see Christ on his throne as the heavens roll away like a scroll, and the angels will gather together his elect from both Earth and heaven. There is deliverance on the Day of Wrath. "Riches profit not in the day of wrath: but righteousness delivereth from death. . . . The righteous is **delivered out of trouble**."[18]

> [In] the **time of trouble,** he shall hide me in his pavilion: In the secret of his tabernacle shall he hide me; **he shall set me up upon a rock.**[19]

His pavilion is a rock, another sphere in the heavens. He "built his sanctuary like high palaces, [the sun and moon[20]] like the earth."[21] The sun, moon and Earth are all spheres. There are many spheres in the heavens, so it makes sense that our heaven is also a sphere.

Why did the Lord say to Israel, "Therefore will I return and take away my corn [*dagan*, grain] in the time thereof, and my wine in the season thereof"?[22] When is the grain's time and the wine's season when the Lord will come to take them?

(1) The grain's time. I believe the grain represents the church saints that are translated on Pentecost, the wheat harvest. It is a definite "time," the Jewish Sivan 6.

(2) The wine's season. The wine, I believe, represents the Tribulation saints that will be translated on the Feast of Trumpets, for the vintage in Israel begins in Elul and continues into Tishri. The vintage is not an exact "time," only a "season" during which the translation will take place. Scripture is painstakingly exact. Every word in the original is God breathed. Like this, time clues are subtle but clear.

Micah spoke as if a Tribulation saint himself. He said,

> Woe is me! for I am as when they have gathered the summer fruits, as the grape-gleanings of the vintage: there is no cluster to eat: my soul desired the firstripe fruit [the time of the firstripe grapes is in Sivan, when the Rapture occurs]. **The good man is perished out of the earth**: and there is none upright among men . . . I will wait for the God of my salvation . . . when I sit in darkness [indicating the end of the age], the LORD shall be a light unto me. **I will bear the indignation of the LORD, because I**

177

**have sinned against him, until he plead
my cause, and execute judgment for me:**
he will bring me forth to the light, and I shall
behold his righteousness.[23]

After the Marriage of the Lamb

The Lord will rescue the Tribulation saints as the rocks
are falling. It looks like it will be after the Marriage of the
Lamb.

Let your loins be girded about, and your lights
burning [i.e., have enough oil as the wise
virgins did]; And **ye yourselves like unto
men that wait for their lord, when he
will return from the wedding** [then the
Bride has already been taken to his father's
house at the Rapture, and the wedding has
taken place]; that when he cometh and knocketh
as to the Laodiceans[24]], they may open unto
him immediately. Blessed are those servants,
whom the lord when he cometh shall find
watching: verily I say unto you, that he shall
gird himself, and make them to sit down to
meat [the Marriage Supper of the Lamb], and
will come forth and serve them.[25]

John saw the Tribulation martyrs in heaven. Rapture II is the
last rank in the first resurrection.

I saw the souls of them that were beheaded for
the witness of Jesus, and for the word of God,
and which had not worshipped the beast,
neither his image, neither had received his mark
upon their foreheads, or in their hands; and
they lived and reigned with Christ a thousand
years. . . . This is the first resurrection.[26]

Translated at the Time of Jacob's Trouble

"There shall be a **time of trouble**," Daniel was told,
"such as never was since there was a nation even to that same

178

time: and **at that time thy people shall be delivered**, every one that shall be found written in the book. And many of them that sleep in the dust of the earth shall awake."[27]

This agrees with Isaiah 26:19-21 (margin):

> Thy dead shall live: my dead bodies shall rise. Awake and sing, ye that dwell in dust . . . earth shall cast out the dead. Come, my people, enter thou into thy chambers, and shut thy doors [a Rapture symbol] about thee: **hide thyself as it were for a little moment, until the indignation be overpast**. For behold, the LORD cometh out of his place to punish the inhabitants of the earth for their iniquity.

Other scriptures make it clear that the translation takes place just prior to the outpouring of God's wrath on "that day" (Tishri 1, 5768, our Thursday, September 13, 2007). "Alas! for **that day** is great, so that none is like it: it is even **the time of Jacob's trouble**, but he shall be **saved out of it**."[28] A day of many names, no other day has so many momentous things happening at the same time. The Translation of the Tribulation Saints, or Rapture II, precedes the Judgment Seat of Christ.

> Our God shall come [the Second Advent is still future] . . . fire shall devour before him [before the Second Advent] . . . He shall call to the heavens [the Church Saints are in heaven] from above, and to the earth [the Translation of the Tribulation Saints at the last trump], **that he may judge** [at the judgment Seat of Christ] his people. **Gather my saints together unto me**; those that have made a covenant with me by sacrifice. And the heavens shall declare his righteousness.[29]

Though a day of darkness on Earth, **all** the saved are gathered in heaven on the Feast of Trumpets, the day our Lord Jesus Christ is crowned King of kings and Lord of lords.

> The sun shall be turned into darkness, and the moon into blood, before the great and terrible

179

day of the LORD come. And it shall come to pass, that **whosoever shall call on the name of the LORD shall be delivered** [*malat*, **escape**]: for in mount Zion and in Jerusalem shall be deliverance.[30]

CLAP your hands . . . shout unto God with the voice of triumph. . . . **God is gone up** [Rapture II] **with a shout** [Come up hither], **the LORD with the sound of a trumpet** [the "last trump" calls the Tribulation saints on the Feast of Trumpets] . . . **God** [Christ] **is the King of all the earth** . . . God sitteth upon the throne of his holiness. The princes of the people are gathered together, even the people of the God of Abraham [Christ was the first and last, both Jehovah and Jesus]: for the shields [i.e., princes] of the earth belong unto God.[31]

The final rank in the first resurrection must be raised on the first day of the Millennium, not seven months later at the Second Advent. According to Revelation 20:6, they "shall reign with him a thousand years." This is the full Millennium, not a thousand years less seven months. The date is locked in place by the 2,300 day shortened Tribulation, which ends on the Jewish Tishri 1, 5768, our September 13, 2007, and the 1,000 year Day of the Lord that begins that very same day.

Chapter 15

Coronation Day

Will Christ marry his Bride before or after he is crowned King of kings? Many place the Marriage of the Lamb immediately after the Rapture, but be careful. The "secrets of wisdom . . . are double to that which is,"[1] and Queen Esther, type of the Church, was not married to the king immediately after the virgins were gathered the first time, but **just before they were gathered the second time**.

Esther means star, hidden, or secret. There is a secret hidden in the book of Esther. Ahasuerus means lion-king, which makes him a type of Christ, who is called "the Lion of the tribe of Juda" in Revelation 5:5.

"Esther was brought also unto the king's house." But, there were "the days of their purifications," before she was brought to the king and **made Queen "in the seventh year."** There was a great **feast** where "he made a release to the provinces, and **gave gifts.**" After that "the virgins were gathered together the second time."[2]

Does this sound familiar? It would fit this scenario. The Church will be brought to the King's house at the Rapture to visit her habitation.[3] During that time, she will make "herself ready,"[4] then go in to the King in the seventh year of the Tribulation and be crowned on the Feast of Trumpets as the Millennium begins. That is when the virgins are gathered the second time (Rapture II), when the rewards are handed out at the Judgment Seat of Christ, and when it is evident that the following year will be the Jubilee, the year of release.

King Solomon, a son of David, was **"crowned . . . on the day of his wedding."**[5] Will this also be true of Jesus Christ, the Son of David? Will he be crowned King then married during the proceedings of the same assembly?

He has earned the right to be King of kings, but is not yet crowned. Maybe the bride will have to wait awhile also. If she is to be brought before the King as Esther was, it cannot be before his coronation. Ahasuerus was already king.

We are "joint-heirs with Christ; if so be that we suffer with him, that we may be also **glorified together**."[6] Since he will be glorified when he is crowned King, we should, as joint-heirs, be glorified with him the day he is crowned.

Preparation Day

On the last day of this age, the day of preparation for the Feast of Trumpets, Christ, Old Testament Saints and Church saints are in heaven. Tribulation saints are on Earth.

A great army from the north and many people with her are moving in on Israel fully determined at last to annihilate her. Scripture says, "Multitudes, multitudes in the valley of decision: for the day of the LORD is near."[7] It is very near. The Day of the Lord starts the very next day, the Day of God's Wrath. This attack is a fatal error. God is furious! This is his land and his people. It "shall come to pass at the same time when Gog ["chief prince of Meshech and Tubal,"[8] "out of the north"[9]] shall come against the land of Israel, saith the Lord GOD, that **my fury shall come up in my face**."[10]

The "battle is the LORD'S."[11] The asteroid Satan lives on (the chariot that he rides), called The Curse[12] and Sword (*chereb*, destroying weapon) of the Lord, is already on a collision course with Earth (the chariot that we ride) on the Day of Preparation because of a whirlwind[13] sent by the Lord.

The Septuagint, the Greek Old Testament, says,

> **[The] reins [controls] of their chariots shall be destroyed in the day of his preparation . . . and the chariots [Earth and the asteroid] shall clash together** . . . their appearance is as lamps of fire.[14]
> Behold, there is an earthquake from the Lord, and **anger proceeds to a convulsion**, it shall come violently [margin: *Gr*. **whirled round as from a sling**] upon the ungodly . . . at the end of the days they shall understand it [we are now living in the time of the end].[15]

Just as David felled the Philistine Goliath with a sling stone, the Son of David will stop the attack of a giant northern army with a rock "**whirled round as from a sling**."

As Christ opens the sixth seal on the Book of Purchase of Earth, the asteroid enters our atmosphere blazing and smoking, causing unnatural darkness. The sixth and seventh seals are broken one right after the other.

When the seventh is broken, the two "chariots shall clash together." A piece will hit the sea. "From the time that it ["the overflowing scourge," or tsunami] goeth forth it shall take you," said the Lord: "for morning by morning shall it pass over, by day and by night: and it shall be a vexation [*zevaah*, fearful agitation] only to understand the report."[16]

Parts of the asteroid will crash into rivers, coals of fire will rain on Jerusalem,[17] but "The sun shall be turned into darkness . . . **before** . . . the terrible day of the LORD come."[18] Thus, darkness will begin on the Day of Preparation, and the LORD'S, "glory shall be seen"[19] as the Day of Preparation ends. The veil that is spread over all nations[20] will be rolled aside like a scroll. When they look up and see the Sign of the Son of man, they will say to the rocks, "Fall on us, and hide us from the face of him that sitteth on the throne, and from the wrath of the Lamb: **For the great day of his wrath is come**."[21] This is the Feast of Trumpets.

The Lord says he will stop the northern army with "an overflowing rain" (shower, i.e., the tidal wave), "and great hailstones, fire, and brimstone. Thus will I magnify myself, and sanctify myself; and I will be known in the eyes of many nations, and **they shall know** that I am the LORD."[22]

He will be seen on day 2,300.[23] Immediately, the sun shall be darkened, and "the powers of the heavens shall be shaken: And then shall appear **the sign of the Son of man** in heaven: and then shall all the tribes of the earth mourn, and they shall **see the Son of man** coming in the clouds of heaven with power and great glory."[24]

No Other Day Like This—Ever

This Feast of Trumpets is Tishri 1, 5768 (our Thursday, September 13, 2007). The Jewish day starts at 6:00 P.M. Wednesday and ends at 6:00 P.M. Thursday.

It is Jesus' birthday, the Jewish New Year, the time of Jacob's trouble, the Day of Darkness, the Day of Indignation and the Day of God's Wrath. It has many more names. This is **"that day,"** so often spoken of in the prophetic Old Testament, the first day of the millennial Day of the Lord.

183

"Alas! for **that day** is great, so that **none is like it:** it is even **the time of Jacob's trouble,** but he shall be saved out of it."[25] The Translation of the Tribulation Saints is that day, and the remnant of Israel will be "born" that day.

It is a day of contrasts, of jubilation in heaven and of terror on Earth. **In heaven, the saints will be rewarded for their faith. On Earth, the transgressors will be rewarded for their unbelief,** breaking the everlasting covenant and laws, worshiping an image and Satan himself.

As Israel blows the trumpet of alarm, the Lord will come to her aid. It "is a **day of wrath,** a day of trouble and distress, a day of wasteness and desolation . . . a day of clouds and thick darkness, A **day of the trumpet** and alarm."[26] Amos said, "Woe unto you that desire the day of the LORD: to what end is it for you? the **day of the LORD** is darkness and not light . . . I despise your feast days [the Feast of Trumpets and the following Day of Atonement]."[27]

Restored by Nebuchadnezzar, Babylon II was destroyed during a feast[28] the day of the handwriting on the wall. Babylon III, fully restored by a future king of Babylon, will be destroyed during another feast, the Feast of Trumpets.

The King of Kings Crowned on his Birthday

The Feast of Trumpets is Jesus' birthday. He came as the "former rain" on Tishri 1. He will also be crowned on Tishri 1, day 2,300 of the Tribulation. With **"the sound of a trumpet . . . God is the King** of all the earth . . . God sitteth upon the throne of his holiness"[29] on the anniversary of the Feast of Trumpets when God began to rule over Adam.

As the Feast of Trumpets begins, an assembly will be called in heaven. Daniel saw the scene.

> I beheld till the thrones were placed and the Ancient of days did sit, whose garment was white as snow, and the hair of his head like the pure wool: his throne was like the fiery flame, and his wheels as burning fire.[30]
> One like the Son of man . . . came to the Ancient of days . . . and there was given him dominion, and **glory,** and a kingdom, that all people, nations . . . should serve him: his dominion is an everlasting dominion.[31]

A glorious "golden crown"[32] is placed on his head. Not only is he King, but also Judge. **The "Father judgeth no man, but hath committed all judgment unto the Son."[33]**

Marriage of the Lamb

The Marriage of the Lamb takes place after the Coronation. Revelation 19 shows the order of events:

the Lord God omnipotent **reigneth.** Let us . . . rejoice, and give honour to him: for the **marriage of the Lamb** is come, and his wife hath made herself ready [as Esther did] . . . Blessed are they which are **called** [Rapture II] unto the marriage supper of the Lamb.

First, Christ is crowned. Next comes the Marriage of the Lamb, then Rapture II. The Tribulation Saints are not called to the wedding, but to the Marriage Supper. The award ceremony follows the assembling of all the saints. Wedding gifts picture our rewards. The Marriage Supper is the reception, when the Laodiceans will sup with him (Revelation 3:20).

Jesus' parable places the wedding before Rapture II.

Let your loins be girded about, and your lights burning: And ye yourselves like unto men that wait for their lord, when he will return **from the wedding**; that when he cometh and knocketh they [Laodiceans[34]] may open unto him immediately. Blessed are those servants, whom the lord when he cometh shall find watching . . . he shall . . . make them to sit down to meat, and will . . . serve them.[35]

Seventh Seal

Christ will break the last seal on the Book of the Purchase of Earth after he is given dominion. For half an hour there will be an awesome silence on Earth before the Seven Trumpets begin to sound.[36] This silence precedes judgment.

O God . . . who may stand in thy sight when once thou art angry? Thou didst cause judgment to be heard from heaven; the **earth feared, and was still**, When God arose to judgment, to save all the meek of the earth.[37]

Keep **silence** before me [the Lord], O islands, and let the people renew their strength: let them come near; then let them speak: let us come near together to judgment.[38]

Seven Trumpet Judgments

After the silence, seven angels are given seven trumpets in the seventh month of the seventh year of the Tribulation, because seven means completion. Another angel will offer incense with the prayers of all saints on the golden altar before the throne. These prayers are about to be answered.

Then he will fill the golden censer with fire from the altar and cast it down to the Earth. This globe shaped censer symbolizes the curse, the asteroid that will impact Earth.

The "curse causeless shall not come. . . . As he that bindeth a stone in a sling, so is he that giveth honour to a fool."[39] If you give honor to the fool, Satan, it is just as if you bind the stone in the sling yourself.

The image of the beast will still be in the temple. Asaph said, "When . . . I went into the sanctuary of God; **then understood I their end.** . . . How are they brought into desolation, as in a moment! they are utterly consumed with terrors . . . O Lord . . . thou shalt despise their image."[40]

As the seven trumpets sound, catastrophes drum the Earth with rapid strokes. Fiery stones rain down. A third of the trees and all green grass are burned up.[41]

At the second trumpet blast, the larger pieces strike. When Moses angrily broke the two tablets of stone to pieces on the ground because Aaron made an image, it demonstrated this vengeance against image worship. One chunk as large as a mountain tumbles at high speed into the NE Mediterranean. A third of all sea creatures die, and a third of all the ships at sea are destroyed.[42] Jesus was scourged. Now Israel will be swept by a tsunami, "the overflowing scourge" (Isaiah 28:18).

When the third trumpet is heard, another piece, a burning "*aster*," asteroid, called Wormwood, impacts on land. A third of all rivers are poisoned by the resulting blast.[43] "I will feed them with wormwood, and make them drink the water of gall: for from the prophets of Jerusalem is profaneness gone forth . . . they speak a vision of their own heart, and not out of the mouth of the LORD. They say still unto them that despise me, The LORD hath said, Ye shall have peace; and they say . . . No evil shall come upon you."[44]

This is like Satan telling Eve, "Ye shall not surely die." The false prophet of Jerusalem, indwelt by Satan, lies like Satan. By peace he will destroy many, and evil will come.

At the fourth trumpet, smoke obscures the sun, moon and stars. One third of the day and night are darkened.[45]

When the fifth angel trumpets, a "star" (*astera*, luminous meteor, asteroid) actually opens hell, the bottomless pit,[46] the pit for the wicked spoken of in Psalm 94:12,13.

> Blessed is the man whom thou chastenest, O
> LORD, and teachest him out of thy law; That
> thou mayest give him [who went in Rapture I]
> rest **from** the days of adversity [Tribulation],
> **until the pit be digged for the wicked**.

The Essene community at Qumran not only understood where hell is, but that the pit would be dug in the day of God's anger. They wrote,

> When the hour of judgment strikes, when the
> lot of God's anger is cast upon the abandoned
> . . . the foundations of the mountains become a
> raging blaze, when granite rocks are turned to
> streams of pitch, when the **flame devours
> down to the Great Abyss**, when all the
> floods of Belial burst forth unto **hell itself**.[47]

As Earth shudders and rocks, smoke shoots out of the pit as if from a blast furnace, spray painting the sky darker and darker around the Earth in a zigzag band. Disturbed winds pull the smoke band wider as the Earth whirls drunkenly.

Demons come up out of the pit to torment men. For five long months afterward, men will seek death and will not be able to find it,[48] but this day the dead lay round the Earth.

187

And the songs of the temple [a feast day] shall be howlings in that day . . . there shall be many dead bodies in every place.[49]

BEHOLD, the LORD maketh the earth empty, and maketh it waste [as in Genesis 1:2], **and turneth it upside down,** and scattereth abroad the inhabitants. . . . **because they have transgressed the laws** [including the Ten Commandments on two tablets of stone], changed the ordinance, broken the everlasting covenant. **Therefore hath the curse devoured the earth,** and they that dwell therein are desolate: therefore the inhabitants of the earth are burned, and few men left.[50]

I will shake the heavens, and the earth shall remove out of her place [because of the asteroid impact], in the wrath of the LORD of hosts [same as "the wrath of the Lamb" in Revelation 6:16; therefore, the LORD of hosts is Christ].[51]

Do you want to be on Earth when it is turned upside down? It will be an awful catastrophe with a world wide earthquake so great it probably cannot be measured. With the oceans out of control and scouring the land, every living soul at sea will die. Those left on land will be few.

Scripture records this. It is not a big secret. Yet Satan will say, "No evil shall come upon you." Will you believe him? Eve did. He is cunningly subtle.

Conditions will be so bad, that if the Lord did not hold the Earth together, it might fly apart as Satan's planet, Rahab, did when the asteroid belt was formed. The Lord promised,

When the earth totters [is knocked out of equilibrium], and all the inhabitants of it, it is I who will poise and keep steady its pillars.[52]

Fear, and the pit, and the snare, are upon thee, O inhabitant of the earth [the pit for the wicked is on earth]. . . . he who fleeth from the noise of the fear shall fall into the pit; and he that cometh up out of the midst of the pit shall be taken in the snare: for the windows from on high are open and the foundations of the earth do shake. . . . the earth is moved exceedingly. The earth shall reel to and fro like a drunkard . . . in that day . . . the LORD shall punish the host of the high ones that are on high [Satan and his fallen angels], and the kings of the earth upon the earth.[53]

Those working on our space program also speak of windows in space through which they can sling a space vehicle into orbit. This works in reverse. When the window is open, a space rock can crash into the Earth.

An army of 200,000,000 slays a third part of mankind as the sixth trumpet sounds. The world is in frantic turmoil. Men's hearts are literally failing them for fear.[54] At this point, there is to be "delay no longer . . . the seventh angel, when he shall begin to sound, the mystery of God should be finished, as he hath declared to his servants the prophets."[55]

And the seventh angel sounded . . . voices in heaven, saying, The kingdoms of this world are become the kingdoms of our Lord, and of his Christ [God was in Christ] . . . And the four and twenty elders . . . worshipped God, Saying, We give thee thanks, O Lord God Almighty, which art, and wast, and **art to come [the Second Advent is still future]**; because thou hast taken to thee thy great power, and **hast reigned**. And the nations were angry, and **thy wrath is come**, and the time of the dead, that they should be judged, and that thou shouldest **give reward unto thy servants the prophets, and to the saints**, and them that fear thy name, small and great; and shouldest **destroy** them which destroy the earth.[56]

Examine those verses carefully. You will see that Christ becomes King in heaven before he returns to Earth. This is not the Second Advent. Here several things happen on the same day. After Christ is crowned, the saints are judged in heaven at the same time the unbelievers on Earth are judged.

Last Trump: Rapture II

When the rewards are being handed out, the Tribulation Saints must be present. Therefore, before the award ceremony, he shall "send his angels, and shall gather together his elect from the four winds, from the uttermost part of the **earth** to the uttermost part of heaven."[57] This is the Translation of the Tribulation Saints, or Rapture II, when the virgins are gathered the second time.

They will be gathered just before the Judgment Seat of Christ convenes: "fire shall devour before him . . . He shall call to the heavens from above, and to the earth, that he may judge his people. Gather my saints together unto me; those that have made a covenant with me by sacrifice."[58]

I looked," John said, "and behold...upon the cloud one sat like unto the Son of man, having on his head a golden crown, and in his hand a sharp sickle." Continuing, he said, "And another angel came out of the temple, crying with a loud voice to him that sat on the cloud, Thrust in thy sickle, and reap: for the time is come for thee to reap; for the harvest of the earth is ripe . . . and the earth was reaped."[59] This sickle reaps the Tribulation saints. The "trumpet shall sound, and the dead shall be raised incorruptible."[60]

These "have washed their robes [they had robes spotted by the flesh], and made them white in the blood of the Lamb [confessed their sins to God[61]]. Therefore are they before the throne of God, and serve him day and night in his temple: and **he that sitteth on the throne** shall dwell among them. They shall hunger no more, neither thirst . . . neither shall the sun light on them, nor any heat. For the Lamb which is in the midst of the throne shall feed them [at the Marriage Supper of the Lamb], and shall lead them unto living fountains of waters: and God shall wipe away all tears."[62]

One reason for their tears is the dreadful things happening on Earth. The sixth seal has already been opened. They say, "**I will bear the indignation** of the LORD, because I have sinned against him, **until he plead my cause, and execute judgment for me**: he will bring me forth to the light, and I shall behold his righteousness."[63]

Can Saints Suffer Tribulation Ten Years?

The Tribulation Saints will be persecuted by the false prophet, who will, I believe, come to power in the Jewish 5758, four years by Jewish inclusive reckoning before the Tribulation proper begins. Therefore, these saints could have tribulation ten years, 5758 (our 1998), 5759, 5760, 5761, 5762, 5763, 5764, 5765, 5766 and 5767 (our 2007).

Because they will suffer persecution, Revelation 2:10 probably addresses them:

> Fear none of those things which thou shalt suffer: behold, the devil shall cast some of you into prison, that ye may be tried; and ye shall have tribulation ten days: be thou faithful unto death [some will be martyrs], and I will give thee a crown of life.

Since days represented years in Genesis 6:3 and Ezekiel 4:6, and there are scriptures where the word for day is translated year because it is obvious that it means year, I believe this is a hint that the Tribulation Saints will have ten years of persecution by the False Prophet. He is Antichrist.

Two groups are translated through the great door in heaven. The ten years between the translations may be indicated by Ezekiel's description of the Millennial Temple. He said that the "breadth of the door was ten cubits."[64] The number ten is the complete earthly number, so it makes sense for the two groups to be gathered during a ten year period.

It looks like the Lord will prove the Laodiceans during ten revolutions of time, just as in Daniel's day. Daniel, whose name means "God is judge," said, "Prove thy servants, I beseech thee, ten days."[65] It could be a hard test. Many will have to choose between worshiping the image and death.

There were ten days between Christ's ascension and the descent of the Holy Spirit on Pentecost. Were the apostles proved ten days at that time? Christ had commanded that they should not depart from Jerusalem, to wait for the promised baptism with the Holy Spirit, and according to Acts, they were **all** together in one place when Pentecost was fully come. If they were being proved ten days, they all passed the test.

The deliverance of the Tribulation Saints was dramatized when Shadrach, Meshach, and Abed-nego refused to worship the image Nebuchadnezzar, who had a beast's mind for seven years, set up. They were cast into the fiery furnace and miraculously saved from it by the Son of God.

The Tribulation Saints will also refuse to worship an image of one who is a beast for seven years. They will be saved from **another fiery furnace** by the Son of God just before God's wrath is poured out on the Earth. After the asteroid impact, smoke will rise out of the pit, "**as the smoke of a great furnace**" (Revelation 9:2).

Judgment Seat of Christ

The "**Lord Jesus Christ . . . shall judge** the quick [living] and the dead at his appearing and his kingdom."[66] His appearing and his kingdom are at the same time. The Sign of the Son of Man appears as he is seated on his throne. Then "the vail that is spread over all nations"[67] will be rolled away like a scroll. Men will look up and see him. As the age ends, his kingdom begins. He will be crowned, and he will judge that same day.

The award ceremony is not first on the agenda of the day. Judging saints for rewards must follow the Translation of the Tribulation saints. All believers must be present by that time.

> Our God shall come . . . a fire shall devour before him [before the Second Advent] . . . He shall call to the heavens **from above** [he's in heaven calling the Bride to the assembly], **and to the earth** [the Translation of the Tribulation Saints], that he may judge his people [at the Judgment Seat of Christ]. **Gather my saints** [all of them] **together unto me; those that have made a covenant with me by sacrifice.**[68]

We must make a covenant with Christ by sacrifice, His sacrifice. There is no other way. We appropriate it by accepting him as our own personal Saviour, being born again. We are first born into our earthly family and then born again into God's family.

After all the saints are gathered, the rewards are handed out. "We must **all** appear before the **judgment seat**

of Christ, that every one may receive the things done in his body, according to that he hath done, whether it be good or bad."[69]

For the saints, this judgment will only be for rewards or loss of rewards. Christ paid the penalty for our sins. They are already taken care of. He took them out of the way as an issue in salvation. Now, the question is. "What think ye of Christ? whose son is he?"[70]

> **Whosoever believeth that Jesus is the Christ is born of God** . . . whatsoever is born of God overcometh the world: and this is the victory that overcometh the world, even our faith. **Who is he that overcometh the world, but he that believeth that Jesus is the Son of God.**[71]

> **[Other] foundation can no man lay than that is laid, which is Jesus Christ:** Now if any man build upon this foundation gold, silver, precious stones, wood, hay, stubble; Every man's work shall be made manifest: for the day shall declare it, because it shall be revealed by fire; and the fire shall try every man's work . . . **If any man's work abide which he hath built thereupon, he shall receive a reward.** If any man's work shall be burned, he shall suffer loss: but he himself shall be saved; yet so as by fire.[72]

Sword of the Lord

As soon as Christ has gathered what is his to himself in heaven, and their judgment is taking place, the remainder on Earth can be pressed down as if in a winepress. Therefore,

> [Another] angel came out of the temple which is in heaven, he also having a sharp sickle. And another angel came out from the altar, which had power over fire: and cried...Thrust in thy sharp sickle, and gather the clusters of the vine of the earth: for her grapes are fully ripe. [It is the Feast of Trumpets, the vintage, a

time when grapes are fully ripe in Israel] And the angel **thrust in his sickle** [the Sword of the Lord, i.e., the asteroid] **into the earth,** and gathered the vine of the earth, and cast it into the great winepress of the wrath of God.[73]

This is the first day of the millennial Day of the Lord. "Howl ye, for **the day of the LORD is at hand; it shall come as a destruction from the Almighty.** . . . he shall destroy the sinners thereof out of it."[74]

The "sword of the LORD shall devour from the one end of the land even to the other end of the land: no flesh shall have peace."[75] This sword was called a flaming sword in Genesis 3:24:

So he drove out the man; and he placed at the east of the garden of Eden Cherubims, and a **flaming sword** which turned every way [it revolves as it orbits], to keep the way of the tree of life.

The Lord said, "For **my sword shall be bathed in heaven** [it is the curse, the asteroid that will slash the Earth] behold, it shall come down upon Idumea [red, Satan's color], and upon the people of **my curse,** to judgment."[76]

According to the Jewish prayer for the New Year, called the *Un'saneh Tokef*, the Feast of Trumpets is the day of God's judgment of the world. They are correct; it will be the day of the Judgment Seat of Christ.

O ye priests . . . if ye will not hear, and . . . give glory unto my name, saith the LORD of hosts, I will even send **a curse** upon you . . . your **solemn feasts;** and **one** [the Feast of Trumpets] **shall take you away with it.**[77]

What will ye do in the solemn day, and **in the day of the feast of the LORD?** For, lo, they are gone because of destruction . . . The days of visitation are come, the days of recompence are come; Israel shall know it: **the prophet** [the False Prophet] **is a fool, the spiritual man** [the Beast] **is mad.**"[78]

"For it is the day [Tishri 1, the Jewish New Year Day] of the LORD'S vengeance, and the year [5768] of recompences for the **controversy of Zion.**"[79] The "LORD hath prepared a sacrifice, he hath bid his guests." You either accept his sacrifice on the cross, or you could be part of this terrible sacrifice. "I will punish the princes," he continued, "and the king's children and all such as are clothed with strange apparel" (no white robes) . . . "**there shall be . . . a great crashing** . . . all the merchant people are cut down . . . They shall plant vineyards, but not drink the wine thereof."[80]

The vintage, when they gather the grapes, is in Tishri, when destruction hits. There will be no time to age wine.

The Northern Army Stopped in Israel

The Lord told Israel, "If ye go to war in your land against the enemy that oppresseth you, then ye shall blow an alarm with the trumpets; and ye shall be remembered before the LORD your God, and ye shall be saved from your enemies."[81] Exactly 2,300 days after the Tribulation begins, this will come true. When Israel blows the alarm on the Feast of Trumpets, she will be saved from the northern army.

Suddenly, "There shall be a great shaking in the land of Israel . . . and **all the men that are upon the face of the earth, shall shake.**"[82] Earth will vibrate like a wet dog slinging off water, liquefying soils and leveling mountains.

A fiery holocaust of almost unbelievable proportions will sear the Earth. God's patience is at an end. His long pent-up anger will explode in furious rebukes upon the disobedient of this planet. Heat will be so intense in one section of our globe that elements in both the atmosphere and Earth will be dissolved at a stroke.

The "day of the Lord will come as a thief in the night; in the which the heavens shall pass away with a great noise, and **the elements shall melt with fervent heat.**"[83]

Babylon is in the Strike Zone

The costliest city the world has probably ever known, will be destroyed so completely that no man will ever again be able to set foot there.[84] Saddam Hussein has started reconstruction and has even rebuilt Nebuchadnezzar's palace. But,

Babylon will be destroyed with a sling stone: "a mighty angel took up a stone like a great millstone, and cast it into the sea, saying, Thus with violence shall that great city Babylon be thrown down, and shall be found no more at all."[85]

The fact that she will no longer exist rules out the theory that Revelation 18's Babylon might refer to Jerusalem. The law will go out from Jerusalem during the Millennium.

Jeremiah also told of Babylon's destruction. "Because of the wrath of the LORD it shall not be inhabited, but it shall be wholly desolate: every one that goeth by Babylon shall be astonished, and hiss at all her plagues."[86]

Jeremiah 46:20 says that "destruction cometh; it cometh out of the north (*tsaphon*, north quarter)." Scorched Earth will scar this planet from the land of Magog, to Ethiopia. "I will send a fire on Magog [region of Gog, in the north], and among them that dwell carelessly in the isles: and they shall know that I am the LORD."[87] Those who have not wanted to know the Lord will find out that he is **the Almighty**.

Idumea, near the Dead Sea, will be hit by a piece. Believers hiding in the Judean mountains and in Petra will be translated before it hits ("saved: yet so as by fire," I Corinthians 3:15). Egypt will not escape. The Lord said, "I will make the land of Egypt utterly waste and desolate, from the tower of Syene even unto the border of Ethiopia. No foot of man shall pass through it, nor foot of beast . . . **neither shall it be inhabited forty years.** And I will make the land of Egypt desolate in the midst of the countries that are desolate . . . I will scatter the Egyptians among the nations."[88]

> **[The] slain of the LORD shall be at that day from one end of the earth even unto the other end of the earth.**[89]

Israel: A Nation Born in a Day

In Israel, two thirds of the people will die. The Lord said, "I will bring the third part through the fire, I will say, It is my people: and they shall say, the LORD is my God."[90] In fact, the remnant of the nation will be born in a day.[91] The Lord said that "the house of Israel shall know that I am the LORD their God from that day and forward."[92]

Let The Sword be Doubled the Third Time

A sword, a sword is sharpened . . . to make a sore slaughter . . . **let the sword be doubled the third time** . . . thou, profane wicked prince of Israel, whose day is come, when iniquity shall have an end . . . take off the crown . . . exalt him that is low [Christ], and abase him that is high [Satan]. **I will overturn, overturn, overturn, it: and it shall be no more, until he come** [on Tishri 1, Christ's return is still future] **whose right it is**; and I will give it him.[93]

The sword is doubled the third time. It causes terrible devastation upon the Earth three times, the last being twice as bad as before. According to Ezekiel 21:16,18 in the Confraternity version, **"God gave this sword "over to the burnisher"** [Lucifer, light bearer, i.e., Satan] and **"the sword has been tested."** An asteroid has hit Earth before.

This "third time" refers us to the three times recorded in Scripture since Adam was created. The first was when Sodom (which means burning) and Gomorrah were destroyed by an asteroid that tore in from the north, split the Earth, and formed the Great Rift Valley. It punched the bedrock down 2,615 feet below sea level. Both east and west of the Dead Sea are sheer cliffs rising 2,500 to 4,000 feet above the lake. Miles of lava near the lower end of the sea bear mute testimony to the severity of that crash. The Earth still shivers there at times.

The second was at Gibeon. On **Joshua's Long Day, "the LORD cast down great stones from heaven** upon them . . . more . . . died with hailstones than they whom the children of Israel slew with the sword" (Joshua 10:11).

Third, Babylon will be wiped out when the asteroid Satan lives on impacts Earth on **Jesus' Long Day**. There will be so few men left "that a child may write them," Isaiah 10:19). It will break though the crust, open hell (the bottomless pit, the molten core of the Earth which has no bottom), and cause the 181.8 mile Lake of Fire.[94] It's smoke will ascend forever.

In Iraq, there are places that burn continually because gas erupts to the surface naturally. The oil fields in that area seem like a powder keg waiting to be ignited by the asteroid.

Come out of her [Babylon], my [the Lord Jesus Christ's] people, that ye be not partakers of her sins, and that ye receive not of her plagues . . . Reward her even as she rewarded you, and double unto her double according to her works . . . her plagues come in one day, death . . . and she shall be utterly burned with fire: for strong is the Lord God who judgeth her.[95]

Seven Vials of the Wrath of God

Before the Wrath of God is poured out, all saints must be in heaven. The scene is in heaven in Revelation 15. The Tribulation Saints, who have gotten the victory over the beast, his image, his mark and the number of his name, are seen there. Then it says, "after that . . . the temple of the tabernacle of the testimony in heaven was opened: And the seven angels came out of the temple, having the seven plagues."

The Tribulation saints will say,

I will bear the indignation of the LORD, because I have sinned against him, until he plead my cause, and execute judgment for me: he will bring me forth to the light, and I shall behold his righteousness. Then she that is mine enemy [Babylon] shall see it [the Curse, Satan's asteroid], and shame shall cover her which said unto me, Where is the LORD thy God? mine eyes shall behold her: now shall she be trodden down as the mire of the streets.[96]

After Rapture II has taken place, the wicked vine is reaped. The "earth bringeth forth fruit of herself; first the blade [the Old Testament saints], then the ear [the Church saints], after that the full corn in the ear [the Tribulation saints]. But when the fruit is brought forth, **immediately** he putteth in the sickle [the Sword of the Lord], because the harvest is come."[97]

After the Translation of the Tribulation Saints, the wrath of God is poured out immediately. The seven golden vials full of the wrath of God are given to the seven angels.

These seven vials describe the final results of the catastrophe. Each is poured out on something different. The first angel pours out his vial on the Earth. Grievous sores break out on those who had the mark of the beast or worshiped the image. This is as the plague on Egypt when Pharaoh would not allow the Israelites to leave.

The second is poured out on the sea. This is truly awful, for "every living soul died in the sea." When the Earth flips upside down, the seas will overflow the land in huge tidal waves. Devastating destruction will result.

The third is poured on the rivers and fountains of waters. They become "blood." John "heard the angel of the waters say, Thou art righteous, O Lord, which art [present tense; while the judgments are being carried out], and wast [at the First Advent], and **shalt be** [future tense; the Second Advent is still future], because thou **hast judged** [past tense; **the Judgment Seat of Christ precedes the Second Advent by seven Jewish months**] thus. For they have shed the blood of saints and prophets, and thou hast given them blood to drink: for they are worthy" (Revelation 16:5,6).

The fourth pours out his vial on the sun. Men are scorched with the great heat, yet some are so stubborn that they will still not repent and give glory to God. The fifth is poured on the throne of the beast. There is thick darkness at Babylon like there was in Egypt in the days of Moses.

The sixth is dashed out over the Euphrates near Babylon. The river dries up so an army of 200,000,000 men coming from the east can cross over easily.

[The] seventh angel poured out his vial into the air; and there came a great voice out of the temple of heaven, from the throne [of Christ], saying, It is done. And there were voices, and thunders, and lightnings; and there was a great earthquake, such as was not since men were upon the earth, so mighty . . . and the cities of the nations fell: and great Babylon came in remembrance before God, to give unto her the cup of the wine of the fierceness of his wrath. And every island fled away, and the mountains were not found. And there fell upon men a great hail out of heaven, every stone about the weight of a talent [around 100 pounds each].[98]

Order of Events in Heaven
on the Feast of Trumpets

Trumpet blown, solemn assembly called, people gathered
    Old Testament Saints and Church Saints present
Congregation sanctified, thrones placed, elders assembled
Ancient of Days seated on His throne like the fiery flame
    Thousand thousands minister to Him
        10,000 x 10,000 rise up before Him
Christ crowned KING OF KINGS AND LORD OF LORDS
    Seated on the throne of his holiness
    Golden Crown put on his head
    Awarded
        Glory
        A kingdom
        Dominion over Earth
    Appointment as judge confirmed
Marriage of the Lamb
    Bride made Joint-heirs with Christ
    Last trumpet call for saints, Tribulation Saints raised
Judgment Seat of Christ
    Judge installed
    All give him glory and worship him
    Judgment set, books opened
    Christ opens 7th Seal on Book of the Purchase of Earth
        One half hour of silence
        Keep silence before me O islands
        Earth fears and is still
    Let the people renew their strength, come near, speak
        Bride probably pleads for Christ to save Israel
    Incense offered with prayers of all saints
    Sentence passed, rewards handed out
        Saints receive rewards for their faith and service
        Unbelievers on Earth receive their just rewards
            Golden Censer filled with fire cast to Earth
                Symbol of crash of Satan's asteroid
            Seven Trumpet Judgments destroy on Earth
            Seven vials of Wrath of God poured out
Marriage Supper of the Lamb
    Bride: Church Saints
    Friends of the Bride: Tribulation Saints
    Friends of the Bridegroom: Old Testament Saints

Chapter 16

Key of the Abyss

Babylon! Babylon! "I will sweep it with the besom of
destruction, saith the LORD of hosts [Christ]."[1]

In the Path of Oblique Impact

Israel will stand, but the broom of destruction will
sweep literal Babylon, on the Euphrates River in Iraq, right
off the map.

Before the Iran-Iraq war, Babylon was being
reconstructed by the Iraqi government as a tourist attraction.
Saddam Hussein continued the project during that war.

As early as 1971, the Los Angeles Times printed an
article, "Tower of Babel May Rise Again" that contained
information about the reconstruction of the city. It mentioned
that sheep and goats, watched over by a black-robed
shepherd, grazed peacefully in the remains of Nebuchadnezzar's palace. That showed that Babylon had not yet
suffered it's final destruction. After it is destroyed this time,
Scripture is very clear that "It shall never be inhabited, neither
shall . . . the shepherds make their fold there."[2]

At that time, there was a small museum containing
relics of the city at its prime. A forty foot tall temple to the
pagan goddess "Nin-Makh," the "Lady of the Heavens," had
been reconstructed in 1960. (The pagan worship of this Lady
of the Heavens carried over in the Roman church as the
worship of Mary, which is never even hinted at in Scripture.)

Invitations were sent out to the world's leading
archaeologists, museums and cultural organizations to take
part in a conference to discuss ideas for the future of the city.

The Tower of Babel and sections of the city walls and
gateways were to be reconstructed in the first phase. The
hanging gardens were to be considered later.[3]

This year, Charles H. Dyer published his book, *The
Rise of Babylon*. He shows photographs of what has already

been constructed, including the "Ninmach" Temple, a half-size reconstruction of the Ishtar Gate, the rebuilt walls of Procession Street, Nebuchadnezzar's palace, a Greek theater that seats 4,000 people, and the Saddam Hussein Guest House in the center of Babylon.

Man does not learn easily. God stopped the building of the Tower of Babel before and has warned of Babylon's destruction in Scripture. Yet they plan to build it. They are brave and have no fear of God. Their problem is: God will have the last say in the matter.

Scripture says, "Behold the land of the Chaldeans; this people was not, till the Assyrian founded it for them that dwell in the wilderness: they set up the towers thereof, they raised up the palaces thereof; and he brought it to ruin."[4] After the coming destruction, it will be impossible to rebuild.[5]

The Bible's warning, **"the nations'** [plural] **labor is only fuel for the flames"**[6] suggests that Babylon will be rebuilt by many nations under the banner of world government. What is there now is just the beginning.

Change of the City

Babylon means confusion. The harlot of Revelation 17 is the Mystery Religion of Babylon. To confuse humanity, Satan instigated this counterfeit religion, started at the Tower of Babel by Cush's son Nimrod, his wife Semiramis, and their son Tammuz. Semiramis, called the queen of heaven, and Tammuz were worshiped as madonna and child. The light brown haired Tammuz was worshiped as the sun god. Semiramis said he was killed by a wild boar and came back to life. Idols, the **high priest's title of Pontifex Maximus**, Vestal virgins, celebrations of Easter with eggs and of Tammuz' birthday on December 25 with evergreen trees were all part of this religion put forth by Satan to steer humans away from faith in Christ. When the languages were confused, the same gods and goddess were worshiped under different names in various countries.

Easily recognized elements of this false religion became mixed with true Christianity when Constantine made Christianity the state religion of the Roman Empire. He saw a blazing cross in the sky with the words "In this sign conquer," so he marched his army right through the river to baptize them, thus bringing Satan worshiping pagans and their customs into the Roman church. When Christians are snatched out of this mixture at Rapture I, what will be left? "MYSTERY, BABYLON THE GREAT, THE MOTHER OF HARLOTS AND ABOMINATIONS OF THE EARTH," and the Lord warns, "Come out of her my people, that ye be not partakers of her sins, and that ye receive not of her plagues."[7]

The headquarters of this harlot church will be moved to Babylon before it is destroyed. Zechariah 5:5-11 describes the move: "Lift up now thine eyes, and see what is this that goeth forth. . . . This is an ephah that goeth forth." An ephah was a large measure for wheat. Since believers are called wheat,[8] this ephah represents a large group of Christians.

"This is their resemblance through **all the earth [it is a united world church]**. . . . and this is a woman [Mystery Babylon, harlot church of Revelation 17] that sitteth in the midst of the ephah [the world church]. And he said, This is wickedness. And he cast it into the midst of the ephah; and he cast the weight of lead [literally, stone lead] upon the mouth thereof [prefiguring day 2,300 of the Tribulation, when the asteroid will be cast at her]. Then lifted I up mine eyes . . . there came out two women [two religious groups] . . . they had wings . . . and they lifted up the ephah between the earth and the heaven. Then said I . . . Whither do these bear the ephah? And he said unto me, To build it an house in the land of Shinar [Babylon, Iraq, where the original Tower of Babel was begun[9]], and it shall be established, and set there upon her own base [*mekunah*, foundation]."

The best clue that the city will be moved is the meaning of Shinar, "**change of the city**." It ties in with Revelation 17:18. The "woman [the harlot church, "MYSTERY, BABY-LON THE GREAT," after the Rapture] which thou sawest is that great city [based in Rome], which reigneth over the kings of the earth" [because her "ancient and honorable . . . head" (Isaiah 9:15) will be chosen leader of world government as the Tribulation begins].

In Revelation 17, the harlot church, "arrayed in purple and scarlet colour, and decked with gold and precious stones and pearls" is Rome.[10] In Revelation 18, the same Mystery Babylon, "clothed in fine linen, and purple, and scarlet, and decked with gold, and precious stones, and pearls,"[11] is in the literal city of Babylon on the Euphrates River[12] in Iraq. She has already moved to her new headquarters in the land of Eden,[13] the country of which the Garden of Eden was a part.

Babylon! Babylon! Destroyed by a Stone

A mighty angel took up a stone like a great millstone [representing an asteroid twice as long as it is wide, Zechariah 5:1-3], and cast it into the sea, saying, Thus with violence shall that great city Babylon be thrown down, and shall be found no more at all."[14]

A heavenly body will collide with the Earth. It will annihilate Babylon and form the volcanic Lake of Fire. This was symbolized in John's vision by an angel who took a globe-shaped vessel for burning incense, filled it with fire and hurled it mightily at the Earth, causing the greatest earthquake since men were put on Earth.[15]

The fiercely blazing stone will impact Earth, explode like an enormous bomb and blast[16] through the earth's crust. Babel means the gate of God, a good clue for Babylon will actually be God's gate to hell.[17]

John's description was accurate. He said, "There fell a great star [astera means a star, a luminous meteor, or an asteroid] from heaven, burning as it were a lamp."[18] It is an asteroid, super heated by friction as it slams into our atmosphere.

Isaiah said, "The LORD shall rise up as in mount Perazim, he shall be wroth **as in the valley of Gibeon**, that he may do **his work, his strange work**; and bring to pass **his act, his strange act**."[19]

Near Gibeon, the Lord "**cast down great stones from heaven** upon them."[20] The Lord's strange act is again casting down great stones from heaven.

Satan's Palace on the Rock

In Revelation 9, John saw a fallen star. Just as Christ is called the morning star, this star symbolizes a being called a day star. **A key was given to him**. John described his vision, saying, "I saw **a star** fall [peptokota, **fallen**, this day star had already fallen] **from heaven** unto the earth." If you compare this with Satan's famous "I will" speech in Isaiah 14:12-15, you will understand that this fallen star is Lucifer (which means "**day star**"), who became Satan ("accuser").

How art thou **fallen from heaven**, O Lucifer ["day star"], son of the morning! how art thou cut down to the ground, which didst weaken the nations [all of them]! For thou hast said in thine heart, I will ascend into heaven; I will exalt my throne above the stars of God: I will sit also upon the mount of the congregation, in the sides of the north: I will ascend above the heights of the clouds, I will be like the most High. Yet thou shalt be brought down to hell, to the sides of the pit.

Satan is the fallen star, "and to him was given the key of the bottomless pit." This key that will open the bottomless pit, abyss, or hell, is **the asteroid that was given to Satan for his home in the heavenlies.**

His asteroid will collide with the Earth and break through the crust opening hell. "And he opened the bottomless pit; and there arose a smoke out of the pit, as the smoke of a great furnace; and the sun [moon and stars] and the air were darkened by reason of the smoke of the pit."[21]

The bottomless pit is the molten center of the Earth where there is no solid bottom and from which every direction is up. As the molten magma rockets through split rock to the surface, a lake of fire covering 1,600 furlongs [181.8 miles) will form.[22] (1 furlong = 400 x 1 1/2' cubit = 600') (600' x 1600 ÷ 5,280' = 181.8 miles)

This will be the greatest natural catastrophe since Adam was created,[23] and probably since the dinosaurs were wiped out. **The Lord will cause this collision on the Day of Wrath.**[24] The prophet Nahum asked, "Who can abide in the fierceness of his anger? his fury is poured out like fire, and **the rocks are thrown down by him.**"[25]

Satan lives on the very rock that will be hurled at the Earth from its whirling sling out there in space. Take a look at Isaiah 22:15-19.

Thus saith the Lord GOD of hosts, Go, get thee unto this treasurer [representing the False Prophet, who won't let you buy or sell without the Mark of the Beast], even unto Shebna ["young," i.e., he won't live out half his days[26]] which is over the house [church,[27] i.e., world church], and say, What hast thou here? and whom hast thou here, that thou hast hewed thee out a sepulchre here, as **he** [the day star] **that heweth him out a sepulchre on high, and that graveth an habitation for himself in a rock**. Behold, the LORD will carry thee away with a mighty captivity, and will surely cover thee. **He** [the Lord] **will surely violently turn and toss thee like a ball** [*duwr*, gyrating circle] **into a large country** [not Israel, she's a small country]: there shalt thou die, and there the chariots of thy glory shall be the shame of thy lord's house. And **I will drive thee from thy station** [*matstsab*, fixed spot].

The question, What hast thou here? is not difficult. The house of the False Prophet will be here on Earth when this collision occurs. At that time, it will become a fiery tomb for anyone who happens to be there during the most deadly holocaust to take place on Earth since Adam was created.

He that "graveth an habitation for himself in a rock" is Satan, the day star and dragon.[28] Though he thought he was building a palace for himself in the heavenlies, it will turn out to be a sepulchre on high. Right now it is whirling along its orbit among the other stones out there in space.

The Lord will throw Satan's home at·the Earth by means of a "destroying wind,"[29] an "east wind,"[30] a whirlwind (Jeremiah 30:23; Isaiah 4:24). "**His device** [also called the Sword of the Lord, the flaming sword, and the curse, all symbols of the asteroid] **is against Babylon, to destroy it**; because it is the vengeance of the LORD"[31] against the "MOTHER OF HARLOTS."[32]

I like the imagery of Isaiah 22:17,18 in the RSV: "the LORD will hurl you away violently . . . He will . . . **whirl you round and round, and throw you like a ball** into a wide land; there you shall die, and there shall be your splendid chariots, **you shame of your master's house**."

"Behold, I am against thee, O destroying mountain, saith the LORD, which destroyest all the earth: and I will stretch out mine hand upon thee, and **roll thee down from the rocks** [planets], and will make thee a burnt mountain."[33]

Harlot Church Sunk in the Lake of Fire

God will destroy two evil houses with one stone. Satan's home in the heavenlies will be demolished as it smashes like a giant sledge hammer into the house of the False Prophet on Earth. Both will become sepulchers, totally submerged in the Lake of Fire as Sodom and Gomorrah have been submerged in the Dead Sea. Only after the headquarters of the harlot world church is moved to Babylon in the land of Shinar, where the original Tower of Babel was built, will it be pulverized by the rock that "cometh out of the north."[34]

The Curse

Satan's rock is The Curse that will enter the house of the False Prophet and consume it. Zechariah said, I "lifted up mine eyes, and looked, and behold a flying roll [*megillah*, rolling thing] . . . the length thereof is twenty cubits, and the breadth thereof ten cubits. . . . **This is the curse that goeth forth over the face of the whole earth.**"[35] This flying rolling thing is twice as long as it is wide. **Its orbit crosses that of this planet as it passes by about twice every year.**

The Flaming Sword

When God expelled Adam from the garden, near the Tigris and Euphrates rivers in Iraq, he meant for man to stay out of that area. "So he drove out the man; and he placed at the east of the garden of Eden Cherubims, and **a flaming sword which turned every way**, to keep the way of the tree of life."[36]

This flaming sword is in the sky. Like the sun, it is seen first in the east as the Earth turns. The word *chereb*, translated "sword" means destroying weapon. **Satan's home in the heavenlies is the Lord's destroying weapon that turns every way. It revolves as it orbits in all four directions.**

This sword will strike Eden before Christ returns. It is the Sword of the Lord. "Thou, profane wicked prince of Israel [the False Prophet], whose day is come, when iniquity shall have an end, This saith the Lord GOD . . . take off the crown [as king of this world] . . . I will overturn, overturn, overturn, it: and it shall be no more, until he come whose right it is [the Second Advent is still future]; and I will give it him. . . . The sword, the sword is drawn: for the slaughter it is furbished, to consume because of the glittering . . . Shall I cause it to return into his sheath? **I will judge thee in the place where thou wast created** [Eden], in the land of thy nativity."[37]

The Lord will not return until after the sword does its work. "The sword of the LORD shall devour from the one end of the land even to the other end of the land: no flesh shall have peace. . . . **Thus saith the LORD against all mine evil neighbours, that touch the inheritance which I have caused my people Israel to inherit; Behold, I will pluck them out of their land,** and pluck out the house of Judah from among them. And it shall come to pass, **after that I have plucked them out I will return.**"[38]

As Goliath was killed with a sling stone, the giant northern army and their allies will be beaten in Israel with a stone slung at the Earth from its orbit in space.

Thus saith the Lord GOD; Behold, I am against thee, O Gog, the chief prince of Meshech and Tubal: And I will turn thee back and will leave but the sixth part of thee, and will cause thee to come up from the north parts, and . . . Thou shalt fall upon the mountains of Israel, thou, and all thy bands, and the people that is with thee . . . And it shall come to pass in that day, that I will give unto Gog a place there of graves in Israel, the valley of the passengers on the east of the sea . . . and they shall call it The valley of Hamon-gog [in the book of Esther, Haman hated and wanted to kill all the Jews, just as this army will want to do].[39]

I will remove far off from you the northern army [those who are able to retreat] **and** will drive him [the remainder] into a land barren and desolate, with his face toward the east sea [the Dead Sea[40]], and his hinder part toward the utmost sea [the Mediterranean Sea,[41] from which a tsunami sweeps the land when a rock as large as a mountain strikes the NE corner].[42]

"Go in between the wheels, even under the cherub, and fill thine hand with coals of fire from between the cherubims, and scatter them over the city."
Ezekiel 10:2

Chapter 17

Between the Cherubim

Satan's present royal palace orbits within our own solar system as did his earlier residence.

Ezekiel saw Satan's base of operations in his visions of the heavenly wheels within wheels in chapters one and ten. The translators obviously did not know what these visions represented. Therefore, the original is easier to understand than the translations. Pray for the Lord's help in seeing through Ezekiel's eyes as you open his first chapter.

Ezekiel's Vision of Wheels Within Wheels

When Ezekiel was 30 years old and at Babylon, "**the heavens were opened**" to him in a vision. He saw the asteroid that will destroy Babylon at the end of our age.

Looking up at the sky, he first saw a whirlwind come out of the north. It quickly fanned out a great doughnut shaped cloud of asteroids around the outside edges, framing an inner picture of four wheels within wheels with one bright fiery hub. The whole scene represented the inner part of our solar system from its center out beyond the orbit of Mars where a former planet exploded and formed our asteroid belt.

In the middle was the radiant sun, "**a fire infolding itself**, and a brightness [*nogah*, **sunlight**] was about it, and out of the midst thereof as the colour of amber."

Spaced at wing tip to wing tip intervals between the sun and the asteroid belt were **four flying planetary bodies** whose orbits formed concentric circles, wheels within wheels, rings, orbs, about the hub where fire flared and fell back on itself. In chapter 10 (margin, New Scofield Bible), Ezekiel called them whirling wheels [*galgal*, heaven, circular, rolling things; i.e., **heavenly planetary orbits**]."[1]

One orbit was "upon the earth." This is the key that unlocked this mysterious puzzle that the translators must not have understood. **One of the flying orbiting bodies is the Earth**. Verse 13 in the New Scofield Bible cinches it: "As for the likeness of **the living creatures, their appearance was like burning coals of fire.**"

Verse 16 says that all "four had one likeness," so **they all look like coals of fire**. All four had "the likeness of a man [*adam*, red earth, i.e., **clay soil**]." Since one is the Earth, all have clay soil, and all orbit between the sun and the asteroid belt, **they are the terrestrial planets, Mercury, Venus, Earth and Mars**, shining in the sunlight.

The word *chajoth*, translated "living creatures," means lively things. These lively things are rotating planetary bodies flying at great speed through space, each in its own orbit.

"And their feet [extremities, limbs; astronomer's call the edge of a celestial disk its limb]; were straight [*yashar*, smooth] feet; and the sole [*kaph*, curve] of their feet [outer edges] was like the sole of a calf's foot [round]; and they sparkled like the colour of burnished brass." In other words, the curve of their outer edges looked smooth and round. **All four planets are round and sparkle in the sunlight**.

"And every one had four faces." The four faces Ezekiel described are those that were on the banners placed at the compass points around the Tabernacle in the desert. They represent the four directions: the eagle north, the man south, the lion east, and the ox west. **Each round flying celestial full orb** [sphere] **faces all four directions**.

And "every one had four wings." Whatever these wings represent, the Earth has them. The same word, *kanaph*, which means quarters, is translated "corners," in Isaiah 11:12: "the four corners of the earth." Green's Interlinear Hebrew/Greek-English Bible has "four wings of the earth." We now have photographic proof of what the wingless Earth looks like from space. Its four "wings" or "corners" are actually quarters. Earth's astronomical symbol is a circle divided into four quarters to help us understand. **Each orbiting planetary sphere has four quarters**.

They had "the hands [*yad*, parts, i.e., elements] of a man [*adam*, red earth] under [*tachath*, used of things which are interchanged: in lieu of, instead of] their wings [*kanaph*, quarters] on their four sides [*reba*, fourth parts]." **Each sphere has elements of clay soil on all quarters**.

Their flight was not erratic, but smooth and regular, each one aligned with the others as they swung around in turn to face the four directions. The Concordant Literal Bible translates verse 17: "When they go, toward one of their four quarters are they going." This is clearly a circular orbit.

IT

Against this background, Ezekiel saw another object. The King James Version says, "like the appearance of lamps: it went up and down among the living creatures." Green's Interlinear is more explicit: "like the appearance of torches. It was **continually circling** [orbiting] among the living creatures [the four planets]."

Between the planets, Ezekiel saw something else orbiting. First, he saw things that looked "like the appearance of lamps" or torches. These are probably the wild asteroids that were shot out into cometary orbits when Satan's former planet exploded and formed the asteroid belt between Mars and Jupiter.

Then Ezekiel narrowed it down to one of these, which he merely called "**it**." In those days before telescopes and photography, it had not yet been discovered. Revelation 8:11 says that "the name of the star (*asteros*) is called Wormwood."

Nahum 2:4 in the Septuagint says of both **it** and the Earth: "**their** appearance is as lamps of fire." All these celestial bodies look like torches or lamps as they shine with reflected sunlight.

Satan's Nest Between the Stars

It is Satan's home. It is "the seat (*shebeth*, abode) of violence."[2] It is Satan's nest on high among the "stars."

The Lord spoke through Edom (which means "red," Satan's color) to proud Satan when he said,

> The **pride** of thine heart hath deceived thee,
> thou that dwellest in the clefts of the rock,
> whose habitation is high; that saith in his heart,
> Who shall bring me down to the ground?
> Though thou exalt thyself as the eagle, and
> though thou set **thy nest among the stars**

[*kokabim*, shining, round, rolling, globes],
thence will I bring thee down, saith the LORD.[3]
Woe to him, that coveteth an evil covetousness
to **his house**, that he may set **his nest on
high**, that he may be delivered from the power
of evil![4]

Cherubim

In Ezekiel 10:20, these four planets are called
"cherubims [*kerubim*]." This makes it much easier to
understand Genesis 3:24, which says, "So he drove out the
man [the flaming sword will destroy at Eden]; and he placed at
the east of the garden of Eden Cherubims [*kerubim*] and a
flaming sword [*chereb*, destroying weapon] which turned
every way, to keep the way of the tree of life."

**This flaming sword is the asteroid that Satan
lives on.** Like the sun, it is seen first in the east as the earth
turns. This rotating orbiting asteroid that turns every way was
placed in the sky to enforce the Lord's commands. He will not
allow evil to gain a foothold in eternity and ruin it for us all.

Between the Cherubim

Satan's home orbits between the cherubim.
God's home is over the cherubim's heads.[5] The first heaven is
our atmosphere. **Satan lives in the second heaven,**
where the planets and stars are. God's is the third heaven, the
heaven of heavens, in the uttermost north above all stars.[6]

Satan said, "I will ascend into heaven, I will exalt my
throne above the stars of God: I will sit also upon the mount
of the congregation [*mowed*, assembly on a feast day, i.e.,
place of the Rapture assembly on a feast day], in the sides
[*yerekah*, remote recesses] of the north: I will ascend above
the heights of the clouds; I will be like the most High."[7]

We can't see God's throne. Its light is hidden by a
dark cloud, probably one our astronomers have discovered. A
friend told me that they say it is either a tunnel through the
stars or a dark galactic blanket hiding all stars in the far north.

Scripture says, "**A cloud is his hiding-place, and
he shall not be seen**; and he passes through the circle of
heaven."[8] "He holdeth back the face of his throne, and

spreadeth his cloud upon it"[9] "With clouds he covereth the light; and commandeth it not to shine by the cloud that cometh betwixt."[10]

This will change as the age ends. "And now men see not the bright light which is in the clouds: but the wind passeth, and cleanseth them."[11] "And he will destroy in this mountain the face of the covering cast over all people, and the vail that is spread over all nations."[12]

As the sixth seal is opened, "the dark cloud"[13] will depart along with other clouds and smoke, "as a scroll when it is rolled together."[14] Men who have not believed in him will see the Sign of the Son of Man, the Lord Jesus Christ "that sitteth on the throne"[15] and receives his crown.

Satan is "the anointed cherub [*kerub*]"[16] that lives on the "sword [*chereb*, destroying weapon]" between the cherubim [*kerubim*]. When his asteroid is hurled at Earth, Jerusalem will have coals of fire cast over her, so **the asteroid will impact Earth somewhere in the Mideast**.

Ezekiel 10:2 says, "Go in **between the wheels** [orbits of the planets], **even under the cherub** [Satan], and fill thine hand with coals of fire from between the cherubims [planets], and scatter them over the city [Jerusalem]."

The Planet Rahab

Satan's asteroid was probably thrown into its elongated cometary orbit when his planet, Rahab, was hit with a rock and fragmented by the explosion. Isaiah 51:9 says,

> Awake, awake, put on strength, **O arm of the LORD** [Christ, Isaiah 53:1]; awake, as in the ancient days, in the generations of old [i.e., He threw a rock at Rahab]. Art thou not it that hath **cut Rahab**, and wounded the dragon?

The Hebrew *chatsab*, which is translated "cut" means split, and of course, the dragon is Satan.[17] The planet Rahab was split in ancient times before Adam. Satan and his demons were dispersed. By "His [the Lord's] understanding He **shattered Rahab**" (Job 26:12 NASB). Psalms 89:10 says,

> Thou hast broken Rahab [which means insolent and proud; like Satan] in pieces, as

one that is slain: thou hast scattered thine
enemies [Satan's forces] with thy strong arm.

We once had ten planets in our solar system: Mercury,
Venus, Earth, Mars, **Rahab**, Jupiter, Saturn, Uranus,
Neptune and Pluto.

Many astronomers think the planets were formed by
the accretion of planetesimals formed from a primordial solar
nebula and are trying to figure out what went awry in the
asteroid belt. Some recognize that there was once a planet in
that area. It has been called Astra. The Lord calls it Rahab and
connects it with Babylon, saying, "I will make mention of
Rahab and Babylon to them that know me."[18] As Satan once
built his palace on Rahab, the Satan indwelt False Prophet will
build himself a palace at Babylon. As Rahab was split by a
rock, Babylon will be destroyed by a rock hurled from space.
"As Babylon hath caused the slain of Israel to fall, so at
Babylon shall fall the slain of all the earth" (Jeremiah 51:49).

Because of Satan's sins, Rahab was shattered, pelting
one side of Mars, forming our asteroid belt and flinging a few
shards into elongated cometary orbits among the planets. One
probably hit the Earth and blasted the material that formed our
moon out into space. Some pieces of the planet Rahab still hit
Earth (and probably Venus, Mars, and the Moon).

According to John H. Reynolds of the department of
Physics of the University of California, Berkeley, the
nickel-iron found in meteorites shows signs of coming from
within a fairly large planet because it cooled and solidified
slowly. Also, the evidence frozen into the crystalline structure
of the metal shows that there was a sudden release of pres-
sure, **proving that the planet exploded.**[19]

Did Life Exist on Rahab?

In *Splendor in the Sky*, Gerald S. Hawkins asked if
life existed on this planet before it split. It is a big surprise, but
it seems that life did exist on it. He said that in 1961, Dr.
Frederick D. Sisler and Dr. Walter Newton coaxed strange
bacteria out of a meteorite that fell in 1950 on Murray,
Kentucky. They sterilized the outside with bichloride of
mercury, hydrogen peroxide and ultraviolet light. After
crushing it in a germ-free lab, they placed it in a nutrient
culture. Later, looking at it under a microscope, they saw

millions of **elongated bacteria, unlike strains found on Earth**.

That same year, scientists at Fordham University, New York, found long hydrocarbon chains, similar to cholesterol and fats, normally thought to be organic, in a meteorite that fell in Orgueil, France in 1864. **They decided a low form of life must have existed on the planet.**[20]

In "Organic Matter on Asteroid 130 Elektra," *Science*, October 9, 1987, D. P. Cruikshank and R. H. Brown reported organics on asteroids 130 Elektra, Orgueil and Murray. They reported **a vast array of complex organics, a group that can include "alkanes, alkenes, purines, and amino acids," on asteroid Murchison**. They could also tell by the clay and "other aqueous alteration products" that **the parent body had been affected by water**.

A Broken Section

Satan's asteroid is a broken section of the planet Rahab. The Lord said that this "iniquity shall be to you as a breach [*perets*, **broken section**] ready to fall, swelling out in a high wall, whose breaking cometh suddenly at an instant. And he shall break it as the breaking of the potters' vessel . . . there shall not be found in the bursting of it a sherd to take fire from the hearth, or to take water withal out of the pit."[21] It will probably be vaporized upon impact.

Calling planets precious stones and "stones of fire," because they reflect the sunlight, the Lord addressed Satan in Ezekiel 28:13-18 as king of Tyrus (rock) because Satan is king of the rock that will annihilate Babylon. He said,

> Thou hast been in Eden the garden of God [as the serpent], every precious stone was thy covering [*mesukkah*, surroundings], the sardius, topaz, and the diamond, the beryl, the onyx, and the jasper, the sapphire, the emerald, and the carbuncle, and gold [ten stones or planets] . . . **Thou art the anointed cherub that covereth [*sakak*, entwines, i.e., the "chariot" he rides on crosses other orbits]; and I have set thee so: thou wast upon the holy mountain of God [when "Satan came . . . to

present himself before the LORD"[22]]; **thou hast walked up and down in the midst of the stones of fire** [Satan's planet, Rahab, was where the asteroid belt is] . . . Thou hast sinned: therefore I will cast thee as profane out of the mountain of God: and I will destroy thee, O covering cherub, from the midst of the stones of fire [the planets] . . . **I will cast thee to the ground . . . I will bring thee to ashes upon the earth**.

A Vexation Just to Understand the Report

What "will ye do in the day of visitation, and in the desolation which shall come from far [*merchaq*, remote distant place, from *rachaq*, to recede far away, i.e., the heavens]?"[23]

And . . . when the overflowing scourge [great tsunami] shall pass through, then ye shall be trodden down by it. From the time that it goeth forth it shall take you [a mountain size piece of rock must hit the northeast corner of the Mediterranean Sea] for morning by morning shall it pass over, by day and by night and it shall be a vexation only to understand the report.[24]
Behold waters rise up out of the north, and shall be an overflowing flood, and shall overflow the land, and all that is therein; the city [even Jerusalem] (Jeremiah 47:2).

"At that day shall a man look to his Maker, and his **eyes** shall have respect to the Holy One of Israel [the Sign of the Son of Man will be seen]. . . . In that day [Tishri 1, our September 13, near summer's end] . . . there shall be desolation. . . . the harvest shall be a heap in the day of grief and of desperate sorrow . . . Woe to . . . the rushing of nations [the invading multi-nation army] . . . God shall rebuke them, and they . . . shall be **chased as the chaff of the mountains before the wind**, and like a rolling thing [*galgal*, heaven, circular, globular, rolling thing; i.e., Satan's asteroid] before the whirlwind. And behold at eveningtide trouble [literally, terror]; and before the morning he is not. This is the portion of them that spoil us, and . . . rob us."[25]

The Lord will send a whirlwind from the east to bring Satan's asteroid into an impact trajectory with Earth. It will come in from the northeast. **"The east wind carried him away, and he goes; and it whirls him out of his place."**[26] Satan is impotent to do anything about it.

The Hammer of the Whole Earth

How is the hammer of the whole earth [Satan's asteroid] cut asunder and broken! . . . **I have laid a snare for thee**, and thou art also taken, O Babylon, and thou wast not aware: thou art . . . caught, because thou hast striven against the LORD. **The LORD hath opened his armoury, and hath brought forth the weapons of his indignation:** for this is the work of the Lord GOD of hosts in the land of the Chaldeans. . . . destroy her utterly . . . declare in Zion the vengeance of the LORD our God, **the vengeance of his temple.**[27]

Many nations will feel the intense destructive force of the blast when this hammer impacts Earth. The Lord said, "I will send a fire . . . I will break also the bar [*beriach*, **flying or piercing object**; a missile with a nuclear warhead?] of Damascus, and cut off the inhabitant from the plain of Aven [Lebanon/Syria;], and him that holdeth the sceptre from the house of Eden."[28] Satan has held the scepter ever since he took dominion away from Adam in the Garden of Eden.

The Vengeance of His Temple

Flee out of the midst of Babylon, and deliver every man his soul: be not cut off in her iniquity; **for this is the time of the LORD'S vengeance** . . . We would have healed Babylon, but she is not healed: forsake her, and let us go every one into his own country; for her judgment reacheth unto heaven . . . **his device is against Babylon**, to destroy it; because it is the vengeance of the LORD, the vengeance of his temple.

> . . . O thou that dwellest upon many waters
> [nations] . . . thine end is come.[29]

Moses demonstrated "the vengeance of his temple" when the Israelites worshiped the golden calf. He came down off Mt. Sinai and angrily dashed to pieces on the Earth two tables of stone on which the ten commandments were written. This could easily picture the two asteroids that would later hammer the Earth. The first slaughtered the enemy at Gibeon on Joshua's Long Day and the latter will smash Babylon on Jesus' Long Day. The stones are cast to the Earth and broken as judgment for breaking God's commandments.

The flying rolling thing is "**the curse that goeth forth over the face of the whole earth**: for every one that stealeth [breaking the commandment] shall be cut off as on this side according to it; and every one that sweareth shall be cut off as on that side according to it."[30]

In the laws of Moses, idolaters were to be stoned. The five kings of the Amorites that Joshua fought at Gibeon were Caananites, who worshipped idols. Babylon will be worse. They will worship an image and Satan himself. When sin comes to a head and Babylon has "become the habitation of devils,"[31] the flaming sword will be hurled at Earth. Without the blood of atonement, God will speak in judgment.

First in the Tabernacle and later in the Temple, were representations or "**patterns of things in the heavens**."[32] The two tablets of stone on which the commandments were written were kept in the ark between the cherubim in the Holy of Holies. Thus, the **two tablets of stone were between the cherubim** in the dark just as the two asteroids that would hit the Earth (one destroying the enemy at Gibeon, the other annihilating Babylon) were between cherubim, the terrestrial planets, in the darkness of space.

Cherubim were also embroidered on the ten curtains in that totally dark cube,[33] evidence that there were originally ten cherubim (planets) in our solar system.

We have read Daniel's "seal the book, even to the time of the end: many shall run to and fro, and knowledge shall be increased."[34] But, little did we know how much knowledge of the meaning of Scripture could increase in this time of the end. **The shock is like opening a book in a foreign language and suddenly understanding it**. Everywhere you look, there are fresh discoveries waiting for you.

NEAs, Near Earth Asteroids

In 1932, the asteroid Apollo was the first Earth-crosser discovered. By 1985, there were 60.[35] *Sky and Telescope* charted 72 by March, 1990. In September, 1990, Eleanor Helin, principal investigator for the Asteroid Project, reported in *The Planetary Report* that 144 NEAs had been documented. NEAs are classed as Apollos, Amors and Atens. All come close to Earth, but only Apollos actually cross our orbit.

In Introduction to Asteroids (1988), Clifford Cunningham listed nine that could hit Earth: Eros [discovered in 1898], Alinda [1918], Ganymed [1924], Ivar [1929], Amor [1932], and Betulia [1950] that do not cross our orbit, plus Toro [1948], Icarus [1949], and Geographos [1951] that do.

In March 1989, the asteroid 1989FC came closer than any other in history up to that time and was discovered too late to try to do anything about it. It was 450,000 miles or six hours from Earth, roughly twice the distance to the Moon. In December, 1989, *Omni* reported that 1989FC's discoverer, Henry Holt, **expects it to impact Earth or the Moon within 30 years**, so I'll add it to our list. It passes by every thirteen months. On July 10, 1990, asteroid 1990MF was among the closest approaches of the last 50 years.

At the public forum, "Is the Sky Falling," presented July 1, 1991 by The Planetary Society and The International Conference on Near-Earth Asteroids, David Morrison said an asteroid is expected to hit Earth in the future. They want more telescopes for detection and a missile system for defense.

Ezekiel saw Satan's asteroid going "up and down" among the four terrestrial planets. If it crossed all four orbits (but maybe it doesn't), the most likely would be Icarus, the only one on our list crossing all four. Walter Baade discovered it in 1949 after Israel became a nation.

Isaiah 18:3 (NASB) says, **"All you inhabitants of the world** and dwellers on earth, As soon as a standard [flag of world government?] is raised on the mountains [nations], you will see it [the asteroid?], And as soon as the trumpet is blown [on the Feast of Trumpets in 2007], you will hear it [the blast of impact will be heard around the world]." The meaning of this verse is obscure. It may not refer to the asteroid at all, but the possibility exists. Since the United Nations was organized in 1945, this could cut our list to those found since then: Toro, Icarus, Betulia, Geographos, and

1989FC. According to Andrew Noymer of the Smithsonian Astrophysical Observatory, no KNOWN asteroid is on a collision course with us during the next 100 years. However the Lord will use a whirlwind to sling it into the Earth.

In mythology, Icarus was the first aeronaut. He attached wings to his body with wax. Not heeding his father's advice, he flew too close the the sun, the wax melted and he crashed into the part of the Aegean Sea called the Icarian Sea where the Island of Patmos is located.[36]

A collision with Icarus is not impossible. It crosses our orbit about twice each year. It was within 3,950,000 miles of us June 14, 1968. Robert S. Richardson, Associate Director of Griffith Observatory and Planetarium, Los Angeles, California, said that it would be possible for the Earth and Icarus to collide if there was a change of only a few degrees in the position of the descending node of the Icarian orbit. The descending node is where Icarus crosses the plane of the Earth's orbit from north to south.[37] (It is to come in from the north too.) Only a small change, he said, in the orbit of Icarus would be necessary to bring it closer on subsequent passages. Because it also orbits near Mercury, he declared that its orbit would change significantly as time goes by.[38] It has a precessing elliptical orbital pattern moving it around the sun a tick more on each pass, so it changes slowly anyway.

If Icarus, 1.7 kilometers average diameter, hit Earth the demolition would be catastrophic. Newsweek said that if it hit on land, the crater would be 40 miles wide and 5 miles deep. If it hit water east of Bermuda, a tidal wave 200 feet high would strike Boston at 400 to 500 miles an hour.[39]

Isaac Asimov called about a half dozen asteroids like Icarus Earth-Grazers. He said that if one came in from outer space, it could destroy a city with one "earth-smashing blow." He said the chances of crash are nil if the orbits stay the same but that they are not necessarily permanent. Passing large bodies can change their orbits. Mars, Venus or Earth could change an orbit just enough to make one an "earth-crasher."[40]

Brian Marsden of the Smithsonian Astrophysical Observatory in Cambridge, Massachusetts estimates that an asteroid impact may happen about once every 1,000 years.[41] This planet is certainly not immune to collision. There are about 100 craters on Earth that are thought to be caused by asteroid impact. Meteorite Crater in Arizona looks like the craters on the moon. It is around 570 feet deep and 3,900 feet

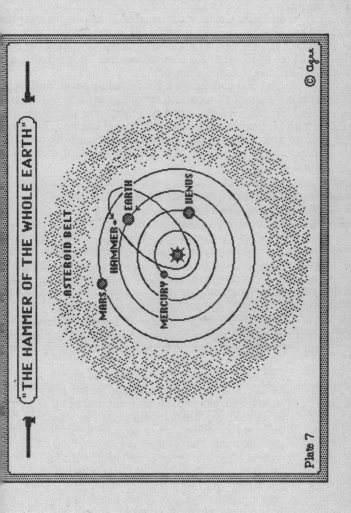

"THE HAMMER OF THE WHOLE EARTH"

ASTEROID BELT

MARS

HAMMER

EARTH

VENUS

MERCURY

© Agee

Plate 7

rim to rim. When it collided with Earth, it exploded like a 5.5 megaton bomb, causing iron rain to fall. The solidified drops of ejecta can be gathered from the surrounding sand with a magnet.

In 1908, a meteor exploded at Tunguska, in northern Siberia. People saw and heard it four hundred miles away. So far, it is the largest to hit us this century. It scorched and knocked down trees for several hundred square miles, all pointed away from the epicenter.

On February 12, 1947, the Sikhote-Alin Mountains in Siberia were hit by a meteorite thought to have been 30 feet in diameter, the second largest to impact our planet in this century. It probably broke up as it crossed Roche Limit, for it caused over 100 holes in the ground. Some were 30 to 40 feet deep and 75 feet wide.[42] A mile wide swath of forest was felled there also.

In the Latter Days ye shall Consider it Perfectly

If Icarus is Satan's asteroid, there is an interesting correlation. On the Jewish Sivan 18, 5728 (June 14, 1968) Icarus made one of its nearest approaches to the Earth. It happened in the 450th Jewish year after the Ottoman Turks took Jerusalem, the Jewish year in which our last 40 years of probation began. They will end in the Jewish 5768.

There is a strange passage in Jeremiah 23:18-20. It describes something not understood in former days that we will understand and teach perfectly in these latter days. It says:

> For who hath stood in the counsel of the
> LORD, and hath perceived and heard his
> word? who hath marked his word, and heard
> it? Behold, a whirlwind of the LORD is gone
> forth in fury, even a grievous whirlwind: it
> shall fall grievously upon the head of the
> wicked [the False Prophet will be blinded in
> his right eye]. The anger of the LORD shall
> not return, until he have executed, and . . .
> performed the thoughts of his heart: **in the
> latter days ye shall consider** [*biyn*, un-
> derstand, teach] **it perfectly.**

We can know what the grievous whirlwind that shall fall on the wicked represents. We are now living in the latter days when we will be able to understand and teach it perfectly.

I understand that an asteroid will hit us, but am not sure which one. There is a problem with picking Icarus. In 5:1-3, Zechariah saw the flying rolling thing, The Curse, as twice as long as wide. When Icarus was first discovered, it was thought to be an irregular chunk from 0.3 to 0.6 kilometers wide. That fit perfectly. However, now they have decided that all the rest of the list are irregular in shape, but that Icarus must be nearly spherical even though its reflected light fluctuates as it rotates. If it is not Icarus, Geographos seems the most likely candidate. It is an Earth-approacher.

Eleanor Helin, of Jet Propulsion Laboratory, said she would "run some orbits" to try to find out which one might be close by on September 13, 2007. The Lord will send a whirlwind to sling it into the Earth, but it will probably be in the vicinity already.

The Sling Stone of the Son of David

Remember how David slew the giant? Goliath was a hybrid, part angel, part man, strong because angels are larger and more powerful than men. It is easy to see that angels are larger in stature than men for in Genesis 6, when the sons of God, angels, took human wives, their children were giants. The bedstead of the last giant, king Og of Bashan, was 13 1/2 feet long. Their power is referred to in Psalms 103:20. "Bless the LORD, ye his angels, that excel in strength."

The battle between David and Goliath will have more than one parallel as the Day of the Lord begins. It is as if the asteroid is in the Son of David's sling, and when he's ready to sling the stone at the king of this world, the Satan possessed False Prophet (an angel-man) and his world government organization, he will simply let go of the thong as David did when he slew Goliath and stopped the attacking Philistine army. With his sling and this stone, he will stop the allied nations attacking Israel.

David chose five smooth stones from the brook. He only whirled one around in his sling and let it go killing the giant. If the one he used represented Satan's asteroid, the unused ones depicted the four terrestrial planets. Ezekiel saw the planets with another stone in cometary orbit between them.

Isaiah 57:3,6 ties this stone in with the seed of the Harlot Church.

> But draw near hither, ye sons of the sorceress,
> the seed of the adulterer and the whore. . . .
> **among the smooth stones of the stream
> is thy portion.**

David picked the sling stone that killed Goliath from among four other stones of the brook. In its parallel, the Lord, the Son of David, will pick the sling stone that will destroy the False Prophet's giant world government and world church at Babylon from among four planetary stones in the orbital stream.

Genesis 3:15 is close to fulfillment. The Lord God said to Satan,

> I will put enmity between thee and the woman,
> and between thy seed [the False Prophet] and
> her seed [Jesus, the seed of Mary]; it [her
> seed] **shall bruise thy head**, and thou shalt
> bruise his heel.

There may be a double meaning here. The word "it" refers to the seed of the woman which is Christ. His heel was bruised when he was nailed to the cross. But, by using "it," the passage also suggests that the false prophet will be bruised by IT, the asteroid Satan lives on.

The seed of Satan is the idol shepherd of Zechariah 11:15-17, the one who commands that people be killed if they will not bow down to the idol of the beast. His head will be bruised when IT impacts Earth. He will lose an eye.

> Woe to the idol shepherd that leaveth the flock!
> [he will move to Babylon Midtribulation] the
> sword shall be upon his arm, and upon his
> right eye: his arm shall be clean dried up, and
> **his right eye shall be utterly darkened.**

"The LORD is in his holy temple," said David, "the LORD'S throne is in heaven: his eyes behold, his eyelids try, the children of men. The LORD trieth the righteous: but the wicked and him that loveth violence his soul hateth. Upon the

224

wicked he shall rain snares [*pachim*, destruction, lightning], fire and brimstone [as on Sodom], and an horrible tempest: **this shall be the portion** of their cup."[43] Their portion among the smooth stones of the orbital stream, **the flaming sword that hangs over their heads**, dumps this well deserved portion of destruction on them as it strikes Earth.

Justice will be done. "For the terrible one [the False Prophet] is brought to nought, and the scorner is consumed, and all that watch for iniquity are cut off: That make a man an offender for a word, and lay a snare for him that reproveth in the gate, and turn aside the just for a thing of nought."[44]

The Gate of Hell

The teachings of the Harlot Church of Babylon are the way to hell, and she will literally sit on the gate of hell. Scripture says, "I have seen the foolish [Satan] taking root: but **suddenly I cursed his habitation** [the asteroid where Satan now resides is the Curse that will destroy the habitation of the Satan indwelt False Prophet]. His children are far from safety, and they are crushed in the gate."[45] The curse will dig the pit for the wicked[46] and open the gate of hell, the molten core of the Earth. Come out of the Harlot Church. "Go not astray in her paths. For she hath cast down many wounded: yea, many strong men have been slain by her. **Her house is the way to hell.**"[47]

> I [the Lord] will rise up against them . . . and cut off from **Babylon** the name, and remnant, and son, and nephew . . . **I will sweep it with the besom of destruction** . . . out of the serpent's root [Satan in Eden] shall come forth a cockatrice [the False Prophet], and his fruit shall be a fiery flying serpent [Satan].[48]

> I will punish Bel [ancient, i.e., Satan in the False Prophet] in Babylon, and **I will bring forth out of his** [the False Prophet's] **mouth that which he hath swallowed up** [Satan[49]]: and the nations [world government] shall not flow together any more unto him . . . My people, go ye out

of the midst of her, and deliver ye every man
his soul from the fierce anger of the LORD. . .
**As Babylon hath caused the slain of
Israel to fall** [both in the past and in this
time of the end], **so at Babylon shall fall
the slain of all the earth.**[50]

Representatives from **all** nations will be present at the
headquarters of world government. They will fall. But, more
than this, Babylon is the gate of hell. The Lake of Fire will be
the door of entry into the fiery bowels of the Earth.

There is a double meaning in the last part of Isaiah
14:29. It could be translated differently: "out of the serpent's
root [Satan in Eden] shall come forth a cockatrice [the False
Prophet], and his fruit [*periy*, reward, as in Psalms 58:11]
shall be a fiery flying serpent [*saraph*, burning, i.e., the
"flaming sword," Satan's home in the heavenlies as it bursts
into flame from the friction of our atmosphere]."

When the Israelites were in the wilderness and bitten
by fiery flying serpents, they were instructed to look up at the
brazen serpent on a pole to be cured. This seems to picture the
last part of the Tribulation when Satan and his demons are all
on Earth tormenting man. At the end of the shortened Tribulation, the Israelites will look up, see Satan's fiery flying
burning home falling and be cured of their unbelief. They will
no longer worship Baal (which means "lord of the planet,"
i.e., Satan). It takes something drastic to make some men
believe in the Lord Jesus Christ. "This shall be with burning
(*serephah*, cremation) and fuel of fire."[51]

**The key of the abyss given to Satan is his
asteroid.** If it is Icarus, which means "island that exterminates," it has an appropriate name for it will exterminate
many. It ties in with Iscariot, which means "he that cuts off or
exterminates a man," and Judas Iscariot betrayed Christ.

I will call for a sword ["*chereb*," a broken
section of the planet, Rahab, that blew up in
the midst of the Cherubim in space] upon all
the inhabitants of the earth, saith the LORD of
hosts. . . . A noise shall come even to the ends
of the earth . . . evil shall go forth from nation
to nation, and a great whirlwind [tornado] shall
be raised up from the coasts of the earth. And

the slain of the LORD shall be at that day from one end of the earth even unto the other end of the earth.[52]

Sodom and Gomorrah were Examples

"Babylon . . . shall be as when God overthrew Sodom and Gomorrah."[53] In 1960, divers under the direction of Dr. Ralph E. Baney of Kansas City, Missouri, announced that they had found Sodom and Gomorrah under water in the Dead Sea. If so, Sodom is in Al Lisan Peninsula Bay. Gomorrah is due west of the northern point of the peninsula.[54]

The Jordan Valley is part of the Great Rift Valley, which extends for some 5,000 miles from Syria to Lake Nyasa in Africa. It is deepest between Israel and Jordan.

The surface of of the water in the Dead Sea is lower than any other on Earth, 1,300 feet below sea level. It is one place where you can fly a thousand feet below sea level.

Before "the Lord rained upon Sodom and upon Gomorrah brimstone and fire from the Lord out of heaven,"[55] the area was a fertile plain. At present, there are mountains, sheer cliffs and steep-sided fissures along the rift. On both east and west sides of the Dead Sea, mountains tower above the water. In the lake, huge blocks of rock were punched down between parallel faults. There is evidence of recent volcanism at the edges where minor outpourings of lava have occurred, but, east of the Dead Sea miles of lava fields testify to the force unleashed on the area. Hot springs are numerous.

The Jewish historian, Josephus, wrote,

The country of Sodom borders upon it [lake Asphaltitis, i.e., the Dead Sea, which has gradually filled up with water]. It was of old a most happy land, both for the fruits it bore and the riches of its cities, although it be now all burnt up. It is related how, for the impiety of its inhabitants, it was burnt by lightning; in consequence of which there are still the remainders of that Divine fire, and the traces of the five cities are still to be seen, as well as the ashes growing in their fruits, which fruits have a colour as if they were fit to be eaten but if you pluck them with your hand, they dissolve into smoke and ashes.[56]

If you look at this great rift valley on a topographic map, you can easily see that this tremendous scar in the Earth could have been caused by a flaming asteroid coming in at a low angle from the north, slashing, ripping, burning and destroying everything in its path.

Like a giant hammer, it broke the bedrock into great fault blocks and depressed those under the upper end of the Dead Sea 2,615 feet below sea level.

What happened there will be repeated at Babylon. Another piece of space rock will come in from the northeast, scorch the Earth from the land of Magog in the northern quarter to Ethiopia and ruin both Babylon and Eden. As pressurized molten lava explodes up through split rock to the surface, the Lake of Fire will spread over 181.8 blood red miles. No man will set foot there again. It's smoke will go up forever.

The Wicked One's Portion on the Feast of Trumpets

"When he is about to fill his belly [a feast, as when Babylon fell the day of the handwriting on the wall], God shall cast the fury of his wrath upon him, and **shall rain it upon him while he is eating** [noon on the Feast of Trumpets]. . . . the glittering sword [the flaming sword of Genesis 3:24] cometh out of his gall: terrors are upon him. . . it shall go ill with him that is left in his tabernacle. The heaven shall reveal his iniquity; and the earth shall rise up against him. The increase of his house shall depart, and his goods shall flow away in the day of his wrath. This is the portion of a wicked man from God."[57]

"I have brought for them a ravager **at noonday** against the mother [mother of harlots, i.e., false religion] of a young man [the False Prophet who will not live out half his days[58]]. I caused to fall on her suddenly anguish and terror. She who has borne seven [Egypt, Assyria, Babylon, Media-Persia, Greece, Rome and its outgrowth, the world government and church of our days]; she has breathed out her life; her sun has gone down while it was yet day."[59]

The end is come [this age is ending] . . . the songs of the temple shall be howlings . . . there shall be many dead bodies . . . I will cause the sun to go down **at noon** . . . And I will turn your **feasts** [on the Feast of Trumpets] into mourning.[60]

[Come] near, ye nations, to hear . . . For the indignation of the LORD is upon **all nations** [world government], and his fury upon **all their armies**: he hath utterly destroyed them . . . and the heavens shall be rolled together as a scroll [so men can see Christ seated on his throne] . . . For my sword shall be bathed in heaven . . . The sword of the LORD . . . it is the day [Tishri 1] of the LORD'S vengeance, and the year [Jewish 5768] of recompenses for the controversy of Zion. And the streams thereof shall be turned into pitch, and the dust thereof into brimstone, and the land thereof shall become burning pitch. It shall not be quenched . . . the smoke thereof shall go up for ever: from generation to generation it shall lie waste; none shall pass through it for ever.[61]

It is as if God said to obey his commandments written on stone *or else*, and nonbelievers are going to get the *or else*. Thank the Lord for giving us a way to escape these things. By decree of the Sovereign God, man must approach Him by sacrifice. Either we accept Christ's sacrifice in our stead or we could be part of this great sacrifice on the altar of Earth.

Take your choice, and you cannot sit on the fence. No decision is a "No" decision.

The Mystery of the Mercy Seat

Hebrews 9:5 says, "And over it [the ark containing the stone tables of the covenant] the **cherubims** of glory shadowing the mercyseat [*hilasterion*, place of propitiation]; **of which we cannot now speak particularly**." What was it that they could not tell about the cherubim? Why not? because the details could not be understood until our days?

In the Septuagint, concerning the day of grief, Amos 9:1 says, "I saw the Lord standing on the altar: and he said, **Smite the mercy-seat** [*hilasterion*], and the porch shall be shaken: and cut through into the heads of all; and I will slay the remnant of them with the sword."

What did he mean, "Smite the mercy-seat"?

The mercy seat was the lid of the ark, made of the same piece of gold as the cherubim (as if it held the stones in their place between the planets). Once a year, on the Day of Atonement, the high priest sprinkled sacrificial blood (representing Christ's sacrifice) on the mercy seat to atone for Israel's sins. If he went in without blood, he died.

The mercy seat speaks of mercy when God's judgment is executed on a sacrifice that is interposed, but when the sacrifice offered is despised, it speaks of judgment.

Picture the mercy seat with its cherubim on the ends, all molded of one piece of gold and resting on top of the ark (the box containing the stone tablets). Imagine quickly slashing through that lid with a sword. What happens? When the holding force of that mercy seat is severed, the heavy gold cherubim fall away, jostling the stone out of its place. If Icarus is the asteroid that will impact Earth, it does not have to be nudged much to cause it to crash into the Earth.

When the asteroid plummets through the atmosphere and hits Earth, coals of fire will rain down on Jerusalem, either from pieces that split off in the atmosphere or from the impact blast. Ezekiel 10:2 describes this figuratively. The Lord said to the man clothed with linen, "Go in between the wheels [planetary orbits], even under the cherub [Satan, Ezekiel 28:13-15], and fill thine hand with coals of fire from between the cherubims [between the terrestrial planets, Mercury, Venus, Earth, and Mars], and scatter them over the city."

Chapter 18

Touchdown

"**The LORD reigneth**; let the earth rejoice; let the multitude of isles be glad thereof. Clouds and **darkness** are round about him: righteousness and **judgment** are the habitation of his throne. A fire goeth **before** him, and burneth up his enemies round about."[1]

The day Christ is crowned is the beginning of the Day of the Lord, the day of darkness, judgment, and trumpets. "Blow ye the trumpet . . . the day of the LORD cometh, for it is nigh at hand; a day of darkness."[2] The fire on that Day of God's Wrath takes place before the Second Advent.

That day of darkness cannot be the day Christ returns to Earth in glory, for at that time,

> **the light shall not be clear, nor dark**: But it shall be one day which shall be **known to the LORD** [he knows when he is coming], not day, nor night: but it shall come to pass, that at evening time it shall be light.[3]

Christ knew when he was coming. He is the Creator. "All things were made by him" (John 1:3). It is inconceivable that he would not know. He was there when the plans were drawn up. He knew the entire Blueprint of Time.

However, sometimes Jesus Christ spoke as man, and other times he spoke as God. When he said, "But of that day and hour knoweth no **man**, no, not the angels of heaven, but my Father only," the Father in him knew but did not want it revealed at that time, so he spoke as a man.

On the dark day, men on Earth will see him sitting on his throne in heaven, but he will not openly return to Earth until later. The Lord said, "I will show them my back and **not my face** in the day of their calamity."[4]

Another reason we know that the Second Advent will not be on the Day of Wrath, Israel is to have no rain on that day. Christ is returning as the latter rain, and Scripture says, **"Thou art the land that is not . . . rained upon in the day of indignation."**[5] There is no ordinary rain in Israel that day, but a great tsunami overflows the land and smites the northern army when a mountain sized piece of the asteroid impacts the northeastern corner of the Mediterranean Sea.

In scripture symbolism, "All flesh is grass."[6] After Rapture II, all the saved will be in heaven. Thus, nonbelievers will be the grass that will be mown down on the Day of Wrath before Christ returns later on as the spring rains begin.

"They shall fear thee as long as the sun and moon endure, throughout all generations. He shall come down like rain upon the mown grass [Day of Wrath is past]; as showers that water the earth. In his days shall the righteous flourish; and abundance of peace so long as the moon endureth. He shall have dominion also from sea to sea, and from the river unto the ends of the earth. . . . all nations shall serve him."[7]

"I will not come in wrath, declared the Lord,"[8] "with fury poured out [past tense], will I rule over you. And I will bring you out from the people, and will gather you out of the countries wherein ye are scattered, with a mighty hand, and with a stretched out arm, and with fury poured out. And I will bring you into the wilderness of the people, and there will I plead with you face to face."[9]

The curse hits before he returns. For "when all these things are come [past tense] upon thee, the blessing and the curse . . . **then the LORD thy God** will turn thy captivity and have compassion upon thee, and **will return.**"[10]

We can see why God was not in the wind, earthquake or fire when he passed by Elijah. He will follow these things when he returns. Elijah was told,

> Go forth, and stand upon the mount before the LORD. And, behold, the LORD passed by, and a great and strong wind [a whirlwind will cause Satan's rock to hit Earth] rent the mountains, and **brake in pieces the rocks before the LORD** [the asteroid is broken in pieces prior to the Lord Jesus Christ's return]; but the LORD was not in the wind . . . the LORD was not in the earthquake . . . the LORD was not in the fire: and **after the fire** a still small voice.[11]

The Lord said, "**after that I have plucked them out I will return** . . . and will bring them again, every man to his heritage, and every man to his land."[12]

In 30 A.D., there was an earthquake. An angel rolled the stone away from the tomb and sat on it before Jesus returned on Sunday, the Lord's day. This was a shadow of things to come. There will be a great earthquake when a stone that an angel, Satan, sat on is rolled away from its place **before** Jesus returns again on Sunday in the Day of the Lord.

The Seven Month Interval

After the fiery slaughter on the Day of Wrath, dead bodies will lay unburied around the world—except in Israel.

> **Seven months shall the house of Israel be burying** of them, that they may cleanse the land. Yea, all the people of the land shall bury them; and **it shall be to them a renown the day that I shall be glorified** [the day he returns as the King of glory].[13]

If Christ returned on the Day of Wrath, there would be dead bodies everywhere. Knocked out of equilibrium, Earth will be reeling "to and fro like a drunkard."[14] On Tishri 1,

> **He stood** [but did not return], and measured the earth: he beheld, and drove asunder the nations . . . The mountains [nations] **saw thee** [Christ on his throne], and they trembled; the overflowing of the water [a tsunami] passed by . . . The sun and moon stood still [**Jesus' long day**] in their habitation [because the planet will rock after the asteroid impact].[15]

Conditions would not allow a very glorious return on that day. It will take seven Jewish months for the Earth to regain its equilibrium and for Israel to be cleansed of dead bodies ready for his return in glory.

God's plans are exquisitely precise. In the sabbatic 5768, there are exactly seven Jewish months between Tishri 1, the Day of Wrath (first day of the 1,000 year Day of the Lord) and Nisan 1, the first day of the Jewish regnal year. The seven months are: Tishri, Cheshvan, Kislev, Teveth, Shevat, Adar, and an extra month, Adar II.

Not every year has seven months between Tishri 1 and Nisan 1. It has to be one of seven leap years in which an intercalary month is added. The Jews add an extra month called Adar II in years 3, 6, 8, 11, 14, 17 and 19 of their 19 year cycle to keep their lunar calendar aligned with the seasons so they will have grain to harvest at the Feast of Firstfruits.

The Second Advent

The Seventieth Week of Daniel, the full 2,520 days, will end on the Feast of Unleavened Bread, Nisan 15, 5768, which is Easter Sunday, April 20, 2008. The seven years begin and end on feast days, the Feast of Weeks and the Feast of Unleavened Bread. It is now easy to see that God established his feasts on dates that coincide with his Timetable.

By the time that day is over, all these things listed by Daniel must be fulfilled: "To finish the transgression, and to make an end of sins, and to make reconciliation for iniquity, and to bring in everlasting righteousness, and to seal up [*chatham*, finish] the vision and prophecy [end the 490 years], and to anoint the most Holy."[16]

"To finish the transgression" refers to the end of Satan's rule. This is to be the 1,260th day since the False Prophet became indwelt by Satan when that old dragon was cast out of heaven.[17]

Since Christ is to take dominion at that time, he must return by that day. Nisan, not only the beginning of the Jewish sacred year but the **beginning of their regnal year**, is the Lord's "appointed season."[18]

As in the chapter Former and Latter Rain, Christ will return as the rain. The Messianic 72nd Psalm says, "**He shall come down like rain**. . . . He shall have dominion also from sea to sea, and from the river unto the ends of the earth."[19]

Hosea said, "He shall come unto us as the rain, as the latter and former rain unto the earth."[20] These are the autumn and the spring rains. Jeremiah said to worship God, "Who gives rain, **both the autumn and the spring rain** in its season."[21] To the Jews, the latter rain is the spring rain. Zechariah said, "Ask of the Lord rain in the time of **the latter or spring rain**."[22] Joel recorded what the Lord will say:

I will remove far off from you the northern army [only one sixth remains, Ezekiel 39:2] . . . rejoice in the LORD your God: for he hath given you the former rain moderately, and he will cause to come down for you the rain, the former rain, and the latter rain in the first month. . . . And ye shall know that I [Christ the Lord] am in the midst of Israel.[23]

The month and day of his return are found in Ezekiel 29. Verse 17 establishes the time, "**In the first month, in the first day of the month**," then verse 21 plainly tells us,

In that day will I cause the horn of the house of Israel to bud forth.

This horn (king[24]) is Christ, as in Psalms 132:17,18. "There will I make **the horn of David** to bud: I have ordained a lamp for **mine anointed**. His enemies will I clothe with shame: but on himself shall **his crown** flourish."

The Beginning of the Regnal Year

It is easy to understand why God had the tabernacle set up "On the first day of the first month" (Nisan)[25] and why the regnal year also began on the first of Nisan. I believe that Christ the Lord, God incarnate, will return as the "King of glory,"[26] on Nisan 1, 5768, exactly seven Jewish months after his coronation in heaven. He will return in a sabbatical year as the "Sun of righteousness"[27] on Sunday, the Lord's day, the beginning of the Jewish sacred year, on April 6, 2008, the anniversary of his crucifixion on April 6, 30 A.D.

When 12, in Nisan, 8 A.D., Jesus went to the Temple. Now, 2,000 years later, "the Lord, whom ye seek, shall suddenly come to his Temple"[28] in Nisan, 2008 A.D. It is easy to see that 2,000 years is one of God's measures of time.

Another clue can be seen in Jesus' statement that in "the third day he shall rise again."[29] Everything dovetails perfectly. He was resurrected in the third 24 hour day. He will return the second time in the third 1,000 year day of heaven, just as Israel was resurrected in their third 1,000 year day (Hosea 6:2).

In Nisan, 30 A.D., when Christ was presented to the Jews on Palm Sunday as king, he was rejected. The next time, he will come again in Nisan **in glory** and be received with delight. It will be Nisan 1, 5758 (our April 6, 2008).

Seven months before this, on Tishri 1, 5768, when **"the day of the LORD** [the Millennium, the seventh 1,000 year day of heaven] cometh . . . I will gather **all nations** [world government's army, including the northern army "and many people with thee," Ezekiel 38:6] against Jerusalem to battle; and the city shall be taken . . . half of the city shall go forth into captivity . . . **Then shall the LORD go forth, and fight against those nations, as when he fought in the day of battle** [when "the LORD fought for Israel"[30] at Gibeon on Joshua's long day].[31]

> And [then, on Nisan 1, 5768] his feet shall stand **in that day** [in the 1,000 year Day of the Lord] upon the mount of Olives . . . and the mount of Olives shall cleave in the midst thereof toward the east and toward the west, and there shall be a very great valley; and half of the mountain shall remove toward the north, and half of it toward the south. And ye shall flee to the valley of the mountains . . . as ye fled from before the earthquake in the days of Uzziah king of Judah: and **the LORD my God** [the Lord Jesus Christ, both God and man] **shall come and all the saints with thee**. And it shall come to pass in that day [Nisan 1], that **the light shall not be clear, nor dark . . . at evening time it shall be light**. . . . living waters shall go out from Jerusalem; half of them toward the former sea, and half of them toward the hinder sea: in summer and in winter shall it be. And **the LORD shall be king** over all the earth: in that day shall there be **one LORD** [Jesus Christ is **"the first and the last"** (Revelation 22:13), Jehovah of the Old Testament and Jesus Christ of the New Testament], and his name one."[32]

During oil exploration, a fault was found in the Mount of Olives. The scene is set for the touch of the Lord's feet.

Chapter 19

The Final Clash of Arms

The Tishri 1 multi-nation attack on Israel is still neither Armageddon nor the end of fighting. At that time, Christ has not yet returned. The Second Advent is seven Jewish months later, on Nisan 1. Armageddon follows that.

Satan and his demons have been in dispute with the Lord since before Adam. R. B. Thieme, Berachah Church, Houston, Texas, calls it the "Angelic Conflict," a good title. Isaiah called it the "controversy of Zion." The Hebrew *riyb* means controversy, conflict, a forensic cause publicly **argued in a court of law. In the final disposition of this court case, Satan will lose the decision.** Then he will fight. Armageddon will be the last war ever fought.

Even after the disaster they suffered in their attack on Israel on Tishri 1, all the remaining armies of the world will regroup and fight against Christ and his army.[2] "Behold, the Lord cometh with ten thousands of his holy saints to execute judgment."[3] The final battle of the Controversy of Zion cannot begin until Christ and his saints are on Earth and the judgment has taken place. Then the saints will execute that judgment.

Judgment of the Nations

The Judgment of the Nations will probably take place the day after the complete 2,520 days of the Seventieth Week of Daniel have run their course. Like Babylonian years, prophetic years often have 360 days. The 2,520th day (360 x 7) is Sunday, Nisan 15, 5768, the Feast of Unleavened Bread. Three feasts occur close together, the Passover, the Feast of Unleavened Bread and the Feast of Firstfruits.

In the fourteenth day of the first month at even is the LORD'S passover. And on the fifteenth

day of the same month is the feast of unleavened bread unto the LORD: seven days ye
must eat unleavened bread. In the first day ye
shall have an holy convocation: ye shall do no
servile work therein.[4]

Since the instructions were to do no servile work on Nisan 15,
it does not seem likely that Christ would sit and judge then.

The false prophet must rule the last three and one half
years of this Seventieth Week of Daniel. "They shall be given
into his hand until a time and times and the dividing of time
[three and a half years]. But the judgment shall sit, and they
shall take away his dominion, to consume and to destroy it
unto the end."[5] Armageddon runs from when this "judgment
shall sit" to "the end" of the war.

I believe Christ will sit to judge the day following
these three and a half years, on the Feast of Firstfruits. If this
is the Judgment of the Nations, and it seems likely that it is,
Christ will also divide sheep from goats that day.

When the son of man shall come . . . then shall
he sit upon the throne of his **glory**: And before
him shall be gathered all nations: and he shall
separate them one from another, as a shepherd
divideth his sheep from the goats: And he shall
set the sheep on his right hand, but the goats
on the left. Then shall the King say unto them
on his right hand, come, ye blessed of my
father, inherit the kingdom prepared for you
from the foundation of the world. . . . Then
shall he say also unto them on the left hand,
Depart from me, ye cursed, into everlasting
fire, prepared for the devil and his angels.[6]

And thou, profane wicked prince of Israel [the
False Prophet] whose day is come, when
iniquity shall have an end, Thus saith the Lord
GOD; **Remove the diadem** [*mitsuepheth*,
miter, headdress of the high priest],
and take off the crown [the end of Satan's
rule as a priest-king]: this shall not be the same:
exalt him that is low [Jesus Christ], and abase
him that is high [Satan, god of this world].[7]

238

It seems that the Judgment of the Nations will take place on Nisan 16, 5768 (Monday, April 21, 2008). If so, **Christ will take dominion on the anniversary of his resurrection** on Nisan 16 in 30 A.D. It would be fitting to turn this world over to him "whose right it is"[8] on **the anniversary of the day he proved he had that right**.

When Christ returns on Nisan 1, the sanctuary must be cleansed. On the first and seventh, a bullock must be sacrificed. Passover is kept on the 14th, "And upon that day shall the prince [resurrected king David] prepare for himself and for all the people of the land a bullock for a sin-offering."[9] The Feast of Unleavened Bread follows. The Judgment of the Nations and the beginning of Armageddon are on the Feast of Firstfruits.

Armageddon

When dominion is taken from Satan, he will fight to try to stay in power. However, "The hope of him is in vain."[10]

In this final conflict, he has done everything in his power to marshal all the armed forces of the nations to fight on his side under the leadership of the False Prophet and the banner of world government. Miracle working demons were sent "forth unto the kings of the earth and of the whole world, to gather them to the battle of that great day of God Almighty. . . . unto a place called in the Hebrew tongue Armageddon."[11]

Armageddon means the hill of Megiddo, which is on the south rim of the plain of Esdraelon, also called the valley of Jezreel, which separates the areas of Galilee and Samaria. It is probably command headquarters for the last fight, with troops assembled in the plain. The survivors must have returned and dug in there after the asteroid blast forced a frantic retreat. In spite of the decimation of his forces, the Satan indwelt False Prophet rallies, shakes his fist at the hill of Jerusalem and aims to take it.

He calls for the attack, but the Lord has other plans. When the battle lines are drawn, Satan and his army against Christ and his army, R. B. Thieme says that each one of us will bump one demon. He could be right. Maybe we are elected to office, displacing these fallen angels in the government of God. The parable of the ten pounds indicates that the good servant is to have authority over ten cities.[12]

Armageddon is the war to end all wars. It is an uneven fight. God's force is stronger than Satan's. John said,

> I saw the beast, and the kings of the earth, and their armies, gathered together to make war against him that sat on the horse [Christ], and against his army. And **the beast was taken, and with him the false prophet** that wrought miracles before him with which he deceived them that had received the mark of the beast, and them that worshipped his image. These **both were cast alive into a lake of fire burning with brimstone.**[13]

After this, Satan, that old serpent, will be bound and cast into the bottomless pit for a thousand years.

The role of Christ's army of saints is described in Psalms 149:5-9:

> Let the saints be joyful in glory: let them sing aloud upon their beds. Let the high praises of God be in their mouth, and a twoedged sword in their hand; To execute vengeance upon the heathen, and punishments upon the people: To bind their kings with chains, and their nobles with fetters of iron: **To execute upon them the judgment written: this honour have all his saints.**

We will carry out the judgment written and assist Christ in setting up the Millennial government. "And the kingdom and dominion, and the greatness of the kingdom under the whole heaven, shall be given to the people of the saints of the most High, whose kingdom is an everlasting kingdom and all dominions shall serve and obey him."[14]

How Long Does Armageddon Last?

In the days of Noah, which appropriately means rest, they went up in the Ark, then there was a seven day wait before it rained 40 days and 40 nights and the waters became the Great Flood. In its modern day parallel, the Church saints will go up in the Rapture to their rest, then the seven year

Tribulation must expire (the full 2,520 days will end Nisan 15) before the armies of the world will come in like a flood for 40 days and 40 nights.

The end of the Beast cannot be with the tidal wave or blast on Tishri 1 because he is still on the scene when Christ returns seven months later. Daniel said of the Beast, the Roman "prince that shall come . . . **the end** thereof shall be with a flood [at Armageddon, the enemy comes in like a flood for 40 days and nights], and unto **the end of the war** [Armageddon] desolations are determined" (Daniel 9:26).

It is fitting that Armageddon lasts 40 days for the number 40 means probation and testing. Satan was allowed to tempt Jesus 40 days and will be allowed to fight 40 days. This is long enough to prove that he cannot win either way. After he is chained in his prison, the bottomless pit,[15] the true Prince of Peace will bring real enduring peace to this tortured planet.

Armageddon begins on Nisan 16, the anniversary of Christ's resurrection on Nisan 16, in 30 A.D. It ends on Iyar 25, the anniversary of his ascension 40 days later, on Iyar 25. Satan will descend on the same month and day on the Jewish calendar that Christ ascended. This is probably why Christ waited 40 days after the Resurrection to ascend to heaven.

On our calendar, the 40th day of Armageddon begins at 6:00 P.M. May 29 and ends at 6:00 P.M. May 30. Thus, the first day of true peace on this planet coincides with the anniversary of the Rapture on our calendar, May 31, 2008.

The Sabbatismos

On the Jewish calendar, peace will begin on the seventh day, the Saturday Sabbath, Iyar 26, 5768. Jesus Christ, Lord of the Sabbath, will reign as the Prince of Peace from that day on. The Greek *sabbaton* means repose, cessation from exertion, rest, a perfect time for lasting peace to begin. This is the time referred to in Hebrews 4:9: "There remaineth therefore a rest [*sabbatismos*] to the people of God." It is the Millennium, the Day of the Lord, the seventh 1,000 year day of the great Week of the Mortality of Man.

After Christ's return, the bodies outside Israel that have lain like dung upon the Earth for seven months will finally be buried. During the seven months preceding the Second Advent, all Israel will bury bodies to cleanse that land.

After Christ returns, certain men will be employed to search for bodies upon the remainder of the Earth. Ezekiel makes this clear.

> And they that dwell in the cities of Israel shall
> ... burn the weapons [maybe made from a
> special laminated wood developed in Holland
> that is as strong as steel] ... seven years ...
> they shall take no wood out of the field ... in
> that day ... I will give unto Gog a place there
> of graves in Israel, the valley of the passengers
> on the east of the sea: and it shall stop the
> noses of the passengers: and there shall they
> bury Gog and all his multitude: and they shall
> call it The valley of Hamon-gog. And seven
> months [the seven between the catastrophe and
> the return of Christ] will the house of Israel be
> burying of them, that they may cleanse the
> land. Yea, all the people of the land shall bury
> them; and it shall be to them a renown the day
> that I shall be glorified [the Second Advent],
> saith the Lord GOD ["God was in Christ,
> reconciling the world unto himself," II Corin-
> thians 5:19]. And they shall sever out men of
> continual employment, passing through the
> land to bury with the passengers those that
> remain upon the face of the earth, to cleanse it:
> after the end of seven months [after Christ's
> return] shall they search.[16]

In Queen Esther's day, Haman, a type of Satan, hated and wanted to kill all the Jews. Instead, Haman was hanged on an implement of destruction, his **own** gallows.

Since the world army will attack Israel to kill the Jews as the age ends, Hamon-gog is a revealing name for their cemetery. Haman means "adversary." Gog means "covering." Satan is the adversary and "the anointed cherub that covereth" (Ezekiel 28:14). The army led by the adversary will be wiped out by an implement of destruction, Satan's **own** asteroid.

"No lion shall be there . . . the redeemed shall walk there: And the ransomed of the LORD shall return, and come to Zion with songs and everlasting joy upon their heads." Isaiah 35:9,10

Chapter 20

The Kingdom Without Lions

Where will we live during the Millennium, in heaven or on Earth? Many teach that our home is heaven, that if we believe in Christ we will go there when we die, that heaven is where we go at the Rapture, and that we will live on Earth during the 1,000 years. Revelation 5:10 in the King James Version clearly says, "[Thou] hast made us unto our God kings and priests: and we shall reign **on the earth**." That settles the question, doesn't it?

However, the Confraternity and Berkeley Versions say, "**over the earth**." That puts it in a different light. What does the original say? Green's Interlinear translates *epi* as "over," and says "we shall reign over the earth." Thayer's Greek-English Lexicon says that *epi* denotes influence upon or over something. It can be translated "above." Interesting, but not really conclusive; it's still an open question.

Those who go to heaven in the Rapture are only there ten years before returning to Earth with Christ as his army. The Tribulation saints are only there seven Jewish months before coming back with him. Christ will be King of kings during the Millennium. We "shall be priests of God and of Christ, and shall reign with him a thousand years."[1] Does that mean that we will have to wait until after the Millennium to go back to our heavenly home? After all, a thousand years is only one of the "days of heaven."[2]

That prospect has no appeal to me. A certain lady I know has actually had her house broken into and robbed, yet she told me that she did not know what heaven was like, that she liked it here and that she liked to watch movies and work. She can havé it, I'd like heaven please, it is a "better country."

"Lay not up for yourselves treasures upon Earth," Matthew said, "where moth and rust doth corrupt, and where thieves break through and steal: But lay up for yourselves treasures in heaven, where neither moth nor rust doth corrupt, and where thieves do not break through nor steal.[3]

Paul said that "ye have in heaven a better and an enduring substance."[4] Peter said that you have "an inheritance incorruptible, and undefiled, and that fadeth not away, reserved in heaven for you."[5] Reserved for when? 1,000+ years from now?

Even Abel, Enoch, Noah, Abraham and Sarah now desire heaven over Earth. "And truly, if they had been mindful of that country from whence they came out, **they might have had opportunity to have returned. But now they desire a better country, that is, an heavenly**: wherefore God is not ashamed to be called their God: for he hath prepared for them a city."[6]

I want to be in the city he has prepared, where "there shall be no more curse: but **the throne of God and of the Lamb shall be in it**; and his servants shall serve him: And they shall see his face."[7] I'm his servant. I want to be there where "there shall be no more death, neither sorrow, nor crying, Neither shall there be any more pain."[8] This does look a little more hopeful, since **Christ's throne will be in the heavenly city**.

On Earth, after the Second Advent, Christ will raise up the tabernacle of David. "And in mercy shall the throne be established: and he shall sit upon it in truth in the tabernacle of David, Judging, and seeking judgment, and hasting righteousness" (Isaiah 16:5).

One consolation is that we will always be with Christ. At the Rapture, "we which are alive and remain shall be caught up together with them in the clouds, to meet the Lord in the air: and so shall we ever be with the Lord. Wherefore comfort one another with these words."[9]

It is a comfort, and most important, we shall always be with Christ as his Bride. Therefore, to find out where we will spend the Millennium, we must determine where he will be during those years.

Two Kingdoms: One Without Lions

On Earth, there will be lions. Isaiah said, "The wolf also shall dwell with the lamb . . . the young lion and the fatling together; and a little child shall lead them . . . **the lion**

shall eat straw . . . the Earth shall be full of the knowledge of the Lord."[10]

In heaven, there will be no lions. Isaiah wrote,

> Then the eyes of the blind shall be opened . . . the lame man leap . . . And an highway shall be there, and a way, and it shall be called The way of holiness; the unclean shall not pass over it . . . **no lion shall be there . . . but the redeemed shall walk there: And the ransomed of the LORD shall return, and come to Zion** with songs and everlasting joy upon their heads: they shall obtain joy and gladness, and sorrow and sighing shall flee away.[11]

The redeemed will be in heaven where there are no lions. Thank you Lord. We **"shall return"** to the heavenly Zion where there is no pain, sorrow, or crying.[12]

Two Jerusalems: Two Zions

There is an earthly Jerusalem and a heavenly Jerusalem, an earthly and a heavenly Zion (Sion in Greek). Hebrews 12:22 refers to the heavenly city at the time of the Rapture: "But ye are come unto mount Sion, and unto the city of the living God, the heavenly Jerusalem."

It is comforting to read that "the throne of God and of the Lamb shall be in it [the heavenly Jerusalem] and his servants shall serve him: And they shall see his face . . . and they shall reign for ever and ever."[13] We are his servants. Christ's throne will be there, we will be there to see him face to face, and we shall **reign with him over the Earth**. We probably won't even need a space shuttle to be able to travel back and forth between the two spheres with ease.

From the Rapture on, we shall "ever be with the Lord," so what happens when Christ returns to the Earth? The simple logical thing—when he comes to the Earth, we will come with him. We are his bride and also his army. When he goes back to heaven, we will return with him. After a marriage, it is customary to go on a honeymoon, to take a trip. Ours will be a little more than the usual; it will be to the Earth.

One Kingdom has a Temple, the Other has None

Scripture's questions are often to make us stop and think. In Isaiah 66:1, the Lord said, "The **heaven is my throne**, and the **Earth is my footstool** [he operates in both]: **where is the house that ye build unto me?**"

This house is the earthly Millennial Temple described by Ezekiel, for **in the heavenly New Jerusalem there will be "no temple** . . . for the Lord God Almighty and the Lamb are the temple of it."[14]

Where is the Matrimonial Abode?

"And," the Lord continued in Isaiah 66:1, "where is the place of my rest [*menuchah*, abode, or matrimonial abode]? The place of Christ's matrimonial abode is the heavenly Jerusalem, where "there shall in no wise enter into it any thing that defileth."[15]

One of "the seven angels which had the seven vials full of the seven last plagues" showed this plainly when he called to John, "Come hither, I will shew thee the bride, the Lamb's wife."

John said, "he carried me away in the spirit to a great and high mountain, and shewed me that great city, the holy Jerusalem, **descending out of heaven** from God."[16]

It looks like Christ will rule from his throne in heaven during the Millennium even though he is King over the Earth. Ephesians 1:20,21 says that he is now seated at God's right hand

> **in the heavenly places**, Far above all principality, and power, and might, and dominion, and every name that is named, **not only in this age, but also in that which is to come.**[17]

He will be in heaven, "not only in this age, but also in that which to come." That is a great relief to me. I want to be with the Lord where moth and rust do not corrupt nor thieves steal.

Revelation 5:10 in the King James Version should be translated, "We shall rule **over** the earth," as it is in the marginal rendering. Evidently, we will come to Earth with Christ, stay until the Millennial government is set up, then return with him to heaven. Later, we will go wherever he sends us to help him rule over the Earth. John 10:9 says we 'shall go in and out." It does sound like we might take over the work of the third of the angels who sided with Satan, doesn't it? In Psalms 47:9, the people of God are called 'shields" (*meginnah*, shields or rulers) that belong to God.

Ascending to the Lord's matrimonial abode is spoken of in the song of ascents in Psalms 132:7-9.

> We will go into his tabernacles [both on Earth and in heaven]: we will worship at his footstool [Earth]. **Arise, O LORD, into thy rest** [*menuchah*, matrimonial abode]; thou and the ark [*aron*, container] of thy strength [i.e., believers, filled with his Holy Spirit]. Let thy priests be clothed with righteousness; and let thy saints **shout for joy**.

Throne of David

While Christ is on the Earth setting up the millennial government, he will sit on the throne of David in Jerusalem, but when he returns to heaven, he will be seated on his own throne in New Jerusalem. The Lord said, "In that day will I raise up the tabernacle of David that is fallen, and close up the breaches thereof; and I will raise up his ruins, and I will build it [earthly Jerusalem] as in the days of old."[18]

Jesus "shall be great, and shall be called the Son of the Highest: and the Lord God shall give unto him the throne of his father David."[19] "In mercy shall the throne be established: and he shall sit upon it in truth in the tabernacle of David, judging, and seeking judgment, and hasting righteousness."[20]

It is David's tabernacle, and he will use it later on, but Christ will use it as headquarters while judging and setting up the millennial government.

After Christ returns to heaven, the resurrected king David will sit on his own throne. The whole world will be ruled from both Jerusalems. Christ is to be King of kings and Lord of lords. He will be the great King, the Son of David who will rule from the heavenly New Jerusalem. He will be over David, the king who will rule from the earthly Jerusalem.

In those days "shall the children of Israel return, and seek the LORD their God, and David their king: and shall fear the LORD and his goodness in the latter days."[21]

They shall serve the LORD their God, and **David their king, whom I will raise up unto them.**[22]

The Jews are promised the Earth. "David my servant shall be king over them . . . And they shall dwell in the land that I have given unto Jacob . . . and they shall dwell therein, even they, and their children, and their children's children for ever: and **my servant David shall be their prince for ever.**"[23] However, we have seen that some of the Old Testament Saints will choose heaven instead.

New Jerusalem

A glorious high throne from the beginning [the original creation of Earth, Genesis 1:1] **is the place of our sanctuary.**[24]

Men have tried to imagine what the heavenly New Jerusalem will look like. **It will be on a celestial rock where there is water.** Isaiah said, "He that walketh righteously . . . shall dwell **on high**: his place of defence shall be the munitions [*metsad*, top, **summit, mountain castle**] on **rocks . . . his waters shall be sure.** Thine eyes shall see the king in his beauty; they shall behold the land that is very far off [heaven]."[25]

Some have thought that the heavenly New Jerusalem will be a cube. Others have decided that it will be a pyramid with a base and height that are equal.

However, it appears to me that New Jerusalem will be a heavenly sphere. It is to come down, so it could orbit the Earth like the moon. It may be a little smaller than the moon. The diameter of the moon is 2,160 miles, one fourth that of the Earth, and if literal, the diameter of the heavenly city is only 1,363.6 miles.

Scripture says, "The city lieth foursquare, and the length is as large as the breadth . . . twelve thousand furlongs." (A furlong was 400 cubits, a cubit 1.5 feet, so a furlong was 600 feet, therefore 12,000 furlongs x 600 ÷ 5,280 = 1,363.6 miles.) "The length and the breadth and the height of it are equal."[26] These dimensions fit a sphere.

Some think the heavenly city is a cube because it "lieth foursquare." However, Scripture also speaks of the "four corners of the earth"[27] or "the four wings of the earth"[28] and we all have seen photographs of the Earth from space showing that it actually is a sphere.

The references to the four corners of the Earth merely indicate the four quarters of the Earth. In Revelation 7:1, the word "*gonias*," translated "corners," also means quarters and is so translated in Revelation 20:8, which says "the four quarters of the earth." This ties in with the astronomical symbol of the Earth, a circle divided into quarters.

The throne of God and of the Lamb shall be in New Jerusalem. Psalms 89:36 speaks of David's seed, which is Christ:

His seed shall endure for ever, and his throne
as the sun before me.

Not only will this sphere be in the sky like the sun, it will also give off light. "The city had no need of the sun, neither of the moon, to shine in it: for the glory of God did lighten it, and the Lamb is the light thereof. And **the nations of them which are saved shall walk in the light of it**."[29]

Not only is the throne of God and the Lamb said to be like the sun, it is also to be like the moon. The next verse says, "It shall be established for ever **as the moon**, and as a faithful witness **in heaven**. Selah [which means pause and calmly think of that]."

If it is in heaven, it cannot be on Earth. It is like the Earth. The 78th Psalm says the Lord "built his sanctuary **like high palaces, like the earth** which he hath established for ever."[30] **If it is like the Earth, it is a sphere.** Since the sun, moon and Earth are all spheres, I believe that the Lord's sanctuary and the high palaces are also spheres.

After the Resurrection, an angel told Mary Magdalene and another Mary to "tell his disciples that he is risen from the dead; and, behold he goeth before you into Galilee," which means a circle. Jesus ascended to the Father that day then returned. This could be a clue that God's heaven is a sphere.

Throne of Christ

In the city will be one throne, occupied by Christ, who is both God and the Lamb for in him "dwelleth all the fullness of the Godhead bodily."[31] In heaven, we will see God in the face of Jesus Christ. "The throne [one throne] of God and of the Lamb shall be in it: and his servants shall serve him [one person]: And they shall see his face [one face]."[32]

On Earth the Holy Spirit of God will tabernacle or dwell with men. The Shechinah glory will be seen again in Israel for the Lord said, "my spirit remaineth among you: fear ye not. . . . I will fill this house with glory . . . The glory of this latter house shall be greater than of the former."[33]

The Flight Home

When will Christ and his bride return to heaven? Maybe this ascension will be on Hanukkah Eve, Sunday, Kislev 24, 5769 (December 21, 2008), the winter solstice, the day the sun turns around to begin its northward journey along the ecliptic. God said he created the lights in the heavens for signs."[34] It would be just like him to use the sun to teach us his truth for Christ is called "the Sun of righteousness."[35]

On Earth, we are "the temple of God,"[36] "built upon the foundation of the apostles and prophets, Jesus Christ himself being the chief corner stone; In whom all the building fitly framed together groweth unto an holy temple in the Lord: In whom ye also are builded together for an habitation of God through the Spirit."[37]

Maybe the day the Lord's temple began to be built in Haggai's day indicates the day of our ascension. Haggai (which appropriately means festive) certainly emphasized over and over that we should pay attention to this day.

As you read, think of types. Christ is the seed of the woman in Genesis 3:15. Galatians 3:16 mentions, "thy seed, which is Christ." The fig tree is Israel, etc.

> And now **I pray you**, **consider** from this day and **upward**, from before a stone was laid upon a stone in the temple of the LORD . . . **Consider** now from this day and **upward**, from the four and twentieth day of the ninth

month [Kislev 24], even from the day that the foundation of the LORD'S temple was laid, **consider it. Is the seed** [Christ[38]] **yet in the barn** [heaven[39]] yea, as yet the vine [Christ[40]] and the fig tree [Israel,[41] i.e., Old Testament saints], and the pomegranate [Church saints[42]] and the olive tree [Tribulation saints[43]], hath not brought forth [*nasa*, **lifted up**,[44] i.e., ascended]: **From this day, I will bless you.**[45]

It is interesting to find that the Hebrew *nasa* means lifted up and our NASA sends vehicles into space. On January 16, 1969, the Orange County Register reported "the stupendous achievement of 1968." Apollo 8 shattered the speed record for **"escaping from the earth on December 21,"** when they traveled 24,916 mph, five times the speed of a rifle bullet. Its strange that this should happen in 1968, when Icarus swung near the Earth just 40 years before an asteroid will impact Earth in the Jewish 5768. On Kislev 24, the Lord will bless someone. I wonder if the bride and bridegroom will end their trip and escape at great speed from the Earth on Kislev 24, 5768, our December 21, 2008.

That December 22nd is Hanukkah. Will we, "the temple of God,"[46] be restored to heaven in time to celebrate this festival of lights, the joyous Feast of the Dedication that commemorates the **restoration of the temple?**

When the sacred candlestick was lit after Judas Maccabeus purified the temple in 165 B.C., only enough pure oil was found to last one day. By a miracle, it lasted eight days.

Eight means new order. We will be established in a new order after returning to heaven. Keep looking for Scripture clues to see if we will celebrate it on Hanukkah or not.

The Kingdom with Lions

All Israel will be saved in a day.[47] I believe it will be the day Christ is crowned King, the day of the catastrophe, Tishri 1, 5768. Then they will finally realize that the scriptures are true, both the Old Testament and the New Testament (Jesus' Last Will and Testament) put in effect by his death.

And it shall come to pass in **that day**, that the remnant of Israel, and such as are escaped of the house of Jacob, shall no more again stay upon him that smote them; but shall stay upon the LORD, the Holy One of Israel, in truth. The remnant shall return . . . unto the mighty God.[48]

They will finally accept Jesus Christ as their Messiah. He is the Lord, both God and man. Scripture says, "the spirit of the LORD shall rest upon him, the spirit of wisdom and understanding, the spirit of counsel and might, the spirit of knowledge and of the fear of the LORD . . . he shall not judge after the sight of his eyes, neither reprove after the hearing of his ears: But with righteousness shall he judge the poor, and reprove with equity for the meek of the earth."[49]

On the Day of Atonement, Tishri 10 (September 22, 2007), they will be sorry and repent, afflicting their souls. "For whatsoever soul it be that shall not be afflicted in that same day, he shall be cut off from among his people."[50]

Between the Day of Wrath and the Second Advent, the Jews might avenge themselves on their enemies that mean to destroy them on the 13th day of the 12th month, Adar (February 19, 2008). During the seven months between the Day of Wrath and the Second Advent, her enemies will be busy regrouping what is left of their armed forces for they will fight Christ when he returns. As soon as possible, they will want to try again to annihilate the Jews. It could easily happen again as it did in Queen Esther's day.[51]

The Bride of Christ could plead for Israel at a time other than when she was called (the "Come up hither" at Rapture I) as Esther did. Israel would prevail and celebrate the feast of Purim with joyful tears of relief. At this point, only one more war would remain, Armageddon, after Christ arrives. The Lord said to Israel,

Thou art my battle axe and weapons of war: for with thee will I break in pieces the nations, and with thee will I destroy kingdoms . . . break in pieces captains and rulers. And I will render unto Babylon and to all the inhabitants of Chaldea all their evil that they have done in Zion in your sight."[52]

After Christ returns on the following Nisan 1 (our April 6, 2008), the world will be ruled forever after from Jerusalem. Israel was told that "the sons of strangers shall build up thy walls, and their kings shall minister unto thee . . . Therefore thy gates shall be open continually . . . that men may bring unto thee the forces of the Gentiles, and that their kings may be brought. For **the nation and kingdom that will not serve thee shall perish.**"[53]

> The wolf also shall dwell with the lamb . . . the young lion and the fatling together; and a little child shall lead them. . . . the lion shall eat straw like the ox. . . . They shall not hurt nor destroy in all my holy mountain: for the earth shall be full of the knowledge of the LORD . . . in that day . . . the Lord shall set his hand **again the second time** [the first time was from the First Zionist Congress in 1897 to 1948] to recover the remnant of his people . . . he shall . . . gather together the dispersed of Judah from the four corners of the earth.[54]

The days Nisan 1 through 15 will see the Temple cleansed, the tabernacle of David set up, sacrifices made, Jews gathered, and the Feast of Passover kept.

> The Lord has [past tense] delivered his people, the remnant of Israel. Behold, I bring them from the north, and will gather them from the end of the earth to the feast of the **passover**: and the people shall beget a great multitude, and they shall return hither.[55]

At the Judgment of the Nations on Nisan 16, Christ will separate the sheep from the goats. There will be 30 days of mourning for the goats because they "shall go away into everlasting punishment."[56]

These days of mourning were customary among the Hebrews. They "mourned for Aaron thirty days, even all the house of Israel."[57] "And the children of Israel wept for Moses in the plains of Moab thirty days."[58]

"In that day shall there be a great mourning in Jerusalem, as the mourning of Hadadrimmon in the valley of

Megiddon. And the land shall mourn, every family apart . . . All the families that remain, every family apart, and their wives apart" (Zechariah 12:11-14).

Isaiah 60:20,21 says that "the **days of thy mourning** shall be ended. Thy people also shall inherit the land for ever." These days of mourning end Iyar 15, (our May 20), the last day of the 1,290 mentioned by Daniel:

> And from the time that the sacrifice shall be taken away, and the abomination that maketh desolate set up, there shall be a thousand two hundred and ninety days.[59]

If Armageddon ends Iyar 25 (our May 30), the anniversary of Christ's ascension on the Jewish Calendar, the millennial peace will begin Iyar 26 (our May 31, the anniversary of the Rapture on our calendar).

Division of the Land

Daniel was told that he would stand in his **lot** 1,335 days from the time the idol, "the abomination that maketh desolate," was set up.[60] This 1,335th day is Friday, Tamuz 1 (**July 4**, 2008). The division of the land will probably be made this day to the twelve tribes of Israel and new governments set up for free men (symbolized for us by July 4). Ezekiel said, "So shall ye divide this land unto you according to the tribes of Israel. . . . divide it by **lot** for an inheritance unto you."[61]

The Jubilee

The Jubilee (or Jubile) is a release from labor. Any of their land that has been sold will revert to the Israelites, and they themselves are all to be free men. Fifty means restoration, and in a Jubilee year, Israel will be restored, "when the times of refreshing shall come."[62]

At Sinai, the Lord gave Moses these instructions: "number seven sabbaths of years . . . seven times seven . . . forty and nine years. Then shalt thou cause the trumpet of the jubile to sound on the tenth day of the **seventh month, in the day of atonement** . . . make the trumpet sound throughout all your land. And ye shall hallow the fiftieth year [which starts Nisan 1], and proclaim liberty throughout all the land . . . ye shall return every man unto his possession."[63]

Many mistakes have been made in figuring the Jubilee. Some thought crops had to grow in the land for 49 years before keeping Jubilee because they were to keep it after they entered the land of Canaan. That doesn't seem necessary.

The Jubilee cycle is 49 years: the 50th year is the first of the next cycle. The cycles began Nisan 1, 2231 (B.C. 1530), the year of the Exodus. Nisan, 5759 (our 1999), the 6,001st year since Adam left Eden, begins the 73rd cycle. Adding nine extra years because this age is extended brings us to Nisan, 5768. The Jubilee year should be announced Tishri 10, 5768 (September 22, 2007) and begin Nisan 1, 5768 (April 6, 2008), the day Christ returns. **Knowing the Jubilee would begin Nisan 1 should have told us a long time ago that Christ would return on Nisan 1.**

If Israel, the fig tree nation, would produce ripe fruit by the Rapture in 1998, the Jubilee probably would be in 1999. The Lord "saw your fathers as the firstripe in the fig tree at her **first** time [members of Rapture I in the spring when figs begin to ripen]: but they went to Baalpeor [where they bowed down to idols as they will during the Tribulation], and separated themselves unto that shame" (Hosea 9:10).

Feast of Tabernacles

On the Feast of Tabernacles following the catastrophe, Thursday, September 27, 2007, they will dwell in booths. Houses will need repair. Because it is a sabbatical year, the law will be read to them publicly as is the custom.

When the next Feast of Tabernacles begins, Tuesday, October 14, 2008, it should be the most joyful feast ever. They will have much to be thankful for: land like the Garden of Eden, a perfect King, Satan chained, and no more war. Men everywhere can rest, each under his vine (Christ) and fig tree (Israel). The world will be governed from the two Jerusalems, the heavenly and the earthly. The Shechinah glory, visible proof of the divine Presence, will shine again on Earth.

Shining with God's light, New Jerusalem will hang above Earth. The "glory of the LORD shall be revealed, and all flesh shall see it together."[64] "The sun shall be no more thy light by day; neither for brightness shall the moon give light unto thee; but the LORD shall be unto thee an everlasting light, and thy God thy glory. Thy sun shall no more go down; neither shall thy moon withdraw itself: for the LORD shall be thine everlasting light, and the days of thy mourning shall be ended. Thy people also shall be all righteous: they [Israel, root and branch] **shall inherit the land for ever**, the branch [as in the Fig Tree Parable] of **my planting** [in 1948], the work of my hands, that I may be glorified."[65]

Some have suggested that modern Israel's gathering in unbelief was not of the Lord, that Christ would gather them after he returned. However, both are of the Lord. One gathering is before the Day of Wrath, the other after it.

The first is spoken of in Zephaniah 2:1-3: "Gather yourselves together, yea, **gather together**, O nation not desired; Before the decree bring forth, before the day pass as the chaff, before the fierce anger of the LORD come upon you, **before the day of the LORD'S anger** come upon you. Seek ye the LORD, all ye meek of the earth, which have wrought his judgment; seek righteousness, seek meekness: it may be ye shall be hid in the day of the LORD'S anger."

Afterward, the Lord will gather them again. Joel 2:31; 3:1,2 says, "The sun shall be turned into darkness, and the moon into blood, before the great and the terrible day of the LORD come. . . . in that time, when I shall bring **again** the captivity of Judah and Jerusalem, I will also gather all nations, and will bring them down into the valley of Jehoshaphat, and will plead with them there . . . for my heritage Israel, whom they have scattered among the nations, and parted my land."

Israel Restored as Wife of Jehovah

"For the LORD hath called thee as a woman forsaken and grieved in spirit, and a wife of youth, when thou wast refused, saith thy God. For a small moment have I forsaken thee; but with great mercies will I gather thee."[66]

"I will even betroth thee unto me in faithfulness: and thou shalt know the LORD . . . And I will sow her unto me **in the earth** . . . I will say to them which were not my people, Thou art my people; and they shall say, Thou art my God."[67]

As I understand it, the Bride will be the wife of Christ in heaven. Israel will be the wife of the Lord on earth.

Chapter 21

Computations

_____

It is not too difficult to figure out God's timetable. I am surprised that more have not done so.

In calculating these things, start with Matthew 24:32-34. In this parable, Jesus answered the question the disciples asked in verse three, "Tell us . . . what shall be the sign of thy coming, and the end of the world [*aionos*, age]?"

Parable of the Fig Tree

> Now learn a parable of the fig tree [Israel, Joel 1:7]; When his branch [a scion broken off for grafting into the old rootstock] is yet tender [young and full of sap], **and putteth forth leaves**, ye know that summer is nigh [it starts June 21]: So likewise ye, when ye shall see all these things [including Israel growing], know that it [the Kingdom of God] is near, even at the doors [symbol of the Raptures]. Verily [importantly] I say unto you, This generation shall not pass, till all these things be fulfilled.

The key words are: "and putteth forth leaves." You have to figure out when the sap started to flow in the new graft making Israel's growth possible. When did she start to grow?

In 1948? No! The new graft had to "take." In 1948, she fought hard just to stay grafted into her old rootstock and to establish her boundaries. In 1956, she tried to put out leaves, but they fell off. It was too soon for God's plan.

In 1967? Yes! In the Six-day War, starting June 5, 1967 (when summer was nigh, beginning June 21), she grew four good sized leaves, the Golan Heights, the Sinai, the Gaza Strip and the West Bank, including the remainder of Jerusalem and her precious Temple area. She ended up the Six-day War with over four times the territory she had before.

Israel's regaining the Temple area suggests that the end of the age is near, for there will be a Temple during the seven year Tribulation. Isn't it possible that this Six-day war was **The Sign of the End of the Age** because it fulfilled the parable? Is there any other year at all that could be considered? That was the first time after she established her boundaries that modern Israel grew leaves that did not drop off.

She was still young, but some time had gone by. There is no way around that fact. Israel is now 43, not so youthful any more. No matter what takes place in the future, the established nation grew her first enduring leaves in 1967.

According to Luke 21:24-28, the Rapture is near when the Times of the Gentiles are fulfilled. It says, "**Jerusalem shall be trodden down of the Gentiles, until the times of the Gentiles be fulfilled** [they were fulfilled in 1967 when Israel took the rest of Jerusalem]. And there shall be signs in the sun . . . moon, and . . . stars; and upon the earth distress of nations . . . Men's hearts failing them for fear, and for looking after those things which are coming on the earth: for the powers of heaven shall be shaken. And then shall they see the Son of man coming . . . And when these things **begin** to come to pass [they began in 1967], then look up, and **lift up your heads** [we will rise up to meet Christ in the air at the Rapture]; **for your redemption draweth nigh**."

When Jesus said that this generation would not pass till all these things were fulfilled, he referred to end time events when the sun will be darkened and "they shall see the Son of man coming . . . And he shall send his angels with a great sound of a trumpet, and they shall gather his elect . . . from one end of heaven to the other [for His coronation]."[1]

Zechariah referred to the same time: "And the LORD shall be seen over them, and his arrow [destroying weapon, the asteroid] shall go forth as the lightning: and the Lord GOD shall blow the trumpet."[2] As the age ends, the darkness will begin, yet "the vail that is spread over all nations"[3] will be rolled away as a scroll.[4] Men will see Christ sitting on his throne in the heavens when he is to receive his crown.

Forty Years from the Sign to the End

All these things [from Israel's taking Jerusalem and putting forth leaves to the asteroid impact] must take place within one 40 year generation. The Jewish 5727 (our 1967) plus 40 years is 5767 (our 2007). The last possible day is the last day of the year, Elul 29 (our September 12). The next day is the Feast of Trumpets, Tishri 1, 5768. Because 5768 is a leap year, it is exactly seven months before the Lord's return on Nisan 1 as required by Ezekiel 39:12,13. Knowing about these seven months and that Christ will return on Nisan 1 as the latter rain locks the end of the age in its proper slot, the last day of 5767. It will actually start at 6:00 P.M. September 11.

Hosea spoke of both the last day of this age, which is the Day of Preparation, and the Feast of Trumpets following it. He asked, "What will ye do in the solemn day [the Day of Preparation for the feast], and in the day of **the feast of the LORD** [the Feast of Trumpets]? For, lo, they are gone because of destruction [from the asteroid impact] . . . The days of **recompence** are come. . . . they shall say to the mountains, Cover us; and to the hills, Fall on us."[5] This corresponds to Revelation, where men say to the rocks, "Fall on us, and hide us from the face of him that sitteth on the throne, and from the wrath of the Lamb."[6]

The Feast of Trumpets when the seven trumpet judgments are meted out, begins at 6:00 P.M., September 12 and ends at 5:59 P.M., September 13, 2007. It is the Jewish New Year, the perfect kickoff for both the sabbatic 5768 and the 1,000 year Day of the Lord we call the Millennium.

Both Joel and Malachi spoke of this Feast of Trumpets. Joel said, "Blow ye the **trumpet** . . . let all the inhabitants of the land tremble: for the **day of the LORD** cometh . . . a day of darkness . . . the sun and the moon shall be dark, and the stars shall withdraw their shining."[7] Malachi said, "**your solemn feasts; and one shall take you away with it.**"[8]

Beginning of the Tribulation

If the Feast of Trumpets is the end of the shortened Tribulation, when will the Tribulation begin? Daniel 8:13,14 gives us the exact number of days it will last.

> How long shall be the vision concerning the daily sacrifice [the first half when the Jews sacrifice in the Temple], and the transgression of desolation, to give both the sanctuary and

the host to be trodden under foot [the last part, when the Israeli False Prophet desecrates the Temple]? And he said unto me, Unto **two thousand and three hundred days.**

Using Jewish reckoning (the first day is counted as number one) count back 2,300 days from the Feast of Trumpets in 2007 (September 13), and you will end on the **Feast of Weeks** (May 28) in 2001. The Feast of Weeks is a perfect time to start the Tribulation. May 28 is even the same day it fell on in 30 A.D. Could you find a better time to start the Seventieth Week of Daniel if you were planning all this?

End of the Tribulation

Now count forward the full 2,520 days of the Seventieth Week of Daniel.[9] As you go, mark the 1,260th day. Revelation 11:3 mentions that the two witnesses will prophesy 1,260 days. This is the first half of the Tribulation, not the last. Because the last half is shortened, there are not 1,260 days left in that segment before the catastrophe takes place.

The Roman Beast "shall confirm the covenant with many for one week: and in the midst of the week he shall cause the sacrifice and the oblation to cease."[10]

The 1,260th day is Cheshvan 23 (Sunday, November 7, 2004), the day the False Prophet will sit in the Temple and claim to be God. The Temple will also be desecrated by an image being placed there. These actions will stop all sacrificing because the Jews know that God is spirit, therefore invisible, and that he commanded, "Thou shalt not make unto thee any graven image." They realize they've been conned.

The Satan indwelt False Prophet "Shall wear out the saints . . . they shall be given into his hand until a time and times and the dividing of time [the last 3 1/2 years of the Tribulation]. But the judgment shall sit [Christ will sit at the Judgment of the Nations the day after the 3 1/2 years are over], and they shall take away his [Satan's] dominion."[11]

These 3 1/2 years are not shortened. (The shortened part concerns the disaster.) These start in the middle of the Tribulation and end on Nisan 15 (Easter Sunday, April 20, 2008). It is the Feast of Unleavened Bread, the end of the seven year Tribulation, and the end of the full 2,520 days.

Christ Must be on Earth by Day 2,521

The next day, Nisan 16, the Feast of Firstfruits, should be the Judgment of the Nations because the false prophet has run out of time. If Christ is to sit and judge, he must return on or before this day. Since "he shall come unto us as the rain, as the latter and former rain unto the earth" (Hosea 6:3), and the latter rains start "in the first month" (Joel 2:23), it seems even more probable that Ezekiel gave us the exact day of the Second Coming. Ezekiel 29:17,21 says,

> [In] the first month, in the first day of the month [**Nisan 1**], the word of the LORD came unto me, saying . . . **In that day will I cause the horn** [king] **of the house of Israel** [Christ] **to bud forth.**

Jesus said that he had foretold us all things. The necessary clues to figure out the time of his return are in the Bible somewhere. I think I have located them. Nisan 1 is our April 6 in 2008, the anniversary of the Crucifixion.

Do you think it is just coincidence that the Jewish year 5768 is a year that has the intercalary month, giving it seven Jewish months instead of the more usual six between the Feast of Trumpets on Tishri 1 and Nisan 1? It ties in with Ezekiel 39:12, which says, "seven months shall the house of Israel be burying of them, that they may cleanse the land. Yea, all the people of the land shall bury them; and it shall be to them a renown the day that I shall be glorified, saith the Lord GOD."

The day that Christ will be glorified is the day of the Second Advent. At that time, "Jesus Christ . . . to him be **glory** and dominion for ever and ever. Amen. Behold, he cometh with clouds; and every eye shall see him."[12]

Peace Follows Armageddon

If the battle of Armageddon starts when Satan is deposed on Nisan 16 (our April 21, 2008), and lasts forty days, it will end with the chaining of Satan on Iyar 25, which is the anniversary of Christ's ascension in 30 A.D. It looks like Christ went up and Satan will go down on the same Jewish date. In 2008, Iyar 25 is our May 30, a **Friday.**

Fry Day

"And the beast was taken, and with him the false prophet that wrought miracles before him, with which he deceived them that had received the mark of the beast, and them that worshipped his image. These **both were cast alive into a lake of fire** burning with brimstone."[13]

Thus peace should begin the next day, the Sabbath, 26 Iyar (May 31). If Rapture I, when we enter rest, takes place on Pentecost in 1998, it will also be on May 31.

God has masterfully aligned our calendar and the Jewish calendar so that they play to each other at the end of this age. We have seen correlations of many kinds.

There is another interesting parallel. On **September 13**, B.C. 4043, the Earth was a chaotic ruin, "and darkness was upon the face of the deep." That day, God said, "Let there be light." On the following days, he restored the Earth to it's pristine state of beauty and made it a fit habitat for man. Soon, he planted the Garden of Eden and put Adam in it.

On **September 13,** 2007, the destruction will be so great that "the elements shall melt with fervent heat, the earth also and the works that are therein shall be burned up."[14] It will also be a day of chaos and darkness. The force released as the asteroid impacts Earth will be twice as great as that which dug the Dead Sea (called by the Arabs Bahr Lut, Sea of Lot) or the one that struck the Amorites on Joshua's Long Day.

After three strikes, Satan [number 13] will be out on the 13th. The first ball destroyed Sodom and Gomorrah and formed the Great Rift Valley. The second struck the Amorites on Joshua's Long Day. The third will destroy the False Prophet's house at Babylon on Jesus' Long Day.

At this time, God will roll away the smoke like a scroll and the Sign of the Son of Man will appear in the sky in a glow of light. Seven Jewish months after the blast, the Lord will again begin to restore the Earth and make it a fit habitat for mankind. Israel will become lush like the Garden of Eden, and her believers will soon be returned to their promised land.

The LORD shall comfort Zion, "make her wilderness **like Eden**, and her desert **like the garden of the LORD**; joy and gladness shall be found therein, thanksgiving, and the voice of melody."[15] Just as the Rapture is as the days of Noah, and the Translation of the Tribulation Saints as the days of Lot, the restoration of the Earth parallels the days of Adam.

"O arm of the LORD; awake, as in the ancient days, in the generations of old. Art thou not it that hath cut Rahab, and wounded the dragon?" Isaiah 51:9

Chapter 22

Blueprint of Time

_____

To recap, time seems to be 7,049 years, a small wave crest on the vast ocean of eternity. Important milestones are marked on the chart "Time" on page 265. The A.H. years (*Anno Hominus*, year of man) date from Adam's creation.

Mankind's time line begins with Adam's creation on the equivalent of the Jewish Elul 29, preparation day for the Feast of Trumpets (our September 18, B.C. 4043) and ends with Elul 29, 7049 A.H. (our 3007 A.D.) the last day of the Millennium. Eternity begins on the Feast of Trumpets just as this *kosmos* began to operate on the Feast of Trumpets.

Ancient days

The term "ancient days" sometimes refers to the dateless past, before Adam was created. In the beginning, before time began for mankind, God planned everything that was going to happen. He designed tests for angels and man and drew up his Blueprint of Time, "definitely appointing the **preestablished periods**" (Acts 17:26, Berkeley Version). Every bit will come true. His counsel will stand.

"Remember the former things of old; for I am God," "he says, "and there is none else . . . and **there is none like me**. Declaring the end from the beginning, and from ancient times the things that are not yet done, saying, **My counsel shall stand**, and I will do all my pleasure."[1]

During ancient times before Adam, the angels were tested. Those that failed were found guilty and sentenced to "everlasting fire, prepared for the devil and his angels."[2] Satan's sentence to prison has not yet been executed, but he does not have many grains of sand in the top of his timepiece.

Evidently, his planet, Rahab, exploded into pieces when he was judged and sentenced. Is it possible to figure out what caused the explosion? Isaiah 51:9 gives us a good clue.

O arm of the LORD; awake, **as in the ancient days**, in the generations of old. Art thou not it that hath cut [split] Rahab, and wounded the dragon [Satan, who lived on Rahab]?

As this age ends, the arm of the Lord (Christ[3])will toss a *chereb*, destroying weapon, "as in the ancient days" when he split Rahab and wounded Satan. Therefore the arm of the Lord split Satan's planet apart by tossing a rock at it too. When he said, "Yet **once more** I shake not the earth only, but also heaven" [Hebrews 12:26], he revealed that **both Earth and heaven have been shaken before**.

"Thou hast broken Rahab in pieces, as one that is slain; thou hast scattered thine enemies with thy strong arm. The heavens are thine [i.e., **Rahab is in the heavens**]."[4]

The destruction of Jericho pictured events at the end of this age. Jericho means "his month," suggesting Tishri 1, when Jesus was born. When Israel marched around the city once each day for six days, it represented the asteroid orbiting Earth for these six 1,000 year days without colliding with it.

On the seventh day, seven priests sounded seven trumpets. Israel marched around seven times. When they shouted, the wall fell. They destroyed the city with the sword and burned it. This suggests the Feast of Trumpets on the first day of the seventh millennium, when Babylon will be destroyed by the Sword of the Lord and the seven Trumpet Judgments.

At Jericho, the harlot Rahab was saved because she helped the Israelites (the nations will also be judged on how they treat the Jews). Her house on the wall fell and broke as Satan's house on a piece of the planet Rahab will swell "out in a high wall," fall, and destroy the harlot's house at Babylon. Psalms 87:4 gives us this tip: "I will make mention of Rahab and Babylon to them that know me." Their destructions are similar. Both the planet Rahab and the house of the harlot at Babylon are destroyed by a sling stone hurtling in from space.

It seems possible that God created man to prove a point of justice to Satan. In spite of seeing God, one third of the angels disobeyed him. After they were judged, Satan must have appealed their sentence, calling their punishment unfair. However, if man, not being able to see God, and having to walk by faith, would still obey him, it would prove the angels' sentence just. Man's seems to be the more difficult test. Our test, by God's sovereign decree, is to walk by faith, not sight.

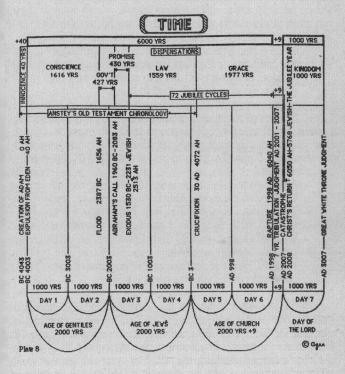

TIME

DISPENSATIONS

INNOCENCE 40 YRS	6000 YRS				+9	1000 YRS
	CONSCIENCE 1616 YRS	PROMISE 430 YRS	LAW 1559 YRS	GRACE 1977 YRS		KINGDOM 1000 YRS
		GOV'T 427 YRS				THE JUBILEE YEAR

72 JUBILEE CYCLES

ANSTEY'S OLD TESTAMENT CHRONOLOGY

- CREATION OF ADAM — 0 AH
- EXPULSION FROM EDEN — 40 AH
- FLOOD 2387 BC — 1656 AH
- ABRAHAM'S CALL 1960 BC — 2083 AH
- EXODUS 1530 BC — 2513 JEWISH 2513 AH
- CRUCIFIXION 30 AD — 4072 AH
- RAPTURE 1998 AD — 6040 AH
- 9 YR. TRIBULATION JUDGMENT AD 2001 – 2007
- CATASTROPHE JUDGMENT AD 2007
- CHRIST'S RETURN — 6050 AH — 5768 JEWISH — THE JUBILEE YEAR
- GREAT WHITE THRONE JUDGMENT

BC 4043
BC 4003

BC 3003

BC 2003

BC 1003

BC 3

AD 998

AD 1998

AD 2007
AD 2008

+9

AD 3007

1000 YRS	1000 YRS	1000 YRS	1000 YRS	1000 YRS	1000 YRS	+9	1000 YRS
DAY 1	DAY 2	DAY 3	DAY 4	DAY 5	DAY 6		DAY 7

AGE OF GENTILES 2000 YRS	AGE OF JEWS 2000 YRS	AGE OF CHURCH 2000 YRS +9	DAY OF THE LORD

Plate 8

© agee

Assembly on the Mount of the Congregation

It is interesting to figure out what God did in the past, but future events grab our attention the most because those things could happen to us. The next event on God's timetable is the Rapture. Will it actually take place on Pentecost?

There are other clues, and more will probably be found. The deeper you dig, the more you find. To him that hath, more will be given. The writer of Hebrews said,

> [Ye] are come unto mount Sion and unto the city of the living God, the heavenly Jerusalem . . . To **the general assembly** and church of the firstborn, which are written in heaven, and to God the Judge of all, and to the spirits of just men made perfect, And to Jesus.[5]

The word translated "general assembly " is *panegurei*, a public festal assembly. This points to the Rapture on a feast day. This assembly may be on the mount of the congregation mentioned by Satan (Lucifer) in his famous "I Will" speech:

> I will ascend into heaven [God's heaven of heavens in the north, above the stars, above the dark galactic cloud that hides his light from man]. I will exalt [set[6]] my throne above the stars of God: I will sit also upon **the mount of the congregation**, in the sides of the north: I will ascend above the heights of the clouds; I will be like the most High.[7]

Satan wants to set up his command post in heaven. This mount of the congregation is "in the sides (*yerekah*, recesses) of the north." It is probably in the apparently empty place in the far north that astronomers have found. They say it is either a tunnel through the stars or covered with a dark galactic blanket. Job 24:7 confirms that "He stretcheth out the north over the empty place." God covered his luminescence from the heaven of heavens with a dark galactic cloud so man could not see it. "With clouds he covereth the light: and commandeth it not to shine by the cloud that cometh betwixt" (Job 36:32). It may be "the covering cast over all people, and the vail that is spread over all nations" of Isaiah 25:7.

The word translated "congregation" in Isaiah 14 is *mowed*, appointment, assembly on a **set solemn feast**, a clue that the Rapture will take place on a feast. We have an appointment to assemble on a set solemn feast day. Is there any feast that could logically apply as well as Pentecost?

The Church era is referred to as the Pentecostal era because it began on Pentecost Sunday, May 28, 30 A.D. Could you think of a better time for the Rapture than Pentecost Sunday, May 31, 1998, the 6,000th year since Adam trudged dismally away from his garden paradise?

The Translation of the Tribulation Saints is at the end of the shortened Tribulation on the Feast of Trumpets. In the "time of trouble . . . at that time thy people shall be delivered, **every one** that shall be found written in the book."[8] By then "**all**" will be present and "**we shall all be changed**. In a moment, in the twinkling of an eye, at the last trump: for the trumpet shall sound, and the dead shall be raised incorruptible, and we shall be changed. For this corruptible must put on incorruption, and this mortal must put on immortality.[9]

Job 14:13,14 hints that a change is associated with the Day of Wrath. "O that thou wouldest hide me in the grave . . . keep me secret, until thy wrath be past, that thou wouldest appoint me a set time, and remember me . . . all the days of my appointed time will I wait, till my **change** come."

The Church is the fifth of the corn taken up in the fifth of the seven good years (1994, 1995, 1996, 1997, **1998**, 1999, 2000) preceding the seven bad years (2001, 2002, 2003, 2004, 2005, 2006, 2007), as in Joseph's interpretation of Pharaoh's dream. The Tribulation saints are taken up near the end of the seven bad years.

In Revelation 6:12, the sixth seal is opened. A parenthetic portion is inserted between the sixth and seventh seals. The Tribulation saints are seen in heaven in the parenthetic portion in 7:9-14, just **before** the seventh seal is broken in 8:1, suggesting this sequence: the sun is darkened, the rocks begin falling, then comes the Translation of the Tribulation Saints just before the Seven trumpet judgments hit Earth.

The Eleven Years of Zedekiah

Jeremiah, a prophet to the nations, dated events according to the eleven years Zedekiah ruled Judah. (In Jewish inclusive reckoning, the first year is counted.) Ezekiel,

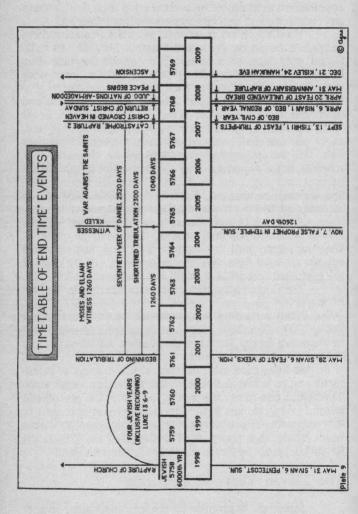

TIMETABLE OF "END TIME" EVENTS

RAPTURE OF CHURCH

FOUR JEWISH YEARS (INCLUSIVE RECKONING) LUKE 13 6-9

BEGINNING OF TRIBULATION

MOSES AND ELIJAH WITNESS 1260 DAYS

WAR AGAINST THE SAINTS

WITNESSES KILLED

SEVENTIETH WEEK OF DANIEL 2520 DAYS

SHORTENED TRIBULATION 2300 DAYS

1260 DAYS

1040 DAYS

CATASTROPHE, RAPTURE 2

CHRIST CROWNED IN HEAVEN

RETURN OF CHRIST, SUNDAY

JUDG OF NATIONS-ARMAGEDDON

PEACE BEGINS

ASCENSION

JEWISH 5758 6000th YR	5759	5760	5761	5762	5763	5764	5765	5766	5767	5768	5769
1998	1999	2000	2001	2002	2003	2004	2005	2006	2007	2008	2009

MAY 31, SIVAN 6, PENTECOST, SUN.

MAY 28, SIVAN 6, FEAST OF WEEKS, MON.

NOV. 7, FALSE PROPHET IN TEMPLE, SUN.

1260th DAY

SEPT. 13, TISHRI 1, FEAST OF TRUMPETS

BEG. OF CIVIL YEAR

APRIL 6, NISAN 1, BEG. OF REGNAL YEAR

APRIL 20 FEAST OF UNLEAVENED BREAD

MAY 31, ANNIVERSARY OF RAPTURE

DEC. 21, KISLEV 24, HANUKAH EVE

© Ogun

Plate 9

a prophet to Israel in exile, dated events according to the year of the exile of Jehoiachin. The eleven years of Zedekiah are the same as the first eleven years of the exile of Jehoiachin for Zedekiah was put in command over Judah in Jehoiachin's place when he was taken to Babylon by Nebuchadnezzar.

The main events of these eleven years seem to parallel things to come during the last eleven years of this age. Even the particular year of the nineteen year Jewish calendar cycle lines up with these. The first year of Zedekiah corresponds with the first year of the Jewish cycle in 5758 (our 1997/8), when the False Prophet takes office after the Rapture. The eleven years are the Jewish 5758, 5759, 5760, 5761, 5762, 5763, 5764, 5765, 5766, 5767, and 5768 (our 2007/8).

Compare past and future events on the chart on page 270. The wicked Zedekiah becoming king when only 21 seems to indicate that the False Prophet will become king of Israel when young. According to Psalms 55:23, the wicked will not live out half their days, and the False Prophet is The Wicked One. Also, Satan said he would be like the Most High, and Jesus was crucified when 33 1/2 years old.

When the Lord put an iron yoke on all nations to serve the king of Babylon in the fourth year, it parallels the beginning of the Tribulation in the fourth year of the reign of the False Prophet. This is when world government's seven year covenant of peace puts all nations under the yoke of the Beast who will move his headquarters from Rome to Babylon.

Jeremiah, who bought land and sealed "**the book of the purchase,**"[10] was also instructed by the Lord to write a scroll about disasters that would come on the nations. I think this is the "book written within and on the backside, sealed with seven seals"[11] seen in Revelation. This **Book of the Purchase of Earth** is sealed with seven seals, which when broken bring plagues on the nations. Ezekiel saw a similar scroll "written within and without: and there was written therein lamentations, and mourning, and woe" (Ezekiel 2:10).

Jeremiah and Ezekiel prophesied of the coming destruction, both dating events. Even this has its parallel. During the first half of the Tribulation, God's two witnesses will also prophecy of the coming destruction, probably explaining Bible chronology.

The blinding of wicked Zedekiah points to the False Prophet. He is the profane wicked prince of Israel whose arm shall be dried up, and whose right eye will be blinded.[12]

"THE SECRETS OF WISDOM.... ARE DOUBLE TO THAT WHICH IS!"

Job 11:6

PAST

Year of Zedekiah and
Year of Exile of Jehoiachin

— Nisan 1, Jewish Regnal Year —

#	Event
1	Wicked Zedekiah became king of Judah when 21 years old.
2	
3	
4	False prophet, Hananiah, lied. The Lord put iron yoke on all nations to serve the king of Babylon. Jeremiah wrote scroll about disasters coming upon Babylon.
5	Both Jeremiah and Ezekiel prophecied of destruction to come and dated events as they took place. Ezekiel saw a vision of The Rock between the cherubim.
6	
7	
8	Zedekiah allied with Egypt, symbol of the world. Judah fell to Babylon, except Jerusalem, Lachish and Azekah. Seige lifted when Babylon marched to meet Pharaoh.
9	Teveth 10: Babylon laid seige to Jerusalem with whole army. King of Babylon camped outside city.
10	
11	Tamuz 9 no food, wall broken through. Zedekiah blinded. Av 10: temple burned Tishri 1: Gedaliah, governor of Judah, assassinated and Tyre, "rock," fell to Babylon.

Plate 10

FUTURE

— Tishri 1, Jewish Civil Year —

Year of Jewish Cycle

#	Year	Event
1	5758 / 1997/8	Wicked False Prophet becomes king of Israel while young, and will not live out half his days.
2	5759 / 1998/9	
3	5760 / 1999/00	
4	5761 / 2000/01	The Tribulation begins. False Prophet lies, signs Covenant putting Israel under yoke of Iran. "Rome" - First seal broken on scroll about disasters coming upon the nations.
5	5762 / 2001/02	Two witnesses prophesy of the coming destruction, probably of when and how it will take place.
6	5763 / 2002/03	
7	5764 / 2003/04	
8	5765 / 2004/05	False Prophet allied with world, now king of this world. Idol in temple 1260th day, war against saints begins, two witnesses killed. "also...Egypt shall not escape."
9	5766 / 2005/06	Will Babylon again lay seige to Jerusalem on Teveth 10? He shall plant the tabernacles of his palace between the seas in the glorious holy mtn.
10	5767 / 2006/07	
11	5768 / 2007/08	This right eye shall be darkened - Tishri: "profane wicked prince of Israel..take off the crown." It's "the vengeance of his temple." The Rock hits Babylon.

When the island of Tyre, which means "rock," fell to Babylon, it could have pictured the rock Icarus, which means "island that exterminates," falling to Babylon, or Icarus may be a type of the rock that will fall. Either way, it will be "a stone like a great millstone . . . Thus with violence shall that great city Babylon be thrown down, and shall be found no more at all."[13]

Reflection of Numerical Meanings

As we examine the dates for the various coming events, more astonishing things become apparent. Even the alignment of the calendars is significant. The sign of the end of the age was in our '67. Forty years later, the age will end in the Jewish '67. It is one of God's miracles that they are now aligned in this manner. Our 2000 is the Jewish 5760. They end with the same numeral until the Jewish New Year in our September or October.

The meaning of Biblical numbers is reflected in the events of end time years. For instance, the number "one" means unity, and in the sabbatical Jewish 5761 (our 2001), when the Tribulation begins, there will be a world government, world bank, world church, and maybe world market.

The number "four" is the number of the Earth. In 5764 (our 2004), in the exact middle of the Tribulation, Satan will be cast down from his home in the heavenlies to Earth.

The number "seven" means completion. In 5767 (our 2007), this age will end. Iniquity will have come to a head.

> Now is the end come . . . the day of trouble is near . . . the rod [the False Prophet] hath blossomed, pride [Satan] hath budded . . . let not the buyer rejoice, nor the seller mourn [who took the 666 to buy and sell]: for wrath is upon all the multitude thereof (Ezekiel 7:2-12).

Number "eight" means new order. Probably in 5758 (our 1998), the Rapture will institute a new order for those who will be translated to heaven. Also, in 5768 (our 2008), Christ will return and set up the new millennial order on Earth.

Thirteen, Satan's number, is reflected in the September 13 date of the asteroid impact. The False Prophet will be wounded just as Satan was wounded when Rahab split apart.

271

Peter was to "watch one hour . . . and pray, lest [he] enter into temptation" (tribulation).[14] Peter could not watch one hour. Can we? One hour of a thousand year day is 41 2/3 years. I expect Christ to return before this hour is up.

Eliminating the Possibilities

Moses spoke of God's wrath in Psalms 90:11. Therefore, his prayer, "Return, O Lord, how long?" in verse 13 refers to the Second Coming following the Day of Wrath.

I believe we can now answer his question. I expect Christ to return Sunday, **April 6, 2008** (Nisan 1, 5768). By the process of elimination, we can determine that **this seems to be the only possible date** for his glorious return.

According to Ezekiel, there will be seven Jewish months between the beginning of the Day of the Lord on Tishri 1 and the return of Christ as King on Nisan 1.[15] Normally, there are six. The year of his return is a leap year.

Since most of the seven year Tribulation must run its course between the Rapture and the Second Advent, and the Rapture has not happened, he cannot return earlier than 1998.

The sign of the end of the age appeared in 1967, and that generation will see him coming (1967 + 40 = 2007). For this search, I have added eight extra years for good measure.

The only years between these dates in which the Jews insert a 13th month are our 2000, 2003, 2005, 2008, 2011 and 2014. Therefore, we have but seven possible years for the Lord's return, and 2008 is among them.

This list can be narrowed down to three possibilities. He must return on **the Lord's day**, Sunday. Dramatizing it for us himself, Jesus was resurrected (came back) on Sunday. He ascended to the Father and returned that same day.[16] In the evening, he reappeared saying, "Peace be unto you," for he will return as King of kings, Lord of lords, and the Prince of Peace. Even when John "became in the spirit on the Lord's day,"[17] playing out the Rapture, Christ was revealed on Sunday. That is "the coming of our Lord Jesus Christ . . . in **the day** of our Lord Jesus Christ."[18] It is His day. He comes on Sunday as the "Sun of righteousness" (Malachi 4:2). He is the Firstfruits, and the Feast of Firstfruits is "on the morrow after the sabbath [the Jewish Saturday sabbath]," Sunday.[19]

Nisan 1 falls on Sunday in our 2001, 2005 and 2008. The year 2001 is eliminated for it does not have an intercalary month. This leaves 2005 and 2008. **This can be cut down to one possibility**. He must return in a sabbatic year. The new moon and sabbath were shadows of his return. Colossians 2:16 says that "the new moon, or . . . the sabbath days . . . are a shadow of things to come; but the body is of Christ." Nisan 1, 5768 (2008) is the new moon in a sabbatic year.

The "Son of man is Lord also of the sabbath,"[20] and he will be crowned King of kings and Lord of lords the first day (the new moon) of the sabbatic year that begins the sabbatic millennium. During that year, seven months after the Coronation, on the new moon, the first day of the Jewish regnal year, I believe he will return and the year of Jubilee begin. After that the Judgment of the Nations and Armageddon will eliminate all unbelievers, Satan and the demons will be chained, and all flesh will worship Christ in truth.

> For as the new heavens and the new earth, which I will make, shall remain before me, saith the LORD, so shall your seed and your name remain. And it shall come to pass, that from **one** new moon [first day of one certain month, Nisan 1] to another, and from **one** sabbath [one sabbatic year, 5768] to another, shall **all** flesh come to worship before me.[21]

The seventieth seven of Daniel,[22] the Tribulation, begins and ends with sabbatic years. The year 2005 is eliminated for it is not a sabbatic year. It seems that we are left with **only one possible year for his return, 2008**.

This date can be proved another way. If we only consider the 2,300 day shortened Tribulation that precedes the Second Advent, we will arrive at exactly the same conclusion.

There are only nine times between 1991 and 2015 that you can add 2,300 days to Sivan 6, the Feast of Weeks, and end on Tishri 1, the Feast of Trumpets. The year following each of these periods is our 1993, 1996, 1997, 2000, 2004, 2008, 2012, 2013 and 2015.

In only two of the years listed does Nisan 1 fall on a Sunday, in 1997 and 2008. The year 1997 has a thirteenth month but is not a sabbatic year, and he can't return before 1998 anyway. **Again 2008 seems to be the only possible year** for the return of our Lord Jesus Christ.

He went to the Temple when he was twelve years old, in 8 A.D. He will come again to the Temple in 2008 A.D.

The Church in the Wilderness Forty Years

Forty years after 30 A.D., when Israel should have recognized the time of the First Advent, destruction hit in 70 A.D. I believe the church also has been given 40 years of probation, and destruction will hit this time in '07 A.D.

Israel is called "the church in the wilderness"[23] to help us relate their experiences to those of the Church.

> Now all these things happened unto them [Israel] for ensamples [*tupoi*, **types**]: and they are written for our admonition, upon whom the ends of the world [*aionon*, ages] are come.[24]

Notice, it literally says "ends of the ages." The last segment of the Age of the Jews runs concurrently with the last of the Age of the Church. One Beast will be of the church, the other a Jew. Also, the fullness of the gentiles is not complete until all Israel is born in a day. Romans 11:25-27 [NASB] says that "a partial hardening has happened to Israel **until** the fullness of the Gentiles has come in [at Rapture II]; and thus all Israel will be saved [born in a day, the same day Rapture II takes place on the Feast of Trumpets in the Jewish 5768]". Probably all three ages, of Gentiles, Jews, and the Church, will have "judgment" extensions and end in a photo finish.

Idolatrous Israel was tested 40 days before Moses came down from Mt. Sinai and smashed the stone tablets.[25] Their armies were tested 40 days before a stone from David's sling killed Goliath,[26] the giant angel-man, and stopped the Philistine army. Is God trying to show us that we have just 40 time periods in which to repent before another angel-man being is deposed, the giant multi-nation army stopped, and the harlot World Church "broken to shivers"[27] by a stone?

The core of this world church exists today. It has both Christian and Babylonian elements dating from the time when Emperor Constantine declared Christianity the state religion. This put pagans in the church of Rome. When the Rapture pulls out the Christians, what is left? Presto! "MYSTERY, BABYLON THE GREAT, THE MOTHER OF HARLOTS AND ABOMINATIONS OF THE EARTH"[28] appears in the forefront.

The Lord says, "Come out of her my people, that ye be not partakers of her sins, and that ye receive not of her plagues."[29]

The majority missed their clues at the First Advent. Today many will do the same, but now and especially during the Tribulation, we need to try our very best to understand Scripture. It won't be needed as much later on. The Lord said that during the millennial Day of the Lord, "they shall all know me, from the least of them unto the greatest of them."[30]

Be sure to look for other developments during these last forty years. Remember, Micah said, "According to the days of thy [Israel's] coming out of the land of Egypt [forty years] will I shew unto him marvellous things. The nations shall see and be confounded at all their [Israel's] might."[31]

These new things we are learning are part of these marvellous things. Already the world has been astonished by the might of tiny Israel. It should be evident that God is helping them. How else could she exist against such odds?

New Eyes to See With

Pray for understanding as you read the scriptures again with this timetable in mind. You will probably enjoy Scripture as never before. Now that your eyes are opened, you will keep finding little skits that will help you see the prophetic picture more clearly. Scattered throughout Scripture like ribbons of silver in the rock are precious pieces of the story that God hid from our eyes for so long. Now you will be able to recognize interlocking pieces and fit them into the puzzle.

The scriptures reflect God's intentions exactly. For instance, the gap of nearly 2,000 years between the birth of Jesus and the birth of the Church was probably pictured for us by the space that was to be left between the children of Israel and the Ark. Jesus was a child of Israel, and the Ark (*aron*, container) was the container of the word of God, just as the Church is the container of The Word, Christ. Yet, it will not be exactly 2,000 years. He was born in B.C. 5 and the Rapture will probably be in 1998. That is 2,002 years. (There is no zero year. Add B.C. and A.D. years and subtract one.)

Scripture is worded very carefully. Joshua 3:4 says, "Yet there shall be a space between you and it, **about** two thousand cubits by measure." The Bible is always correct down to the tiniest details. It is literally "about" 2,000 years.

Over and over, simple details of Israel's history are recorded so that the order of events of the end times that they prefigure are kept in their proper order. For example:

> Jacob went on his journey . . . behold a well . . . three flocks of sheep lying by it . . . thither were all the flocks gathered: and they rolled the stone from the well's mouth, and watered the sheep, and put the stone again upon the well's mouth in his place. . . . Jacob said . . . water ye the sheep . . . they said, We cannot, until **all the flocks be gathered together**.[32]

In typology, believers are sheep and Christ is the shepherd who gave his life for the sheep.[33] There are three flocks, Old Testament saints, Church saints, and Tribulation saints. All three are to be gathered to Christ in heaven. The first rank to arrive must wait on the last, then **all** will receive their rewards together. At that time, a stone that is rolled out of its place will hit the mouth of the abyss in the earth that's prepared for the devil and his angels. The correlation is good.

It is not hard to see end time events in the story of David (type of Christ), Nabal ("man of Belial") and Abigail (Bride of Christ). She spoke as if speaking to Christ:

> **I pray** thee, forgive the trespass of thine handmaid [prays for forgiveness for sin] . . . **my lord** [she accepts the Lord] fighteth the battles of the LORD, and evil hath not been found in thee all thy days. Yet a man [Nabal, i.e., the Satanic False Prophet] is risen to pursue thee [he rises to power when the Rapture takes place], and to seek thy soul: but **the soul of my lord shall be bound in the bundle of life with the LORD thy God**; and the souls of **thine enemies . . . shall he sling out, as out of the middle of a sling** [as when the asteroid is slung at Christ's enemies]. . . . when the LORD . . . shall have **appointed thee ruler over Israel** [on the Feast of Trumpets] . . . then remember thine handmaid [the Marriage of the Lamb takes place on the Feast of Trumpets]. And David

said . . . **blessed be thou** [the blessed hope] . . . **Go up in peace to thine house** [Rapture I]; see, **I have hearkened to thy voice, and have accepted thy person**. . . . Nabal . . . held a **feast** [the False Prophet comes to power following the Rapture at midnight on the Feast of Pentecost] . . . he was very drunken . . . in the morning . . . his heart died within him, and he became as a stone. And it came to pass about **ten days after**, that the LORD smote Nabal, and he died [it is about ten years between Rapture I and the Day of Wrath]. And . . . David . . . communed with Abigail, to **take her to him to wife** [the Marriage of the Lamb is that same day].[34]

After Rapture I, "then shall that Wicked be revealed... Even him, whose coming is after the working of Satan."[35] He will be smitten and the Bride of Christ married about ten years later. About ten years from the Rapture on May 31, 1998 is September 13, 2008, when Christ becomes King and the stone is slung at the earth as if from a sling.

The account of Solomon, the son of David, being anointed king is a type of Christ's Coronation Day:

[Make] his [son of David's, i.e., Christ's] throne greater than the throne of my lord king David. . . . the priest took an horn of oil out of the tabernacle, and anointed Solomon. And they blew the **trumpet** [Feast of Trumpets]; and all the people said, God save king Solomon. And **all** the people **came up** [Rapture II] after him, and the people piped with pipes, and rejoiced with **great joy** [the saints receive their rewards on the Feast of Trumpets], so that **the earth rent** with the sound of them.[36]

Jesus, the son of David, will have in heaven a throne greater than the throne of king David on earth. He will be crowned on the Feast of Trumpets, a day of joy in heaven, but also the day when with great noise the earth will be split and knocked upside down. Only God could plant such good clues.

Isaac is the best type of Christ we have. He was **married when he was 40 years old**, a hint that Christ will be married in the 40th year of our probation.

When Abraham's servant went to get a wife for Isaac, Rebekah's "brother and her mother said, Let the damsel abide with us a few days, at the least **ten**, after that she shall go." The servant was anxious to be on his way, so they called the beautiful Rebekah and asked her.

She answered, **"I will go,"** and was taken to another country. There the son of promise took her into his mother's tent (Sarah had died when he was 37), and Rebekah became his wife when he was 40 years old.[37]

The ten days after which she could go suggest the ten years after which the Tribulation Saints can go to heaven. Rebekah went at the first call, as the Bride of Christ will do. She could have waited ten days and then gone, but she did not. At the Rapture, we will be taken to a place Christ has prepared for us, where the dead in Christ dwell. There we will be married to Christ in the 40th year of probation and testing.

Picturing this 40 years of probation and the Marriage of the Lamb for us, Jesus was tested in the wilderness 40 days then went to the marriage at Cana, where he made water wine. After the Last Supper, Jesus told his disciples that he would not drink any more of the fruit of the vine until he would drink it new with them **in his Father's kingdom**. These things help us understand the full import of the marriage at Cana.

> And the **third day** [i.e., the Day of the Lord] there was a marriage in Cana [erect, i.e., high] of Galilee [circuit, circle, i.e., a heavenly orbiting sphere] . . . **Jesus was called, and his disciples, to the marriage**. And when they wanted wine, the mother of Jesus saith unto him, They have no wine. . . . there were . . . six waterpots of **stone**, after the manner of the **purifying** of the Jews . . . Jesus saith . . . Fill the waterpots with water. . . . Draw out now, and bear unto the governor. . . . When the ruler of the feast had tasted the water that was made wine . . . the governor of the **feast** called the bridegroom, And saith . . . thou hast kept the good wine until now. This beginning of miracles did Jesus in Cana of Galilee, and

> **manifested forth his glory**; and his
> disciples believed on him. **After this he
> went down** to Capernaum [which means to
> make reconciliation].[38]

This is a foreview of the Marriage of the Lamb on a heavenly
sphere in the third 1,000 year day since his first advent. The
Old Testament Saints, including his mother, are there. Jesus is
called before his Father to receive his crown, and the Church
Saints are called to the marriage. It is the Feast of Trumpets,
the day when Jesus will manifest his glory, drink the best
wine with them anew in his Father's kingdom and purify the
earth with a stone. After seven more months, he will go down
to reconcile things on earth.

Rapture II is as the days of Lot.

> **Just after sunrise** Lot entered Zoar. Then
> the LORD rained sulphur and **fire from heaven,**
> from the LORD on Sodom and Gomorrah . . .
> **Early in the morning** Abraham **went up** to
> the spot where he had stood in the LORD's
> presence. As he **looked down** upon . . . that
> whole valley, he saw the smoke of the country
> rising like the smoke from a furnace. . . .
> **God . . . led Lot out of the catastrophe,**
> when He was over-turning the cities.[39]

This suggests that the translation will occur just after sunrise.
No wonder Psalms 30:5 says, "For his anger endureth but a
moment; in his favour is life: weeping may endure for a night,
but joy cometh in the morning." Evidently, the catastrophe
will strike at noon, and Rapture II must take place before that.

Amos 8:9,10 says, "I will cause the sun to go down at
noon, and I will darken the earth in the clear day: And I will
turn your **feasts** into mourning."

God was to work a work that unbelievers would not
believe until they saw it happening. It had not yet been fulfilled when Luke quoted the prophets in Acts:13:40,41.

He said, "Beware therefore, lest that come upon you,
which is spoken of in the prophets; Behold, ye despisers, and
wonder, and perish: for I work a work in your days [our
days, the fifth and sixth 1,000 year days], a work which ye
shall in no wise believe, though a man declare it unto you."

Habakkuk 1:5-10 probably began to come to pass when Iraq took Kuwait on August 2, 1990. It says,

> Behold ye among the heathen . . . I will work a work in your days, which ye will not believe, though it be told you. For, lo, I raise up the Chaldeans, that bitter and hasty nation, which shall march through the breadth of the land, to possess the dwellingplaces that are not their's. They are terrible . . . their judgment and their dignity shall proceed of themselves. Their horses also are swifter than the leopards [they took control quickly] . . . and their horsemen [the military] . . . shall fly as the eagle that hasteth to eat [in fast airplanes]. They shall come all for violence . . . they shall scoff at the kings . . . they shall deride every strong hold; for they shall heap dust [hurried troop movements in the desert stirs up dust] and take it.

Nebuchadnezzar made Babylon the most splendid capitol city of antiquity. This will repeat in our days, but the seventh head of the great red dragon will be different. Instead of one nation overrunning the world, it looks like **world government itself "shall devour the whole earth."**

Scripture indicates that Babylon will become the headquarters of world government. Iraq has begun its restoration as a tourist attraction, but soon, the nations will join in rebuilding the magnificent city. It will be very costly—and all for nothing. The nations' labor is only fuel for the flames.

We may now (in 1991) have only seven years until the Rapture. Are you ready?

Do you have family and friends that you want to talk to about Christ before it is too late. Now is the time to make sure that every member of your family has accepted our Lord and Saviour Jesus Christ. You don't want to be separated from your loved ones for eternity if you can help it.

I pray "That the God of our Lord Jesus Christ, the Father of glory, may give unto you [the reader of this book] the spirit of wisdom and revelation in the knowledge of him: **The eyes of your understanding being enlightened;** that ye may know what is the hope of his calling."[40]

Take heed of God's word. Pray. Watch, walk worthy, and win the prize of the upward call of God in Christ Jesus, for the Lord said,

> I will shake the heavens [including Satan's asteroid] and the earth; And I will overthrow the throne of kingdoms [seat of the leader of world government], and I will destroy the strength [armies] of the kingdoms of the heathen [*goyim*, nations]; and I will overthrow the chariots [the asteroid that Satan rides and the Earth that we ride], and those that ride in them; and the horses [of Revelation 6] and their riders [the Beast and False Prophet] shall come down.[41]

> In that day the LORD with his sore [*qasheh*, sharp, hard] and great and strong sword [destroying weapon] shall punish leviathan the piercing serpent [Satan in the False Prophet] . . . and he shall slay the dragon [the world government] that is in the sea [the nations].[42]

Notes

Introduction
1. Daniel 12:4
2. 1 Corinthians 13:12
3. Matthew 13:12
4. 1 Thessalonians 5:21

Chapter 1: The Wise Shall Understand
1. 2 Peter 3:8
2. Matthew 24:21,22
3. Luke 12:56
4. Daniel 12:10
5. Mark 13:37
6. Revelation 3:3
7. 1 Thessalonians 4:16,17
8. Titus 2:13
9. Hebrews 11:5
10. 1 Corinthians 10:32
11. Hebrews 5:12
12. Hebrews 5:14
13. Isaiah 28:9
14. Acts 1:7,8
15. Luke 12:42
16. Ecclesiastes 3:1
17. 1 John 2:18 Green's Interlinear Hebrew/Greek-English Bible
18. 2 Peter 3:8
19. Psalms 89:29
20. 1 John 2:20,27
21. Mark 13:23
22. 1 Peter 1:10-12
23. Acts 16:30,31
24. Romans 10:9,10
25. Psalms 12:6
26. Isaiah 28:13
27. 1 Corinthians 2:14
28. Proverbs 1:23
29. Proverbs 2:3-5
30. Jeremiah 23:19, 20
31. James 1:5-7
32. Job 8:8-10
33. Colossians 2:16,17
34. Matthew 24:36

35. Matthew 25:13
36. Matthew 26:40
37. Matthew 26:41
38. Revelation 13:17
39. Revelation 14:9-11
40. Amos 3:7
41. 2 Corinthians 5:19
42. Job 28:11
43. Ecclesiastes 8:5

Chapter 2: A Pacific Moon?

1. Psalms 33:6-9
2. Psalms 8:3,4
3. Isaiah 45:18
4. Pananides, Nicholas A.. *Introductory Astronomy*. (Reading, Mass.: Addison-Wesley Publ. Co., Inc., 1973) p. 120-123.
5. "Did Comets Kill the Dinosaurs?" *Time*, May 6, 1985, p. 72-83.
6. Trefil, James S.. *Space Time Infinity*. (Washington, D.C.: Smithsonian Institution) p. 164-167.
7. "Huge asteroid hit the Pacific eons ago, UCLA study says," *The Register*, July 12,1988, p. C-9.
8. Morris, Henry M.. *Scientific Creationism*. (CLP Publishers, 1974) p. 158-165.
9. Whitcomb, John C. and De Young, Donald. *The Moon, It's Creation, Form and Significance*. (Winona Lake, Indiana: BMH Books, 1978) p. 59-61.
10. Poinar, George O. , Jr.. "The Amber Ark," *Natural History*, Dec., 1988, p. 45.
11. Bearak, Barry. "Archeological Discovery in Florida, Bones of Prehistoric Man, Animals Found Together," *Los Angeles Times*, Jan. 15, 1986, part 1, p. 10.
12. Bearak, *ibid*.
13. Revelation 6:12, Joel 2:10
14. Anstey, Martin. *The Romance of Bible Chronology*. (London: Marshall Bros., 1913) Vol. 1.
15. Genesis 2:5
16. Unger, Merrill F. *Unger's Bible Dictionary*. (Chicago: Moody Press, 1957) p. 350.
17. Genesis 2:14
18. 1 Corinthians 15:39
19. Genesis 1:28

Chapter 3: Seven Part Test

1. Numbers 14:34
2. Jeremiah 30:9
3. Estep, Bullinger, etc.
4. 1 Corinthians 2:9
5. Amos 1:5
6. Genesis 3:24
7. Jeremiah 12:12
8. Genesis 7:19
9. Jude 6
10. Deuteronomy 3:11
11. Genesis 6:9
12. Genesis 10:32
13. Daniel 12:4
14. Wooley, Leonard, *Ur: The First Phases*. (London: Penguin Books Limited, 1946) p. 12.
15. Halley, Henry H.. *Halley's Bible Handbook*. (Minneapolis: Zondervan, 1964 edition) p. 40,41.
16. Genesis 6:3,13
17. Genesis 10:25
18. Genesis 11:1-9
19. Genesis 12:2,3
20. Genesis 16:2
21. Genesis 17:2-17
22. Genesis 17:21
23. Genesis 18:32
24. Genesis 18:14
25. Isaiah 66:8
26. Genesis15:18
27. Genesis 15:13
28. Exodus 12:40
29. Jeremiah 25:11
30. Daniel 9:2
31. Anstey, *op. cit.*, Vol. 1, p. 278-293.
32. Jeremiah 27:7
33. Colossians 2:14
34. Galatians 3:24
35. Romans 1:20
36. 1 Corinthians 15:45-49

Chapter 4: Days of Heaven

1. Psalms 89:29
2. Tatford, Frederick A.. *Will There be a Millennium?* (Sussex: Prophetic Witness Publ. House, 1969) p. 17-21.

3.   Larkin, Clarence. *Dispensational Truth*. (Philadelphia: Larkin, 1918) p. 16.
4.   Job 24:1
5.   Revelation 20:4
6.   1 Corinthians 15:45

Chapter 5: Ages of Time

1.   1 Corinthians 2:7
2.   Revelation 19:13
3.   John 1:1-3,14
4.   Ephesians 3:6-11
5.   1 Corinthians 10:32
6.   Hebrews 11:3
7.   Heb 1:2
8.   Genesis 1:14
9.   Daniel 8:13,14
10.   1 Corinthians 10:11
11.   Matthew 12:32 Green's Interlinear Hebrew/Greek-English Bible
12.   2 Timothy 2:15
13.   1 Corinthians 10:32
14.   Ezekiel 18:31
15.   Ecclesiastes 8:5
16.   Job 7:18
17.   Isaiah 28:17-22
18.   Joshua 10:11
19.   Revelation 16:21
20.   Joshua 10:13
21.   2 Kings 20:9-11
22.   Matthew 13:39-42
23.   Malachi 4:5,6
24.   2 Timothy 2:15

Chapter 6:   Former and Latter Rain

1.   Matthew 23:39
2.   2 Corinthians 5:19
3.   1 Corinthians 15:45,47
4.   Luke 3:38
5.   Romans 10:9
6.   John 14:7-10
7.   John 8:58
8.   Isaiah 45:21-23
9.   1 Timothy 3:16
10.   Philippians 2:9-11
11.   Revelation 22:16

12. Revelation 22:13
13. Matthew 1:23
14. Isaiah 9:6
15. Psalms72:6
16. Psalms 65:9
17. Jeremiah 2:13; 17:13
18. Job 37:6
19. Hosea 14:5-9
20. James 5:7
21. Jeremiah 5:24
22. "Christmas." *World Book Ency.* 1966, Vol. 3, p. 416.
23. Joel 2:23,27
24. Psalms 12:6
25. Psalms 132:17,18; Luke 1:68,69
26. Malachi 3:1
27. Ezekiel 45:18,19
28. Luke 6:5

Chapter 7: Day of the Cross

1. Isaiah 44:28; 45:13
2. Whiston, William. *The Works of Flavius Josephus.* (Phila.: Henry T. Coates and Co., n. d.) Book XI, Ch. 1.1.
3. Anstey, *op. cit.*, p. 278-293.
4. Luke 3:23
5. John 1:48
6. John 2:20
7. Whiston's Josephus, Book XV, Ch. XI. 1.
8. Turner, C. H.. "Adversaria Chronologica," *Journal of Theological Studies.* Oct., 1901, 3:110-123.
9. John 4:35
10. Deuteronomy 16:16; Luke 22:1
11. Andrews, Samuel J.. *The Life of our Lord upon Earth.* (Grand Rapids: Zondervan, 1954) p. 37,38.
12. Luke 3:1
13. Ramsey, *Was Christ Born in Bethlehem.* (London: Hodder and Stoughton, 1898) p. 200.
14. John 11:9
15. John 12:1,2,12,13
16. John 12:13
17. Luke 19:42
18. Mark 11:11
19. Mark 11:12
20. Genesis 1:5
21. Mark 11:19,20,27

22. Mark 13:1
23. Luke 21:37,38
24. Mark 14:8
25. Mark 14:1,2
26. John 18:28
27. John 13:29
28. John 13:30
29. Mark 14:12
30. John 19:14
31. Exodus. 12:18
32. John 19:14-16
33. Hebrews 9:22
34. John 19:31
35. 1 Corinthians 5:7
36. Exodus 12:6, literal translation. Green's Interlinear Hebrew/Greek-English Bible says "between the evenings."
37. Deuteronomy 16:6
38. Malachi 4:2
39. Ephesians 4:9
40. Matthew 12:40
41. Luke 23:43
42. John 2:19
43. Luke 24:20,21
44. Matthew 27:62,66
45. Luke 23:50-56; 24:1,2
46. Mark 16:1-6
47. Goudoever, J. Van. *Biblical Calendars.* (Lieden, Netherlands: E. J. Brill, 1959) p. 162.
48. Nehemiah 2:11,12
49. A. N. Sherman-White. *Fifty Letters of Pliny.* (N. Y.: Oxford University Press, 1967) 10.94.
50. *The Complete Works of Tacitus.* (N. Y. Random House, 1942) transl. by Alfred John Church and William Jackson Brodribb. 15.44, p. 380.
51. "Jesus Grew to Manhood Amidst Violence, Struggle and Peril," *The Register*, Dec. 20, 1969. p. A4.
52. *Halley's Bible Handbook*, p. 443.
53. Herford, Robert Travers. *Christianity in Talmud and Midrash.* (N. J. Reference Book Publishers, 1966) p. 48,62,83,348.

Chapter 8: Sign of the End of the Age

1. Matthew 24:3
2. Matthew 24:32,33
3. Hosea 9:10; Joel 1:6,7; Ezekiel 36:8

4. Luke 21:31
5. Matthew 24:30
6. Micah 7:15
7. Daniel 9:27
8. Daniel 9:24-27

Chapter 9: Modern Parallels

1. Job 11:6
2. Jeremiah 23:7,8
3. Job 8:8-10
4. Genesis 15:13; Acts 7:6,7
5. Exodus 12:40,41; Galatians 3:17,18
6. Acts 13:19,20
7. 1 Kings 6:1
8. Daniel 9;25,26
9. Daniel 9:24
10. Acts 7:6,7; Genesis 15:13
11. Webber, David, and Hutchings, Noah. *Is This the Last Century?* (Nashville: Thomas Nelson Publ.) p. 130, 131.
12. *Look,* "Israel," 4-30-68. p. 35.
13. "Luther, Martin," *Encyclopedia Americana*, 1949, XVII, 717.
14. 1 Samuel 15:23
15. 1 Samuel 29:1; 31:3-5
16. Mark 10:47
17. 1 Kings 6:1
18. 1 Corinthians 3:16
19. Daniel 9:25
20. Daniel 9:24
21. Galatians 4:22-26
22. Genesis 17:17
23. Romans 9:9
24. Song of Solomon 3:11
25. Genesis 25:20
26. Leviticus 23:10,11,16,1

Chapter 10: The Prize

1. Revelation 3:3
2. Romans 15:12
3. Genesis 5:24
4. Revelation 3:8-13
5. Matthew 25:30
6. 2 Thessalonians 2:3
7. John 14:2,3
8. 1 Thessalonians 4:16,17

9.   1 Thessalonians 5:4-11
10. Titus 2:13
11. Job 5:19-24
12. John 21:20,24
13. John 20:17-19
14. Matthew 22:30
15. Revelation 1:19
16. Psalms 118:20
17. Revelation 4:1
18. 1 Thessalonians 4:16
19. Revelation 1:11
20. Revelation 4:1
21. Revelation 5:9,10
22. Matthew 19:28
23. Luke 21:34-36
24. Acts 2:6
25. Exodus 23:16
26. Exodus 34:22
27. James 1:18
28. Matthew 13:24,25,38
29. Leviticus 23:17
30. Hebrews 12:18-25
31. Exodus 19:1
32. Deuteronomy 10:4
33. Nehemiah 10:35,36
34. Isaiah 61:3
35. James 1:18
36. Numbers 28:26
37. 1 Corinthians 16:8,9
38. Acts 20:16,22
39. Revelation 5:9
40. 1 Corinthians 10:4
41. Song of Solomon 2:10-14
42. Numbers 13:20,21
43. Luke 13:6-9
44. Exodus 4:22
45. Hebrews 11:39,40
46. Matthew 24:37-42
47. Genesis 7:6
48. Genesis 7:10
49. Philippians 3:8-14
50. 1 Corinthians 9:24-27
51. 2 Timothy 4:7,8

Chapter 11: Foolish Virgins

1. Matthew 5:13
2. John 15:1,2
3. Galatians 5:22,23
4. Leviticus 23:22
5. Numbers 13:20
6. Obadiah 5
7. Deuteronomy 24:19-21; Leviticus 19:9,10
8. John 6:39
9. Numbers 10:4
10. 2 Peter 1:5-11
11. 1 John 1:9
12. Philippians 1:9-11
13. Colossians 1:18
14. Ephesians 2:8,9
15. Ephesians 4:30
16. Revelation 3:19
17. Hebrews 12:6
18. Matthew 24:42-51
19. Revelation 3:3
20. Matthew 24:48-51
21. Luke 12:42-46
22. Revelation 1:16
23. Revelation 2:12-17
24. Matthew 25:30
25. Revelation 19:8, margin
26. Matthew 22:11-13
27. Matthew 8:11,12
28. Revelation 3:17
29. Revelation 16:15
30. Hebrews 12:11-14
31. Jude 23
32. Revelation 7:14
33. Revelation 3:4,5
34. Revelation 3:18
35. Revelation 3:16
36. Revelation 3:21
37. Revelation 3:11
38. Revelation 3:18
39. Revelation 3:19
40. Revelation 4:1
41. Matthew 25:1-12
42. Galatians 4:4-7

43. Philippians 2:14,15
44. Colossians 2:18 ASV
45. Matthew 25:11,12
46. Matthew 7:21
47. 1 John 3:23
48. Galatians 5:22
49. 1 John 4:8
50. 1 John 4:12
51. Ephesians 5:17,18
52. Ephesians 4:30-32
53. 1 John 1:6-9
54. John 13:8
55. John 6:44
56. 1 Corinthians 10:12
57. Esther 2:17
58. Matthew 22:2-14
59. Revelation 19:8, margin
60. Ephesians 5:25-27
61. Luke 11:5-13
62. Revelation 2:10
63. Revelation 17:14

Chapter 12: Seventieth Week of Daniel

1. Daniel 9:24-27
2. Ptolemaic dates are out of sync with the Bible by 82 years.
3. Daniel 4:32
4. Matthew 3:12
5. Daniel 3:1-6
6. Revelation 13:18
7. Daniel 2:31-45
8. Revelation 17:15
9. Revelation 13:3; Daniel 2:40-44
10. Zechariah 11:8
11. Revelation 17:13
12. Revelation 17:11,12
13. Revelation 17:14
14. Daniel 9:26
15. Daniel 11:21
16. Revelation 16:13,14
17. Revelation 17:15
18. Daniel 9:26
19. Ezekiel 21:25
20. Zechariah 11:17
21. Habakkuk 2:5

22. Daniel 11:21
23. Job 11:6
24. Jeremiah 25:1
25. Daniel 11:21
26. Revelation 19:20
27. Revelation 13:5
28. Revelation 2:13; 13:2,4; 17:6,9,18
29. Psalms 55:23
30. Isaiah 9:14,15
31. Daniel 9:26
32. Revelation 13:2
33. Daniel 2:37
34. Daniel 4:29,30
35. Zechariah 5:5-11
36. Revelation 18:21
37. Revelation 11:6
38. Jeremiah 25:1
39. Ezra 4:24; 6:15
40. Isaiah 14:14
41. Isaiah 10:14
42. Zechariah 5:4
43. 1 Peter 4:17
44. Revelation 6:8
45. Jeremiah 14:13
46. Jeremiah 14:14,15
47. Isaiah 28:15,18
48. Habakkuk 2:5,6
49. 2 John 7, margin
50. Psalms 55:23; Jeremiah 17:11; Job 21:21
51. Isaiah 14:14
52. Genesis 49:17
53. Daniel 7:25
54. Daniel 7:8,20,21; Revelation 13:7,12
55. Daniel 7:9-11
56. Revelation 12:4
57. Revelation 12:7-9
58. 2 Thessalonians 2:3-9
59. Isaiah 32:7
60. Psalms 10:7
61. Zechariah 11:16,17
62. Isaiah 32:14
63. Daniel 11:36-39
64. Joel 3:2

65. John 12:6
66. Isaiah 22:15
67. Isaiah 10:13,14
68. Habakkuk 2:5
69. Proverbs 29:6
70. 1 Corinthians 10:13
71. Ezekiel 17:4
72. Revelation 18:11-19
73. Revelation 18:2
74. Luke 12:18
75. Jeremiah 51:44,45
76. Revelation 18:11,15,19

Chapter 13: The Final Crescendo Begins

1. Revelation 11:3-12
2. Hebrews 11:5
3. Isaiah 54:5
4. Matthew 17:2,3
5. Colossians 4:10
6. Revelation 11:6
7. Revelation 17:11
8. James 5:17,18; cf. 1 Kings 17:1
9. Revelation 6:5,6
10. Genesis 41:26,27
11. Matthew 13:24-30
12. Numbers 10:4
13. John 5:43
14. Revelation 11:6
15. Isaiah 14:17
16. Revelation 11:3
17. Revelation 20:2
18. Revelation 12:4
19. Revelation 12:7
20. Revelation 13:11
21. Daniel 9:27
22. Psalms 94:20
23. Hosea 9:7,8
24. Isaiah 22:15, a type
25. 2 Chronicles 9:13
26. Revelation 14:9-11
27. Revelation 11:7; 20:3; 17:8,11
28. Revelation 11:8
29. Matthew 24:15-23
30. Revelation 12:14

31. Revelation 12:15
32. Revelation 11:3
33. Revelation 12:13,14
34. Revelation 11:12
35. Revelation 11:13
36. Revelation 19:20
37. Isaiah 33:8, Amplified (the Dead Sea Scrolls say "the witnesses"); cf. RSV and Confraternity
38. Revelation 12:17
39. 1 Thessalonians 5:23
40. Romans 8:9,10
41. Revelation 5:9-11
42. Isaiah 25:7
43. Ezekiel 7:2-8
44. Ezekiel 7:10,11
45. Revelation 6:16,17
46. Ezekiel 38:22,23
47. Ezekiel 22:24
48. Revelation 8:8
49. Isaiah 28:18
50. Jeremiah 51:42,43
51. Isaiah 24:1,5,6
52. Ezekiel 7:17

Chapter 14: The Last Trump

1. Matthew 24:31
2. Mark 13:24-27
3. Isaiah 40:31
4. Matthew 24:28
5. Luke 17:28-37
6. 1 Corinthians 15:51-53
7. Numbers 10:2-4
8. 1 Corinthians 15:22,23
9. Ephesians 4:4-6
10. John 6:37-39
11. James 1:18
12. 2 Chronicles 31:7
13. Joel 2:15-20
14. Revelation 4:4
15. Revelation 1:6
16. Mark 13:23-27
17. Revelation 6:16,17
18. Proverbs 11:4,8
19. Psalms 27:5

20. Psalms 89:36,37
21. Psalms 78:69
22. Hosea 2:9
23. Micah 7:1-9
24. Revelation 3:20
25. Luke 12:35-37
26. Revelation 20:4,5
27. Daniel 12:1,2
28. Jeremiah 30:7
29. Psalms 50:3-6
30. Joel 2:31,32
31. Psalms 47:1-9

Chapter 15: Coronation Day

1. Job 11:6
2. Esther 2:8-19
3. Job 5:24
4. Revelation 19:7
5. Song of Solomon 3:11, Amplified
6. Romans 8:17
7. Joel 3:14
8. Ezekiel 38:2
9. Ezekiel 38:15
10. Ezekiel 38:18
11. 1 Samuel 17:47
12. Zechariah 5:3
13. Jeremiah 30:23,24
14. Nahum 2:3,4 (LXX)
15. Jeremiah 23:19,20 (LXX)
16. Isaiah 28:19
17. Ezekiel 10:2
18. Joel 2:31
19. Isaiah 60:2
20. Isaiah 25:7
21. Revelation 6:16,17
22. Ezekiel 38:22,23
23. Daniel 8:14
24. Matthew 24:29,30
25. Jeremiah 30:7
26. Zephaniah 1:15,16
27. Amos 5:18,21
28. Daniel 5:1,31
29. Psalms 47:5-8
30. Daniel 7:9,10 margin

31. Daniel 7:13,14
32. Revelation 14:14
33. John 5:22
34. Revelation 3:20
35. Luke 12:35-37
36. Revelation 8:1
37. Psalm 76:6-9
38. Isaiah 41:1
39. Proverbs 26:2,8
40. Psalm 73:16-20
41. Revelation 8:7
42. Revelation 8:8,9
43. Revelation 8:10,11
44. Jeremiah 23:15-17
45. Revelation 8:12
46. Revelation 9:1,2
47. Kraeling, C. H.. *John the Baptist*. (N. Y.: Scribner's, 1951) p. 117.
48. Revelation 9:2-6
49. Amos 8:3
50. Isaiah 24:1,5,6
51. Isaiah 13:13
52. Psalms 75:3, Amplified
53. Isaiah 24:17-21
54. Luke 21:26
55. Revelation 10:6,7 margin
56. Revelation 11:15-18
57. Mark 13:27
58. Psalms 50:3-5
59. Revelation 14:14-16
60. 1 Corinthians 15:51-54
61. 1 John 1:9
62. Revelation 7:14-17
63. Micah 7:9
64. Ezekiel 41:2
65. Daniel 1:12
66. 2 Timothy 4:1
67. Isaiah 25:7
68. Psalms 50:3-5
69. 2 Corinthians 5:10
70. Matthew 22:42
71. 1 John 5:1-5
72. 1 Corinthians 3:11-15

73. Revelation 14:17-19
74. Isaiah 13:6-9
75. Jeremiah 12:12
76. Isaiah 34:5
77. Malachi 2:1-3
78. Hosea 9:5-7
79. Isaiah 34:8
80. Zephaniah 1:7-13
81. Numbers 10:9
82. Ezekiel 38:19,20
83. 2 Peter 3:10
84. Isaiah 13:20
85. Revelation 18:21
86. Jeremiah 50:13
87. Ezekiel 39:6
88. Ezekiel 29:10-12
89. Jeremiah 25:33
90. Zechariah 13:8,9
91. Isaiah 66:8
92. Ezekiel 39:22
93. Ezekiel 21:9,10,14,25-27
94. Revelation 14:20
95. Revelation 18:2-8
96. Micah 7:7-10
97. Mark 4:28,29
98. Revelation 16:17-21

Chapter 16: Key of the Abyss

1. Isaiah 14:23; compare Isaiah 13:13 with Revelation 6:16
2. Isaiah 13:20
3. "Tower of Babel May Rise Again," *Los Angeles Times*, Dec. 3, 1971, Part 1-A, p. 6.
4. Isaiah 23:13
5. Revelation 18:22,23
6. Jeremiah 51:58 (NIV)
7. Revelation 18:4; Revelation 17:5
8. Matthew 13:25,38
9. Genesis 11:2-4
10. Revelation 17:4
11. Revelation 18:16
12. Jeremiah 46:10; 51:63; Revelation 16:12
13. Ezekiel 21:30;31:18; Joel 2:3
14. Revelation 18:21,22
15. Revelation 8:5; Revelation 16:18

16. 2 Kings 19:7; Isaiah 37:7; Deuteronomy 28:22; Amos 4:9
17. Proverbs 7:27; Matthew 7:13; 16:18
18. Revelation 8:10
19. Isaiah 28:21
20. Joshua 10:10,11
21. Revelation 9:1,2
22. Revelation 14:20
23. Revelation 16:18
24. Jeremiah 10:10
25. Nahum 1:6
26. Psalms 55:23
27. Hebrews 3:6
28. Revelation 12:3
29. Jeremiah 51:1
30. Job 27:21
31. Jeremiah 51:11
32. Revelation 17:5
33. Jeremiah 51:25
34. Jeremiah 46:10,20
35. Zechariah 5:1-3
36. Genesis 3:24
37. Ezekiel 21:25-30
38. Jeremiah 12:12-15
39. Ezekiel 39:1-4,11
40. Ezekiel 47:18
41. Deuteronomy 11:24
42. Joel 2:20

Chapter 17: Between the Cherubim

1. Ezekiel 10:13
2. Amos 6:3
3. Obadiah 1:3,4
4. Habakkuk 2:9
5. Ezekiel 1:26-28
6. 2 Corinthians 12:2
7. Isaiah 14:13,14
8. Job 22:14 (LXX)
9. Job 26:9
10. Job 36:32
11. Job 37:21
12. Isaiah 25:7
13. Job 22:13
14. Revelation 6:14
15. Revelation 6:16

16. Ezekiel 28:14
17. Revelation 20:2
18. Psalms 87:4
19. Langewiesche, Wolfgang, "*The Thing That Hit Us From Outer Space*," Reader's Digest, Apr., 1963, p. 85.
20. Hawkins, Gerald S., *Splendor in the Sky*, (N.Y.: Harper and Brothers, 1961) p. 213,214. (emphasis mine)
21. Isaiah 30:13,14
22. Job 2:1
23. Isaiah 10:3
24. Isaiah 28:19
25. Isaiah 17:7-14
26. Job 27:13,20,21 Green's Interlinear Hebrew/Greek-Ehglish Bible
27. Jeremiah 50:23-28
28. Amos 1:4,5
29. Jeremiah 51:6-13
30. Zechariah 5:3
31. Revelation 18:2
32. Hebrews 9:23
33. Exodus 26:1
34. Daniel 12:4
35. "Did Comets Kill the Dinosaurs?" *Time*, May 6, 1985, p. 72.
36. Richardson, Robert S.. *The Fascinating World of Astronomy*. (New York: McGraw-Hill, 1960) p. 159.
37. Richardson, Robert S.. "Here Comes Icarus," *Science Digest*, June, 1968, p. 14.
38. Richardson, Robert S.. "The Discovery of Icarus," *Scientific American*, Apr., 1965, p. 109. (emphasis mine)
39. "Science and Space," *Newsweek*, June 24, 1968, p. 74.
40. Asimov, Isaac. "Earth Grazers: 'H-Bombs' in Space,"*Scientific Digest*, Nov., 1959, p. 77. (emphasis mine)
41. *Newsweek*, p. 74.
42. Langewiesche, p. 82-84.
43. Psalms 11:4-6
44. Isaiah 29:20,21
45. Job 5:3,4
46. Psalms 94:13
47. Proverbs 7:24-27
48. Isaiah 14:22-29
49. Revelation 16:13,14
50. Jeremiah 51:44-49
51. Isaiah 9:5

52. Jeremiah 25:29-33
53. Isaiah 13:19
54. "U. S. Divers 'Find' Biblical Sodom and Gomorrah," *Los Angeles Examiner*, Apr. 29, 1960, p. 1.
55. Genesis 19:24,25
56. Josephus,*Wars of the Jews*, Book IV, Ch. VIII, sect. 4.
57. Job 20:23-29
58. Psalms 55:23
59. Jeremiah 15:8,9 Green's Interlinear Hebrew/Greek-English Bible
60. Amos 8:2,9,10
61. Isaiah 34:1-10

Chapter 18: Touchdown

1. Psalms 97:1-3
2. Joel 2:1,2
3. Zechariah 14:6,7
4. Jeremiah 18:17;33:5; Isaiah 54:8
5. Ezekiel 22:24
6. Isaiah 40:6,7; 1 Peter 1:24
7. Psalms 72:5-11
8. Hosea 11:9, Amplified
9. Ezekiel 20:33-35
10. Deuteronomy 30:1,3
11. 1 Kings 19:1-13
12. Jeremiah 12:15
13. Ezekiel 39:12,13
14. Isaiah 24:20
15. Habakkuk 3:6-11
16. Daniel 9:24
17. Revelation 12:6,7
18. Numbers 9:2,7, cf. Exodus 13:1,10
19. Psalms 72:6,8
20. Hosea 6:3
21. Jeremiah 5:24, Amplified
22. Zechariah 10:1, Amplified
23. Joel 2:20,23,27
24. Revelation 17:12
25. Exodus 40.2,17
26. Psalms 24:10
27. Malachi 4:2
28. Malachi 3:1
29. Matthew 20:19
30. Joshua 10:14

23. Ezekiel 37:24,25
24. Jeremiah 17:12
25. Isaiah 33:15-17
26. Revelation 21:16
27. Revelation 7:1; Isaiah 11:12
28. Isaiah 11:12, Green's Interlinear Hebrew/Greek-English Bible
29. Revelation 21:23,24
30. Psalms 78:69
31. Colossians 2:9
32. Revelation 22:3-5
33. Haggai 2:5-9
34. Genesis 1:14
35. Malachi 4:2
36. 1 Corinthians 3:16
37. Ephesians 2:19-22
38. 2 Timothy 2:8
39. Matthew 13:30
40. John 15:1
41. Hosea 9:10; Joel 1:6,7
42. Song of Solomon 4:3,13
43. Psalms 128:3
44. as in Isaiah 51:6
45. Haggai 2:15,18,19
46. 1 Corinthians 3:16
47. Isaiah 66:8
48. Isaiah 10:20,21
49. Isaiah 11:2-4
50. Leviticus 23:29
51. Esther 9:5
52. Jeremiah 51:20-24
53. Isaiah 60:10-12
54. Isaiah 11:6-12
55. Jeremiah 38:7,8 (LXX) (31:7,8 in KJV)
56. Matthew 25:46
57. Numbers 20:29
58. Deuteronomy 34:8
59. Daniel 12:11
60. Daniel 12:11-13
61. Ezekiel 47:21,22
62. Acts 3:19
63. Leviticus 25:8-10
64. Isaiah 40:5
65. Isaiah 60:19,21

24.   1 Corinthians 10:11,12
25.   Deuteronomy 9:11-17
26.   1 Samuel 17:16
27.   Revelation 2:27
28.   Revelation 17:5
29.   Revelation 18:4
30.   Jeremiah 31:34
31.   Micah 7:15
32.   Genesis 29:1-8
33.   John 10:15
34.   1 Samuel 25:28-39
35.   2 Thessalonians 2:9
36.   1 Kings 1:37-40
37.   Genesis 24:55-58
38.   John 2:1-12
39.   Genesis 19:22-29 (Berkeley Version)
40.   Ephesians 1:17,18
41.   Haggai 2:21-22
42.   Isaiah 27:1

Selected Bibliography

Alnow, William M. *Soothsayers of the Second Advent.* (Old Tappan, N. J.: Fleming H. Revell Co., 1989)

Amplified Bible. (Grand Rapids: Zondervan Publishing House, 1962)

Aldrich, J. K.. "The Crucifixion on Thursday Not Friday," *Bibliotheca Sacra*, 27:401-429, July, 1870.

Allen, Roy M.. *Three Days in the Grave.* (N. Y.: Loizeaux Brothers, 1942)

Alvarez, Luis W.; Alvarez, Walter; Asaro, F. and Michel, Helen V. "Extraterrestrial Cause for the Cretaceous-Tertiary Extinction." *Science*, Vol. 208, June 6, 1980, pp. 1095-2108.

Alvarez, Walter, *et al.* "The End of the Cretaceous: Sharp Boundary or Gradual Transition?" *Science*, Vol. 223, Mar. 16, 1984, pp. 1183-1186.

_____ "Impact Theory of Mass Extinctions and the Invertebrate Fossil Record." *Science*, Vol. 223, Mar. 16, 1984, pp. 1135-1141.

Anderson, Sir Robert. *The Coming Prince.* (Grand Rapids: Kregel Publ., 17th edition, 1969; first published 1895)

Andrews, Samuel J.. *The Life of Our Lord Upon Earth.* (Grand Rapids: Zondervan Publishing House, 1954; first published 1891)

Anstey, Martin. *The Romance of Bible Chronology.* (London: Marshall Bros., 1913, Vol. I and II)

Asimov, Isaac, "Earth-Grazers: 'H-Bombs' in Space," *Scientific Digest*, Nov.1959.

Ballard, Robert D., *et al.* "Crustal Processes of the Mid-Ocean Ridge." *Science*, Vol. 213, July 3, 1981, p. 31.

Barclay, William. *The New Testament, A New Translation*, Vol. I, The Gospels and the Acts of the Apostles. (London: Collins, 1968)

Barnhouse, Donald Grey, *Revelation.* (Grand Rapids: Zondervan Publishing House, 1971)

Baxter, J. Sidlow. *Studies in Problem Texts* (Grand Rapids: Zondervan Publishing House, 1960.

Bearak, Barry. "Archeological Discovery in Florida, Bones of Prehistoric Man, Animals Found Together," *Los Angeles Times*, Jan. 15, 1986, part 1.

Bedford, Arthur. *The Scripture Chronology.* (London: James and John Knapton, 1730)

The Bible, Revised Standard Version. (N. Y.: American Bible Society, 1952)

Bishop, Jim. *The Day Christ Died.* (N. Y.: Pocket Books, Inc., 1957)

Bloomfield, Arthur E. *The End of the Days, A Study of Daniel's Visions*. (Minneapolis: Bethany Fellowship, Inc., 1961)

Bohor, Bruce F., *et al*. "Shocked Quartz in the Cretaceous-Tertiary Boundary Clays: Evidence for a Global Distribution." *Science*, Vol. 236, May 8, 1987, pp. 705-710.

Bond, John. *Handy-Book of Rules and Tables for Verifying Dates with the Christian Era*. (New York: Russell & Russell, 1966)

Brenton, Sir Lancelot C. L.. *Septuagint Version: Greek and English, with Apocrypha*. (Grand Rapids: Zondervan Publishing House, originally published 1851)

Brouwers, Elisabeth M., *et al*. "Dinosaurs on the North Slope, Alaska: High Latitude, Latest Cretaceous Environments." *Science*, Vol. 237, Sept. 25, 1987, p. 1608.

Brown, O. M.. *Bible Chronology Vindicated*. (Cleveland: Christian Messenger Publ. Co., 1901)

Burton, Ernest DeWitt and Goodspeed, Edgar Johnson. *A Harmony of the Synoptic Gospels for Historical and Critical Study*. (New York: Charles Scribner's Sons, 1929)

Chafer, L. S. *Systematic Theology*. (Dallas: Dallas Seminary Press, 1947)

"Christmas," *World Book Encyclopedia*, 1966.

Concordant Literal Bible. (Canyon Country, California: Concordant Publishing Concern, published in parts with different dates)

Cooper, David L.. *Messiah: His First Coming Scheduled*. (Los Angeles: Biblical Research Society, 1939)

Courtillot, Vincent and Beese, Jean. "Magnetic Field Reversals, Polar Wander, and Core-Mantle Coupling." *Science*, Vol. 237, Sept. 4, 1987, pp. 1140-1147.

Cruikshank, D. P. and Brown, R. H. "Organic Matter on Asteroid 130 Elektra." *Science*, Vol. 238, Oct. 9, 1987, pp. 183ff.

Cunningham, William. *A Vindication of the True Date of the Passion*. (London: Seeley, Burnside, and Seeley, 1846)

De Haan, M. R.. *Revelation: 35 Simple Studies on the Major Themes in Revelation*. (Grand Rapids: Zondervan Publishing House, 1946)

Deal, Colin Hoyle. *Armageddon & the 21st Century*. (Rutherford College, N. C.: Colin H. Deal, 1988)

"Did Comets Kill the Dinosaurs?" *Time*. May 6,1985, p. 72-83.

Dimont, Max I. *Jews, God and History*. (New York: The New American Library of World Literature, Inc., 1964)

Eerdmans' Handbook to the Bible, edited by David and Pat Alexander. (Grand Rapids: Wm. B. Eerdmans Publishing Co., 1973)

Edersheim, Alfred. *The Life and Times of Jesus the Messiah*. (London, 1886)

Ehlert, Arnold D. *Syllabus of Bible Chronology*. (La Mirada, California: unpublished ms. at Bible Institute of Los Angeles, 1946)

Div. of Information, Ministry for Foreign Affairs. *Facts About Israel*. (Jerusalem: Keter Publishing House, 1972)

Feinberg, Charles L. *Premillennialism and Amillennialism*. (Grand Rapids: Zondervan Publishing House, 1936)

Fotheringham, J. K. "Astronomical Evidence for the Date of the Crucifixion." *The Journal of Theological Studies*, 12:120-27, Oct., 1910)

French, Bevan M. *The Moon Book*. (N. Y.: Penguin Books, 1978)

Gaebelein, Arno C. *The Prophet Daniel*. (Grand Rapids: Kregel Publications, 1955)

_____ *The Revelation*. (New York: Our Hope Publication Office, 1915)

Ganapathy, R. "A Major Meteorite Impact on the Earth 65 Million Years Ago: Evidence from the Cretaceous-Tertiary Boundary Clay." *Science*, Vol. 209, Aug. 22, 1980, pp. 921-923.

Gilmore, James, *et al.* "Nonmarine Iridium Anomaly Linked to Extinctions." *Science*, Vol. 212, June 19, 1981, p. 1376.

Girdlestone, Robert B.. *The Divine Programme: Suggestions for its Study*. (London: Chas. J. Thynne, 1915)

Goodenow, Smith B.. *Bible Chronology Carefully Unfolded*. (N. Y.: Fleming R. Revell Co., 1896)

Goudoever, *Biblical Calendars*. (Leiden, Netherlands: E. J. Brill, 1959)

Greek, Latin, English New Testament Students' Workbook. (Collegeville, Minn.: The Liturgical Press, 1963)

Green, Jay. *The Interlinear Hebrew/Greek-English Bible*. (Evansville, Indiana: Associated Publishers and Authors, 1978)

Hand, John Raymond. Why I Accept the Genesis Record, An Answer to Evolution. (Lincoln, Nebraska: Back to the Bible Publishers, 1959)

Hawkins, Gerald S.. *Splendor in the Sky*. (N. Y.: Harper and Brothers, 1961)

Heider, Franz, *et al.* "Magnetic Properties of Hydrothermally Recrystallized Magnetite Crystals." *Science*, Vol. 236, June 5, 1987, p. 1987.

Hislop, Alexander. *The Two Babylons*, third ed. (New York: Loizeaux Brothers, 1943)

Hocking, David. *The Coming World Leader, Understanding the Book of Revelation*. (Portland: Multnomah Press, 1988)

Hoehner, Harold W.. *Chronological Aspects of the Life of Christ*. (Grand Rapids: Zondervan Publishing House, 1973)

Holy Bible, The Berkeley Version. (Grand Rapids: Zondervan Publishing House, 1959)

Holy Bible, Confraternity Version. (N. Y.: Catholic Book Publishing Co.,1963)

Imbrie, John and Imbrie, Katherine Palmer. *Ice Ages, Solving the Mystery.* (Short Hills, N. J.: Enslow Publishers, 1979)

"Is There Any Such Thing as a Gift of Prophecy?" *The Daily Breeze,* Family Weekly magazine section, Feb. 20, 1977.

Jamieson, Robert; Faussett, A. R. and Brown, David. *A Commentary Critical, Experimental, and Practical on the Old and New Testaments.* (Grand Rapids: Wm. B. Eerdmans Publishing Co., 1945)

"Jerusalém Is Talking About Rebuilding the Temple." *San Francisco Chronicle,* Sept. 10, 1964.

"Jesus Grew to Manhood Amidst Violence, Struggle and Peril," *The Register,* Dec. 20, 1969.

Kee, Howard Clark. *Jesus in History, An Approach to the Study of the Gospels.* (N. Y.: Harcourt Brace Jovanovich, Inc., 1977)

Keller, Werner, translated by William Neil. *The Bible as History, A Confirmation of The Book of Books.* (N. Y.: Bantam Books, 1974)

Kerr, Richard A. "Asteroid Impact Gets More Support." *Science,* Vol. 236, May 8, 1987, pp. 666-668.

_____ "Asteroid Theory of Extinctions Strengthened." *Science,* Vol. 210, Oct. 31, 1980, pp. 514-517.

_____ "The Great Asteroid Roast: Was It Rare or Well-Done? *Science,* Vol. 247, Feb. 2, 1990, pp. 528,9.

_____ "How Is New Ocean Crust Formed? *Science,* Vol. 205, Sept. 14, 1979, pp. 1115-1118.

_____ "Making the Moon, Remaking Earth." *Science,* Vol. 243, Mar. 17, 1989, pp. 1433-1435.

_____ "Ocean Drilling Details Steps to an Icy World." *Science,* Vol. 236, May 22, 1987, pp. 912,913.

_____ "Plate Tectonics Is the Key to the Distant Past." *Science,* Vol. 234, Nov. 7, 1986, pp. 670-672.

_____ "Tracking the Wandering Poles of Ancient Earth." *Science,* Vol. 236, Apr. 10, 1987, p. 148.

Kirban, Salem. *The Day Israel Dies!* (Old Tappan, N. J.: Fleming H. Revell Co., 1975)

Kraeling, C. H.. *John the Baptist.* (N. Y.: Scribner's, 1951).

Kurten, Bjorn. *The Ice Age.* (N. Y.: G. P. Putnam's sons, 1972)

Kuyper, Abraham. *The Revelation of St. John.* translated by John Hendrik de Vries. (Grand Rapids: Wm. B. Eerdmans Publishing Co., 1935)

Kyte, Frank T. and Wasson, John T. "Accretion Rate of Extraterrestrial Matter: Iridium Deposited 33 to 67 Million Years Ago." *Science*, Vol. 232, June 6, 1986, pp. 1225-1229.

Kyte, Frank T., *et al*. "New Evidence on the Size and Possible Effects of a Late Pliocene Oceanic Asteroid Impact." *Science*, Vol. 241, July 1, 1988, p. 64.

Langewiesche, Wolfgang. "The Thing That Hit Us From Outer Space," *Reader's Digest*, Apr., 1963.

Larkin, Clarence. *Dispensational Truth*. (Philadelphia: Larkin, 1918)

LaHaye, Tim F. *Revelation Illustrated and Made Plain*. (Grand Rapids: Zondervan Publishing House, 1981)

Lewin, Roger. "Mountain Goat Horn: A Clue to Extinction?" *Science*, Vol. 232, Apr. 25, 1986, p. 450.

Lindsay, Hal. *The Late Great Planet Earth*. (Grand Rapids: Zondervan Publishing House, 1970)

_____ *The 1980's: Countdown to Armageddon*. (King of Prussia, Pennsylvania: Westgate Press Inc., 1980)

_____ *The Rapture: Truth or Consequences*. (New York: Bantam Books, 1983)

_____ *A Prophetical Walk Through the Holy Land*. (Eugene, Oregon: Harvest House Publishers, 1983)

_____ *There's a New World Coming*. (Santa Ana, California: Vision House Publishers, 1973)

"Luther, Martin," *Encyclopedia Americana*, 1949, XVII.

Madison, Leslie P.. *Problems of Chronology in the Life of Christ.*, unpubl. Th.D thesis. (Dallas Theological Seminary, 1963)

McBirnie, William Steuart. *AntiChrist*. (Dallas: Acclaimed Books, 1978)

McGee, J. Vernon. *Reveling Through Revelation*. (Los Angeles: Thru the Bible Books Foundation, 1962)

Meldau, Fred John. *Messiah in Both Testaments*. (Denver: The Christian Victory Publishing Co., 1956)

Morris, Henry M. *The Bible and Modern Science*. (Chicago: Moody Press, 1951)

Nave's Compact Topical Bible. (Grand Rapids: Zondervan Publishing House, 1972)

New American Standard Bible. (Nashville, Camden, N. Y.: Thomas Nelson, Publishers, 1977)

The New English Bible, New Testament. (U. S.: Oxford University Press and Cambridge University Press, 1961)

New International Version of The Holy Bible. (Grand Rapids: Zondervan Publishing House, 1973)

New Testament and Wycliffe Bible Commentary. (Chicago: Moody Press, 1971)

The New Testament of The Jerusalem Bible. editor, Jones, Alexander. (Garden City, N. Y.: Doubleday & Co., Inc., 1969)

Ogg, George. *The Chronology of the Public Ministry of Jesus*. (Cambridge, 1940)

Olmstead, A. T.. "The Chronology of Jesus' Life," *Anglican Theological Review*, 24:1-26, Jan., 1942.

Page, William M. *New Light from Old Eclipses*. (St. Louis: C. R. Barns Publ. Co., 1890)

Pananides, Nicholas A.. *Introductory Astronomy*.. (Reading, Mass.: Addison-Wesley Publ. Co., 1973)

Patten, Donald Wesley. *Catastrophism and the Old Testament*. (Pacific Meridian Publishing Co., 1988)

Pentecost, J. D.. *Things to Come*. (Findley, Ohio: Dunham Publ. Co., 1958)

Pfeiffer, Charles F. *Baker's Bible Atlas*, revised edition (Grand Rapids: Baker Book House, 1979)

Poinar, George O., Jr.. "The Amber Ark," *Natural History*, Dec., 1988. _____ and Cannatella, David C. "An Upper Eocene Frog from the Dominican Republic and Its Implication for Caribbean Biogeography." *Science*, Vol. 237, Sept. 4, 1987, pp. 1215,16.

Power, Matthew. *Anglo-Jewish Calendar*. (London: Sands and Co., 1902)

Price, Ira Maurice. *The Monuments and the Old Testament, Light from the Near East on the Scriptures*. (Philadelphia: The Judson Press, 1925)

Ra`anan, Uri, *et al.*, *History from 1880*. (Israel: Keter Books, 1973)

Ramsey, William Mitchell. *Was Christ Born in Bethlehem?* (New York: G. P. Putnam's Sons, 1898)

Raup, David M. "Biological Extinction in Earth History." *Science*, Vol. 231, Mar. 28, 1986, pp. 1528-1533.

Redfern, Ron. *The Making of a Continent*. (N. Y.: The New York Times Book Co., Inc., 1983)

Richardson, Robert S., "Here Comes Icarus," *Science Digest*, June, 1968. _____ The Discovery of Icarus," *Scientific American*, April, 1965. _____ *The Fascinating World of Astronomy*. (New York: McGraw Hill, 1960)

Robinson, James Harvey; Breasted, James Henry; Smith, Emma Peters. *History of Civilization, Earlier Ages*. (Boston: Ginn and Company 1951)

Rosen, Ruth, editor. *Jesus For Jews*. (San Francisco: A Messianic Jewish Perspective, 1987)

Runcorn, S. K. "The Ancient Lunar Core Dynamo." *Science*, Vol. 199, Feb. 17, 1978, pp. 771-773.

Rusk, Roger. "The Day He Died," *Christianity Today*, Mar. 29, 1974, pp. 4-6.

Ryrie, Charles Caldwell. *Revelation*. (Chicago: Moody Press, 1968)

"Science and Space," *Newsweek*, June 24, 1968.

Scofield, C. I.. *Scofield Reference Bible*. (New York: Oxford University Press, 1917)

_____ *New Scofield Reference Bible*. (New York: Oxford University Press, 1967)

Sciss, Joseph A. *The Apocalypse, Exposition of the Book of Revelation*. (Grand Rapids: Kregel Publications, 1987)

Shimer, John A. *This Sculptured Earth: The Landscape of America*. (New York: Columbia University Press, 1959)

Slemming, Charles W. *The Bible Digest*. (Grand Rapids: Kregel Publications, 1960)

Strauss, Lehman. *The Book of Revelation*. (Neptune, N. J.: Loizeaux Brothers, 1964)

Strong, James. *The Exhaustive Concordance of the Bible*. (New York: Abingdon Press, 1894)

Swindoll, Charles R. *Daniel, God's Pattern for the Future*. (R. R. Donnelley & Sons Co., 1986)

Talbot, Louis T. *An Exposition of the Book of Revelation*. (Grand Rapids: Wm. B. Eerdmans Publishing Co., 1937)

Tarduno, J. A., *et al.* "Southern Hemisphere Origin of the Cretaceous Laytonville Limestone of California." *Science*, Vol. 231, Mar. 21, 1986, pp. 1425-1428.

Tatford, Frederick A.. *Will There be a Millennium?* (Sussex: Prophetic Witness Publ. House, 1969)

Taylor, Charles R. *Get all Excited--Jesus is Coming Soon!* (Redondo Beach, California: Today in Bible Prophecy, Inc., 1975)

Thayer, Joseph Henry. *Thayer's Greek-English Lexicon of the New Testament*. (Grand Rapids: Associated Publishers and Authors, n. d.)

Thieme, R. B., Jr. *Armageddon*. (Houston: Berachah Tapes & Publications, 1974)

_____ *Daniel, Chapter Two*. (Houston: Berachah Tapes & Publications, 1973)

_____ *The Faith-Rest Life*. (Houston: Berachah Tapes & Publications, 1961)

_____ *Super-Grace Life*. (Houston: Berachah Tapes & Publications, 1973)

Tomas, Andrew. *We Are Not The First, Riddles of Ancient Science.* (New York: G. P. Putnam's Sons, 1971)

Torrey, Reuben A. "Was Jesus Really Three Days and Three Nights in the Heart of the Earth?" *The King's Business*, magazine published by Bible Institute of Los Angeles, Apr. 1961, pp. 12,13.

"Tower of Babel May Rise Again," *Los Angeles Times*, Dec. 2, 1971, Part I-A.

Trefil, James S.. *Space Time Infinity.* (Washington, D. C.: Smithsonian Inst., 1985)

Tregelles, Samuel Prideaux. *Gesenius' Hebrew and Chaldee Lexicon to the Old Testament Scriptures.* (Grand Rapids: Baker Book House, 1979)

Turner, C. H.. Adversaria Chronologica," *Journal of Theological Studies*, Oct. 1901, p. 3.

"U. S. Divers 'Find' Biblical Sodom and Gomorrah," *Los Angeles Examiner*, Apr. 29, 1960.

Unger, Merrill F.. *Unger's Bible Dictionary.* (Chicago: Moody Press,1957)

Vandeman, George E. *Showdown in the Middle East.* (Mountain View, California: Pacific Press Publishing Assoc., 1980)

Velikovsky, Immanuel. *Ages in Chaos.* (N. Y.: Doubleday, 1952)
_____ *Worlds in Collision.* (N. Y.: Doubleday, 1951)

Walvoord, John F. *The Rapture Question.* (Grand Rapids: Zondervan Publishing House, 1957)
_____ *The Revelation of Jesus Christ.* (Chicago: Moody Press, 1966)

Webber, David, and Hutchings, Noah. *Is This the Last Century?* (Nashville: Thomas Nelson Publ.)

Weihaupt, John G. *Exploration of the Oceans, An Introduction to Oceanography.* (New York: Macmillan Publishing Co., Inc., 1979)

Westcott, Brooke Foss. *An Introduction to the Study of the Gospels*, 6th ed.. (London, 1881)

Whisenant, Edgar C. *88 Reasons Why the Rapture Could Be in 1988.* (Nashville: World Bible Society, 1988)

Whiston, William. *The Works of Flavius Josephus.* (Philadelphia: Henry T. Coates and Co., n. d.)

Whitcomb, John C. and De Young, Donald. *The Moon, It's Creation, Form and Significance.* (Winona Lake, Indiana: BMH Books, 1978)

Woodrow, Ralph. *His Truth is Marching On.* (Riverside, California: Ralph Woodrow Evangelistic Assoc., 1977)

Wooley, Leonard. *Ur: The First Phases.* (London: Penguin Books Limited, 1946)

Young, Robert. *Young's Analytical Concordance.* (Grand Rapids: Associated Publishers and Authors, n. d.)

Index